THE LEGEND OF STOR

BY FRED STOREY

Suite 300 - 990 Fort St
Victoria, BC, Canada, V8V 3K2
www.friesenpress.com

Copyright © 2015 by Fred Storey
First Edition — 2015

All rights reserved.

No part of this publication may be reproduced in any form, or by any means, electronic or mechanical, including photocopying, recording, or any information browsing, storage, or retrieval system, without permission in writing from the publisher.

ISBN
978-1-4602-6299-3 (Hardcover)
978-1-4602-6300-6 (Paperback)
978-1-4602-6301-3 (eBook)

1. Biography & Autobiography, Historical

Distributed to the trade by The Ingram Book Company

TABLE OF CONTENTS

AUTHOR'S NOTE..................................... IX

ACKNOWLEDGEMENTS XIII

PRELUDE
LINDISFARNE XXI

PART ONE
| THE LABOUR | 1

CHAPTER 1
DEATH OF THE KINGDOM OF CUMBRIA............ 3

CHAPTER 2
THE MANDATE......................................23

CHAPTER 3
STOREYE...43

CHAPTER 4
WAR AGAINST PAGANISM............................51

CHAPTER 5
VALHALLA..61

CHAPTER 6
ROUGH JUSTICE.....................................71

CHAPTER 7
JORVIK..81

CHAPTER 8
STRANGER IN PARADISE.............................97

CHAPTER 9
FOR OTHER MEN'S GLORY...........................115

CHAPTER 10
HEIR TO STOREYE 129

CHAPTER 11
THE LAST KING OF YORK 133

CHAPTER 12
THE STORK 141

CHAPTER 13
THE HOSTAGE OF WESSEX 151

PART 2
| THE BIRTH | 163

CHAPTER 14
FAIRNESS FOR NORTHUMBERLAND 165

CHAPTER 15
EDGAR: KING OF ALL ENGLAND 181

CHAPTER 16
WHEN COWARDS DIE 199

CHAPTER 17
ENGLAND HER OWN 205

PART 3
| INFANCY | 229

CHAPTER 18
PIRATES AND TRAITORS 231

CHAPTER 19
VENGEANCE DENIED 243

CHAPTER 20
A WOUNDED WARRIOR 251

CHAPTER 21
THE VIPER STRIKES 257

CHAPTER 22
THE PALATINE ARCHBISHOPRIC 267

CHAPTER 23
SIGEN AND UHTRED 277

CHAPTER 24
A RESTING PLACE FOR A SAINT 283

CHAPTER 25
THE HORN OF ULPHUS 291

PART 4
| A COMING OF AGE | 297

CHAPTER 26
TREACHERY AND MURDER 299

CHAPTER 27
THE VIKING KING 307

CHAPTER 28
COMES THE CONQUEROR 311

CHAPTER 29
NORTHUMBRIAN REVOLT 315

EPILOGUE 327

ABOUT THE AUTHOR
FRED STOREY 333

Dedicated to the memory of my son, Ronald.

AUTHOR'S NOTE

Over a century ago a group of people, whose surname I share, set about gathering information regarding their ancestors who were also named Storey. They worked diligently through documents, records and cemeteries and then began corresponding with all those people named Storey whom they had found. Out of this endeavor, they came to conclude that all those people who share this name of ours, whether spelt Storey, Storeye, Story, Storrie and even Sturey and Sturis, in all likelihood shared a common ancestor named Stor (sometimes spelt Styr). They compiled all of their data into a volume called *Storeys of Old*.

I combed through this work, on some occasions using their work directly and on other occasions using clues which I gleaned from them. I then began my own research until I was able to compile what I believe is an accurate genealogy of the male members of my family tracing us back to that same Stor. I also began committing my findings to the written word, but the more I dug, the more I discovered and eventually I realized that the story of Stor and his immediate family was sufficiently fascinating to warrant a book in its own right. I was not content to simply dwell on the bare facts, or rumours, of the life of Stor and those people with whom he interacted. These people lived, loved, hated, procreated and died. Their lives coincided with an epoch in the emergence of the country we call England and they played their role in that emergence. And so I found myself writing, not just about them, but about the birth of England itself.

This story also emerges out of that period of time known as the Dark Ages. While they were indeed dark, they were not without some illumination. Chroniclers such as Bede had meticulously attempted to record the history of Britain as best they could. Towns and castles were named for their owners and coins were minted bearing the likenesses of kings who oversaw their issue. The beginning of surnames was underway and the recording of legal transactions had begun. From these I was able to glean an outline of this story. But I was not content with that. These people had real lives and relationships. As a result, I often and liberally resorted to my own imagination in order to breathe life into those ancient personalities.

For those who hold accuracy in historical accounts more firmly than I, this note is an attempt to allow them to separate fact from fiction.

Stor's existence is confirmed by a simple piece of writing in which he transfers a piece of land to the Bishop of Lindisfarne. This led me into a myriad of questions. Stor is a Norwegian word and therefore he was undoubtedly related to the pagan Norse Vikings that swept across England from Dublin and placed their king on the Throne of Jorvik. So who was this Stor who owned land in England? Why did this Viking give land to the Bishop? And why was this transaction sufficiently significant to warrant its registration? These questions drove my research.

History records that a certain Styr was recognized, in the presence of King AEthelred, to have made this land grant and a Danish horn, known as the Horn of Ulphus, hangs today in York Minister commemorating this event. Things began to come together for me when I realized that

THE LEGEND OF STOR

Styr was in fact the Anglo Saxon spelling of Stor. Ulphus, son of Torald and father of Norman and Achill are all also real. When William the Conqueror commissioned his *Doomsday Book* it showed Norman still residing at Toraldsby.

It is also documented that Sigen Storsdotter, Daughter of Stor was the second of three wives of Uhtred of Bamburgh and bore him two sons, Eadulf and Cospatric. History also records that in a blood feud initiated by Stor, Uhtred was murdered by Thurbrand of the Hold. He in turn was killed by Uhtred's eldest son, EAldred who in turn was killed by Carl Thurbrandson. Carl and his two sons were killed by Waltheof. These rounds of vengeance took place over a seventy-two year period, making it the longest, continuously running, blood-feud in English history.

All of the members of the House of Bamburgh and those of the House of Wessex are as described and did the things which this book attributes to them. The same is true of the ancient Rheged Kingdom and the MacAlpine kings of Scotland. Amdarch did burn Cuillen to death in retaliation for the rape and murder of his daughter. The kings of Jorvik (York), Both Danish and Norwegian, were also as described.

Historians do not completely agree on whether or not Eric Bloodaxe even existed, however, coins of that period were minted with the inscription *Eric Rex*. To the extent that he did actually live and rule York, he also fought a huge battle and defeated the House of Bamburgh. And he did die violently and alone at Stainmore.

The children and grandchildren of Uhtred and Sigen provided the last Anglo-Saxon resistance to William the Conqueror and Waltheof did pay the ultimate price for this resistance as the book describes.

Much of the rest of this book is a product of my interpretations of the words and actions which must have occurred in order to have yielded the outcomes which they did.

Credit for accuracy belongs to those people who troubled themselves to record these events. Errors, on the other hand, are all mine.

Respectfully,
Fred Storey

ACKNOWLEDGEMENTS

This work could not have been carried out without the tremendous effort of those unidentified people, who, over a century ago, diligently gathered every genealogy, story, antidote and record pertaining to those families who bore the name Storey and its divergent spellings. They collated their findings and published them under the name *Storeys of Old* , Preston: Exors. Of C.W.Whithead, Printers and Bookbinders, Avenham Street Mill, 1920.

The affirmation of the existence of Stor, his relationship to Sigen and subsequently to Uhtred of Bamburgh was recorded in a very ancient document by the scribe, Simeon of Durham, within the lifetime of Stor. His writings have been transcribed in *On the Origins of the Church of Durham, Northumbria, 500 to 1100 AD*, Oxford Medieval Texts, Claredon Press. Richard Fletcher, in *Bloodfeud: Murder and Revenge in Anglo-Saxon England* (2004), expanded on Simeon's writing and describes the blood feud that raged between Stor and the house of Bamburgh on the one side and Thurbrand of the Hold and his family on the other. Michael Wood's, *In Search of the Dark Ages* (BBC Books, London, 1981) provided a wealth of background on Britain as it emerged from the Dark Ages.

The Woodsworth poem has been reprinted in many publications and in particularly in *The Almanack . the inheritage journal of history, travel and lore*, produced by Inheitage. Likewise

, Thorkill's poem appears in numerous publications, most notably in Anglo-Norman Studies: XIX Proceedings of the Battle Conference, 1996. Ed. Christopher Harper-Bell, The Baydell Press, Woodbridge, 1997

Contributors to the internet provided numerous antidotes and confirmations of the best historical judgments on the struggles of Anglo-Saxons, Vikings, Scots and Celts as they fought over the land which would become England, at a time in which the historical record is scanty, biased and contradictory.

Ruth Steeves was my inspiration, mentor, taskmaster, editor and friend, without whom this book would never have been completed.

All of the artwork flows from the hand of Bob English.

THE LEGEND OF STOR

***

FRED STOREY

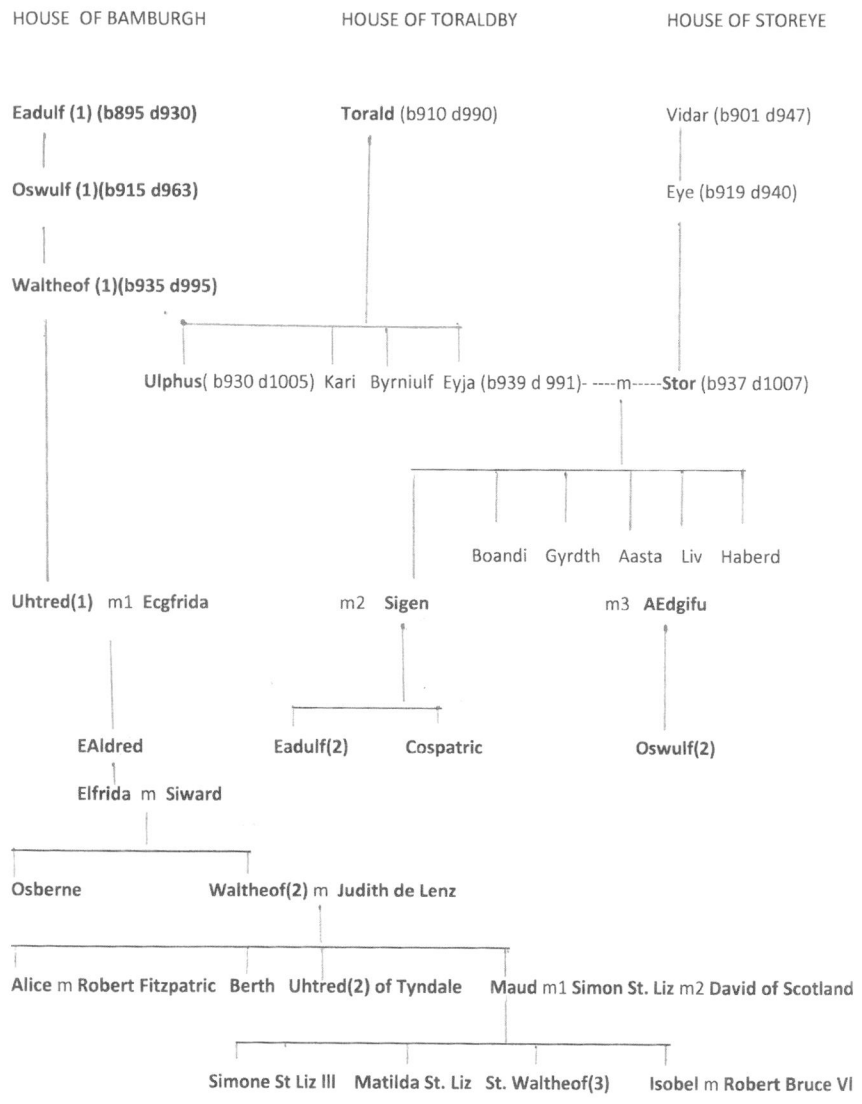

Bolding denotes historically real people

THE LEGEND OF STOR

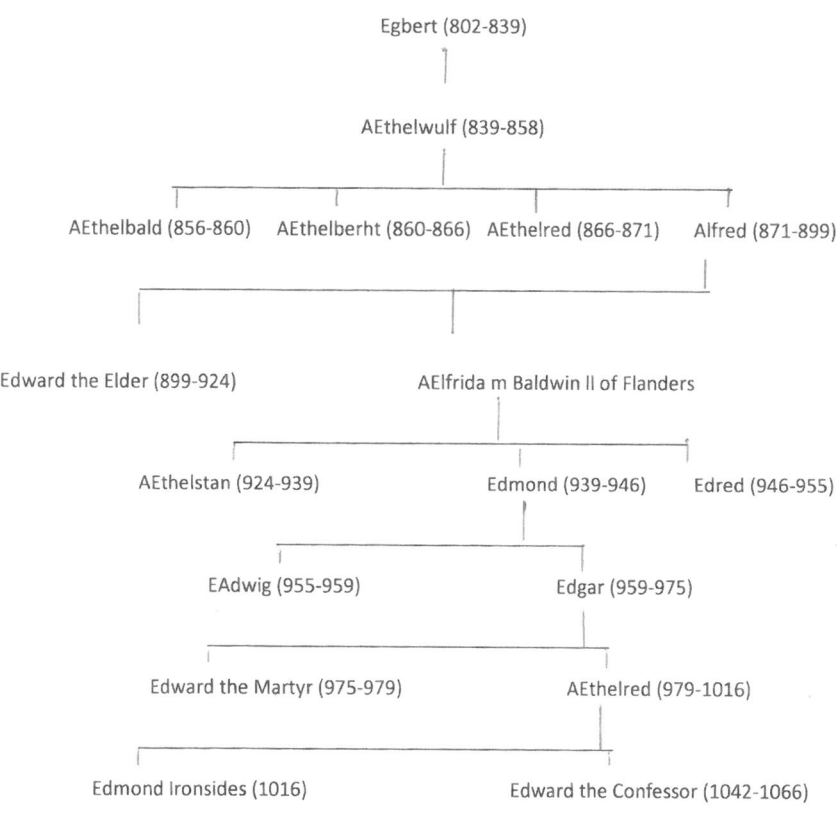

BRITAIN 793 AD

THE LEGEND OF STOR

ENGLAND 945 AD

PRELUDE
LINDISFARNE

LINDISFARNE, JUNE 8, 793 AD

The soft breeze that rippled the long grasses surrounding him gently caressed his skin and playfully tousled his hair, as the young monk sat on rocky outcrop contemplating the wonders of God's creation. The sun hung warm and heavy in a cloudless sky on that tranquil summer afternoon. Aldwyn gazed out across the expansive sea which would become known to men as the North Sea. His task this day was a simple one and one which he enjoyed. He simply had to watch over the abbey's flock of sheep as they grazed peacefully on the grasses in the meadows which surrounded him.

Below him, stretching out into the sea lay the Abbey of Lindisfarne. It was situated on a piece of land which protruded off the coast out into the ocean which, at high tide, when the waves lapped ever higher against the shore, they slowly formed a barrier of water between the abbey and the coast. Then it became an island. For hundreds of miles, people knew it as the Holy Island. But, at this hour, the land continued to connect him to the abbey below. He casually checked the angle of the sun and unconsciously decided that he had at least another hour before the waters began to rise and he would have to begin to herd the sheep back across the land bridge to the safety of the island.

His work at the abbey was not always this easy. Except at harvest time, which required the involvement of the whole abbey, Aldwyn worked with the sheep and the wool which they produced. The sheep had been sheared of their rich winter coats which were now in the hands of the spinners and weavers. Until the coarse cloth was woven, Aldwyn had little to do, aside from tending the flock and participating in the daily prayer rituals of the abbey. The weaving would soon be producing rough cloth. Then the hard work of fulling the cloth would begin for Aldwyn.

The fulling was all done by hand. The liquid laden material was very heavy and the work was hard, but Aldwyn did not mind. He was content with his lot in life. He had been orphaned nine years before, when a marauding band of bandits had swept into his small village, killing most of the inhabitants, carrying off all that they could carry, including his younger sister, and putting the remains to the torch. He had hidden, terrified, in the nearby forest until a kindly stranger had found him and brought him to Lindisfarne. The monks had taken him in and raised him. Now, in the fourteenth year of his life, memories of those early horrors had faded and been eventually replaced by a more quiet contentment.

* * *

The glorious summer day, which Aldwyn was now enjoying, was not common to this part of the world. Located on the shore of North Sea, Lindisfarne more often experienced a gloomy overcast, if not the vicious gales which regularly assaulted the shoreline. Earlier that year, great lightning storms had been so intense across Northumbria that they were later described in the chronicles as fiery dragons dancing across the heavens. These storms were followed by an extensive drought which many attributed as being a portent from the "Fiery Dragons".

Today, however, as Aldwyn sat on that rocky crag, under a warm sunny sky, surrounded by his contented flock and taking in the beauty and wonderment that his Lord had given him, he felt certain unease. It was nothing that he could put his hand on; just uneasiness, a quiet sense of foreboding. He had known nothing but security here at Lindisfarne, with the impregnable Bamburgh Castle just down the beach, housing the might of the Kingdom of Northumbria. Aldwyn would have no knowledge of the inner turmoil which had brought the kingdom to the edge of its destruction and now challenged its ability to defend its territory.

* * *

Following Rome's withdrawal from Britain in 410 AD it left behind roads, fortresses and other civic works but it took with it all vestiges law, order and governance. The isolated bands of mostly Christian Celtic inhabitants, who were left to deal with this void, were besieged by waves of pagan Angle, Saxon and Jute invaders. Many of these people were brought to the island, from the continent, as mercenaries to protect Celtic communities from each other and from other invaders. Others came as invaders. Out of the ensuing battles and conquests, the successes of the Anglo warrior, Ida Flamebearer, of a little known kingdom called Bernicia, arose the beginnings of what would become the most substantial of Anglo-Saxon kingdoms, the Kingdom of Northumbria. Ida established his capital in an old, but substantial Roman castle. Ida's grandson, AEthelfrith, built on the conquests of his grandfather. He also refurbished the castle and presented it to his wife, Bebba, who named it for herself.

Down the beach from Bebbanburgh Castle, and clearly visible from its ramparts, was the island of Ynys Metcaut with its small stone castle. It was the last stronghold of the surviving independent Britons who resided in this part of Britain. Their island was connected to the mainland during low tide and, on one such low tide AEthelfrith's troops crossed that land bridge, conquered its inhabitants and changed its name to Lindis Feorna, later to come to be known as Lindisfarne.

The Kingdom of Northumbria reached its zenith in both power and wealth by 634 through conquest and marriage. Its boundaries stretched from shore to shore and from the Firth of Forth in the north to the Thames in the south. The new king of Northumbria was Oswald and he was a Christian. He brought a monk named Aiden from the Monastery of Iona, made him a bishop, and gave him the task of Christianizing his kingdom. Aiden was installed in a newly erected monastery at Lindisfarne, while Oswald ruled from his magnificent, but impregnable castle just down the beach, now known as Bamburgh.

The bishopric at Lindisfarne would come to be known as the Holy Island. Lindisfarne and Bamburgh were now the centres of religious and secular authority for the kingdom. It was also the center of great wealth after generations of Anglo traders had contributed treasures from all over Europe.

After a century now, the once powerful Kingdom of Northumbria had fallen into a state of turmoil and decay on all fronts. Its external neighbours were becoming less and less intimidated by its military might. The earlier kingdoms which had been incorporated into the greater Northumbria Kingdom were more and more demanding their independence. The throne itself was under continual challenge from feuding royal relatives. Not only were there external challenges, but also challenges from the rival Anglo-Saxon Kingdoms of Wessex and East Anglia but also the Scots and Picts to the north. Internally, the incorporated kingdoms of Mercia, Deidre, Bernicia, Cumbria, and Strathclyde were all in open revolt.

THE LEGEND OF STOR

* * *

The ships did not immediately appear on the horizon. They slowly emerged from the sun's glare over the expanse of ocean and gradually took on recognizable forms. Ships, in themselves, were not a cause for alarm. For centuries seagoing traders had plied their trade along the coast of Britain and from across the sea, bringing all manners of goods from continental Europe, and beyond, to seek out the lucrative market in the ports of Northumbria. But what Aldwyn was seeing today came as a yet unidentified fear of something greatly amiss. Aldwyn rose immediately and began rounding up his sheep. As he was doing so, it dawned on him; there were far too many ships. Traders travelled alone or sometimes in pairs and even in fleets as large as six vessels. This armada involved at least thirty wind powered vessels. Their large sails glided them across the water, directly towards Lindisfarne. As they rapidly drew nearer, Aldwyn could see that they were not only being driven by the wind, but dozens of oars protruding from the sides of each ship propelling their headlong progress. Aldwyn had only just broken into a run when the ships drew close enough for him to see that the occupants of the ships were all fully armed with glittering swords and fearsome axes and from their gunwales hung wildly painted war shields, as if to proclaim their ill intentions.

The fiery dragons were not only a portent of famine. They were a portent of an invasion which would change forever the way of life in Anglo-Saxon Britain. Aldwyn opened his mouth and screamed.

As Aldwyn dashed down the gentle slope that lead to the land bridge connecting Lindisfarne Island to the coast, all thoughts of his sheep were gone. He had but one mission and that was to warn the inhabitants of the abbey of the impending danger. As he ran, the ships drew nearer. He could now clearly see that these were not the ships of traders. Instead of the short, wide draught merchant ships, these were long, sleek vessels which skimmed the water rapidly driven by wind and oars. Their prows were adorned with massive carved replicas of fearsome beast. There were dragons, wolves, eagles and assorted serpents, all with mouths full of terrifying fangs, poised to inflict serious wounds to those who might oppose them.

On the nearest ships, Aldwyn could make out rough-clad men wearing chain mail armour. Their leather helmets, which were coated with metal, caught the sunlight and created a glimmering spectacle. This spectacle was further enhanced by the huge metal axes and swords which were waved aloft by these specters. They were large, rough looking men, whose golden hair danced in the wind where it protruded from beneath their mail studded leather helmets. Along the gunnels of their ships hung multi-coloured shields bearing the likeness of dragons, bears, wolves and other fearsome creatures, complimenting the fearsome beasts on each prow.

Aldwyn was now on the land bridge, closer now to the monastery with its collection of out buildings and fenced corrals. His shouts were being heard and monks were beginning to stream out of the buildings to discover the source of the commotion. They were, for the most part, poorly armed, content in the peace and security that had long prevailed on the Holy Island.

* * *

The assault on Lindisfarne was swift and brutal. The Vikings quickly leapt from their boats into knee deep waters and raced up the shore before the monks could muster any semblance of a defense. The attack was a complete surprise. While it would be followed by centuries of relentless Viking attacks on the inhabitants of Britain, this was the first. Some of the monks had attempted to hold their ground. They formed a wall behind their shields and raised their swords against the onslaught of the invaders. The Vikings, too, formed a shield wall, which proceeded methodically forward towards the waiting defenders, screaming cries of certain victory and setting up a terrifying frenzy by clashing their war swords and axes against their shields.

A shield wall was a fearsome thing to see. The opponents hold their shields in a manner that each man's shield is touching the shield of his comrades on either side in order to protect both themselves and those in the ranks behind them. When the two walls meet there is a mighty crash. The sounds of shouting and clattering of weapons against shields is replaced by a grunting as men on each side pushed against their opponent's wall, attempting to create a breach. The killing is limited as long as the respective walls hold. But if a wall falters and is breeched, the slaughter begins in earnest.

When the two shield walls collided, Viking superiority became overwhelmingly apparent. Christian swords broke and shields splintered. While the monks were competent to thwart attacks from small bands of marauding bandits, they were neither armed nor trained to face such an assault as this. Their primitive weapons clanged harmlessly against the Viking shields and the mighty barbarian sword and axes quickly felled all resistance. The monks' wall of resistance faltered then broke. All who did not retreat were slaughtered immediately. Many of the others were chased down and slain as they fled. The end of the battle came swiftly and absolutely.

Once subduing the defenders, the raiders swarmed into the buildings in search of loot. The Kingdom of

Northumbria had, by now, emerged as one of the wealthiest kingdoms of Europe and Lindisfarne was a treasure trove of art, precious minerals and gems. These were quickly claimed by the invaders who then turned their attention to wanton destruction. Furniture was smashed. Several blows of axes demolished the chapel's main altar. The precious remains of the departed saints of the Holy Island were dragged from their shrines, strewn about the litter and stomped upon. When the destruction was complete, the raiders gathered their loot. With a dozen healthy young captives in chains and as much livestock as they could readily corral, the raiders casually returned to the vessels which had brought them, and sailed back over the horizon from which they had appeared, leaving Lindisfarne in flames.

The Viking raid on the Holy Island of Lindisfarne shocked and horrified all of Christian Europe. These raiders were from a part of Scandinavia now called Denmark. They did not call themselves Vikings. That was the name given to them by their victims. It meant raiders or pirates. But they were the first of a wave of Scandinavian invaders and colonizers who would terrorize the British Isles and much of continental Europe for centuries to come. The Viking era had arrived.

* * *

As consciousness return to Aldwyn, he was not sure where he was or what had happened. He did not even know if he was dead or alive or how long he had been in this condition. He raised his head slightly, only to see the pool of blood on the ground and covering the sleeve of his tunic. Rapid investigation revealed that it was his blood and that it was flowing from the top of his head and coagulating in his matted hair. This revelation brought with it the realization that he was indeed alive and that a searing pain felt as if it were splitting his head apart.

As awareness expanded, he began to comprehend that his injuries were not as severe as he initially feared. Memories began to slowly emerge. He had not yet reached the monastery when the first wave of raiders descended upon it. Closest to him was a burly beast with a golden mane, a massive sword, hard, cold blue eyes and a chilling merciless smile that was only interrupted by a bloodcurdling, incomprehensible scream which shattered the air around them. The savage raised his fearsome sword above his head as he ran at Aldwyn. Aldwyn was armed only with a wooden stave but he was resolved to hold his ground. He raised the stave and swung with all of his strength, but the stave crashed harmlessly against the raider's shield. The Viking, caught in the mid-swing of his massive sword, was taken off-guard and stumbled slightly sideways. Not enough, however, for the sword to miss its target. Fortunately, in stumbling, the sword turned in his grip and, instead of cleaving Aldwyn's skull, the Viking slammed the flat side of the blade against Aldwyn's head. It connected solidly and rendered Aldwyn unconscious before his body reached the ground. Blackness had engulfed him. Assuming him dead, the Viking turned his attention to other targets for his hungry sword.

Aldwyn did not dwell long on his condition. Around him swirled the disheveled retreat of the survivors of the Viking attack. The raiders were preoccupied with loading the prizes from their rampaging and getting under sail before warriors from Bamburgh Castle could arrive. Over all of the shouting and commotion Aldwyn could hear Bishop Higbald imploring the survivors to protect the remains of St. Cuthbert.

* * *

In the year 685 AD a humble and devout Christian monk, with a solid reputation for healing the sick and causing other miracles to occur, was appointed Bishop of Lindisfarne. His name was Cuthbert. Part of his mandate was to convert Northumbria from a colloquial form of Ionian Christianity to that of the Church of Rome. His incorruptible piousness presented little threat to the country's rulers and therefore it became generally accepted that the Church of Rome would possess the ultimate Christian authority, but would consult with the Royal Court prior to appointing bishops. Likewise the Court would consult with the Church before enacting laws or taxes which would impact the church.

In his role as bishop, Cuthbert's stature continued to grow to the point that, upon his death and canonization, he became the most revered saint in Britain. Thousands made pilgrimages to Lindisfarne to pray before his coffin and many miracles were credited to such prayer. Lindisfarne flourished as a centre of religion and its grand library made it a centre of learning throughout the kingdom. Even the noted Anglo-Saxon chronicler, Bede, came to Lindisfarne to write and study. Lindisfarne became the Holy Island and St. Cuthbert became Britain's most adored saint.

* * *

The attack on Lindisfarne, therefore, was not only the most substantial attack on Britain since the establishment of Anglo-Saxon hegemony, but it was an attack both on the centre of Anglo-Saxon Christian spirituality and on the centre of Anglo-Saxon material wealth. Many still refer to this attack as the beginning of the Viking era in English history. While this may be true in many respects, this era became the forge in which the Britain was transformed into the English Nation. It was also from these flames that a man emerged who, along with his family, became entwined in the

THE LEGEND OF STOR

struggle that created England. His name was Stor, son of Eye, and his descendants would be known throughout the world as Storey.

VIKING SHIPS

PART ONE

| THE LABOUR |

CHAPTER 1
DEATH OF THE KINGDOM OF CUMBRIA

The horses cautiously pursue
Their way, without mishap or fault;
And now have reached that pile of stones
Heaped over brave Dunmail's bones;
His who had once supreme command,
Last king of rocky Cumberland;
His bones and those of all his power
Slain here in a disastrous hour!
-William Woodsworth, 1819

INTERLUDE

The attack by the Danish Vikings at Lindisfarne in 793 was the first of relentless attacks all along the Eastern and Southern coast of Britain. The initial attacks for plunder and slaves evolved into invasions for the purpose of colonization. Finally, in 866, a Dane, Ivar the Boneless, and his brothers, Halfdene and Hubba, led Danish invasion which successfully colonized East Anglia. The following year they swept through Northumbria. The old, already crumbling, Kingdom of Northumbria was completely destroyed and replaced with the new Danish Kingdom of Jorvik, which would eventually be known as York. The pagan Danes actively colonized York, Deira and Lancaster, but, while conquering Bernicia, and central and western Northumbria, they left the Anglo-Saxons in possession of their lands.

Halfdene succeeded his brother on Ivar's death in 873. He conquered Mercia and East Anglia and almost completed a sweep of the island by conquering most of Wessex. But a young King Alfred of Wessex delivered Halfdene a striking defeat. Alfred parlayed this victory into successes in East Anglia and Mercia and established his rule over the southern part of the island. Between Alfred of Wessex and Halfdene of York, the whole of Britain, as far north as Edinburg, was divided into England south of the Humber River and the Kingdom of York, which was known to the Anglo-Saxons as the Danelaw, in the north.

In 877, Halfdene died and was succeeded by Guthred. Guthred immediately led his army north into the land of the Scots, defeated them in battle and killed their king, Constantine I. With his northern frontier completely secure he then broke the peace and invaded the territory of King Alfred. However, in this venture he was defeated. Alfred successfully demanded that Guthred recognize the House of Wessex as the over-authority of York and all of its client kings. In exchange Alfred allowed Guthred to retain control over his extended Kingdom of York as a client king of Wessex. While Alfred's hold over these northern territories was very tentative, with the Danes continuing to do much as they pleased, Alfred did become the first king of all of what would become England.

This fragile pact ended in 899, when, in that same year, both Alfred and Guthred died. Alfred's heir, Edward, did not have his father's reputation and status. Guthred left no heirs whatsoever. Edward died in 913 and his sons began a contest for succession. The land was without a strong leader.

THE LEGEND OF STOR

***

CARLISLE, CUMBRIA, 945 AD

The Assembly was not due to commence for another hour. The group of young boys, about twenty in all, ranging in age from six to ten, had expended their initial energy chasing about in the boisterous play of children. They now sat in the dirt, carrying on a relaxed conversation. One of them asked, "So what has become of old King Dunmail? I hear that they murdered him."

Wanting to be part of the conversation I was quick to answer, "Edmund killed him with his own sword. And then they forced his soldiers to bury him under a cairn of stones."

"I heard that he escaped and his soldiers built the cairn of stones so that the Saxons would believe that he was dead. And then they spirited him into hiding." Another offered.

"What of his sons?" yet another intervened. "My father told me that they blinded them with a hot poker and then gelded them like steers."

"That's right. One of them was seen on the road south, black holes where his eyes had been."

"I think the King is still alive. His own soldiers took his crown and threw it into the lake, Grizdale Tarn, so that the Saxons could not find it. One day he will return and fetch it and reclaim his kingdom."

And so it continued, spinning conflicting myths, which, like so many other myths arising out of the soil of Cumbria, remains unresolved, but celebrated, to this day. Indeed the spot was remembered and the cairn still remains undisturbed.

I was only seven years old when Cumbria was conquered and Dunmail was slain, but I remember well that day in Carlyle. *What he could not, at the time, comprehend was that he was witnessing the final chapter of a saga which, during his lifetime, would bring political hegemony to a country which would become England. It would also result in the creation of a clan that would bear his name.*

* * *

My name is Stor. I was born in 937 in York, of a Norse sword Viking named Eye, which, in the Norse language means "*sea*". My name, Stor, means "*vast*". My mother was Jenz, "*God's grace*". She was an Anglo-Saxon, born in Bernicia, north of York, in 920. She descended from a monk from Lindisfarne named Aldwyn whose descendants had gained considerable fame as master sword-makers. My mother died giving birth to me. I was her only offspring.

I spent the first three years of my life being nursed and raised in Bernicia by kinfolk of my mother. Just days after my third birthday, my father was slain in a battle to reclaim the throne of York for Olfa Guthricson. Upon his death, his father, my grandfather, Vidar, took charge of me and moved me to Deira in the Kingdom of York.

Vidar, my grandfather, is the only member of my family that I really remember. I recall his first telling me that, like my father, he too was a sword Viking. He had come here from Norway at the beckoning of Ivar ll, the king of Dublin, a Hiberno-Norse kingdom in Ireland. Ivar offered land in exchange for loyal sword arms to Vikings from Norway. Vidar, his four brothers and their families, were amongst those who answered this call. They received extensive land holdings in Cumbria, but at a terrible price.

War and disease have now taken Vidar's entire family save for me. And now, here we are together in Carlyle to discover whether it was all for naught.

THE LEGEND OF STOR

* * *

The official portion of assembly, which had drawn all of these people together, was scheduled for the morrow, when our new king, Duhb, of the House of Alpine, Crown Prince of Scotland, would announce his intentions upon his becoming ruler of Cumbria and Strathclyde. Today, however, the real work of negotiations would conclude and on the morrow King Duhb will simply be formalizing the results of these discussions.

We were all assembled in the large stone hall which, I have since learned, had once been part of the ancient Roman fortress of Luguvalium. The Romans had built this fortress to house their garrison at the western end of Hadrian's Wall. After their departure, a succession of Cumbrian kings had used it as the capital of their kingdom, but wars between invading Anglos, Saxons, Scots and other Celtic regimes had left much of the fortress in ruin. The Church of St. Cuthbert and the large hall still remained intact and serviceable.

The representatives of the victorious forces of England and Scotland numbered only two dozen men, half of them dressed in their drab black cleric gowns, the other half dressed in the finery of Scottish and English nobility. Although facing a much larger number of those whom they had fought against just days ago, they appeared confident and comfortable. And well they should be. Stationed outside the hall were segments of the English forces along with almost all of the Scottish warriors who had fought and subdued us and slain our king. Vidar and I sat amongst approximately 100 men clad in heavy brown and grey woolen coats covering leggings and tunics of a similar material. We were of mixed backgrounds of Celtic, Norse, Danish, Scottish and Anglo and Saxon backgrounds. We represented the largest landholders in Cumbria and we were the defeated. Our king was dead and his court had fled. We were here to plead our case and await a declaration of our fate.

We all knew each other. The days leading up to this session had been occupied by extensive introductions by both sides, including who we were, what land we held and who we represented. The victors were led by a Kenneth Mac Innes, a large burly man with a thick crop of red hair, wildly framing his weathered face and a bushy red beard to match. He wore a skirt of various brown and grey plaids with thin strips of blue running intermittently through it in a regular pattern. His tunic was covered with an immense fur cloak, fastened with a large silver broach engraved with elaborate design. Kenneth stared challengingly at the assembled Cumbrians and snarled a self introduction.

"I represent both King Malcolm of Scotland and King Edmund of England who came together in common cause to put an end to the aggressive, uncivilized, and wanton calumny which has run rampant through this region. We have been successful. I would now like to hear from you as to why we should not foreclose your lands and hang you all as the filthy traitors that you are." As he lowered his haunches back onto the sturdy wooden bench, a hush of both fear and astonishment swept through the hall.

As they gathered their wits, our fellows began to find their voice to plead their innocence or for mercy. Finally a more dignified voice, dressed in priestly robes and crowned with his tonsure of holy identity was heard. Father Leo rose to his full height and in a soft, but firm, voice began, "Carlyle is my parish and these men here are the sheep of my fold. I am here to speak on their behalf and to ensure that the historical information which frames this discussion reflects the reality to which we all strive.

"For a millennium, armies have marched through Cumbria, but few have stayed. The barren windy climate, the weak soil and the ferocity of the Cumber inhabitants were not inviting. It was the home of the ancient Celtic people who called themselves the Cumber. Rome conquered Cumbria and reduced it to a client state, but they left the ancient kingdom intact. When, in 420, the Romans withdrew, and their empire collapsed, Coel Hen, known as Cole the Old was Rome's client king. (*His name gave rise to the contemporary children's poem, "Old King Cole".*) He simply continued on as king,

"The subsequent Anglo and Saxon invasions of Britain resulted in years of warfare which drove the Celts to the eastern fringes of Britain. But the Cumber successfully defended their domain, battling back not only the invading Anglos and Saxons and Scots, but also other Celtic kingdoms. In 530 AD a descendant of Coel Hen, Urien emerged as ruler of the northern portion of the old Celtic kingdom with a territory corresponding closely to the present Cumbria. Through the marriage of Urien's granddaughter, Riemmelth, to King Oswey of Northumbria, the independent Kingdom came under the rule of Anglo-Saxon Northumbria. Urien's descendants, however, carried on as client rulers of Cumbria. As the Kingdom of Northumbria began to unravel, Cumbria gained greater and greater independence. Although first, the Danes of York, then the Saxons of Wessex, claimed Cumbria as part of their respective kingdoms, the descendants of Cole Hen continued to rule with very little real challenge. The final holder of this kingdom was Dunmail, descended directly from Cole Hen, who ruled until you so recently deposed him.

"In short, Cumbria has been under the continuous rule of the descendants of Cole Hen since before the breakup of the Roman Empire, since before the creation of either Scotland or England, and therefore it is ludicrous to describe the supporters of Dunmail as traitors to either Scotland or England."

I was amazed at the depth and breadth of Father Leo's knowledge and his willingness to put it to use in this tense situation. He was obviously a very learned man.

Several other speakers rose to speak. Then, after some back and forth shouting, my grandfather rose to his feet. He was a tall, well-proportioned man with a long golden mane. While much of his hair was now white, it seemed more to highlight his blond locks rather than reveal aging. His mouth was framed by a bushy mustache that draped down his chin and matched the rest of his hair. Unlike his fellow petitioners, he wore his highly polished silver breast plate which gleamed as if in defiance of the conquerors. Even without his massive war axe (weapons were not allowed in the hall) he cut an imposing figure. I felt a shiver of pride flow through me knowing that this was my grandfather.

"I am Vidar of Norway." He stood tall and matched Mac Innes's challenge with a calm but confident demeanor. His voice was powerful and resonated clearly throughout the hall. "I, accompanied by my four brothers, came from Norway in the year 904, by your way of counting. At that time, an agreement existed between the Norse King Ivar of Dublin and Oswain, the king of Cumbria and Strathclyde through which the latter would welcome Norse sword Vikings to settle land in Cumbria and Strathclyde in exchange for pledging their swords in defense of Cumbria and Strathclyde. For doing so we each received twenty hides of land along the north banks of the River Eske. "

After each statement, Vidar paused and scanned the assembly to ensure that he was being heard and his words comprehended. "In 913, Ragnald, the King of Dublin, called upon our swords in order to establish an orderly government in Jorvik. Jorvik had been in chaos since the death of King Guthred in 899. At the invitation of the inhabitants of Jorvik, Ragnald took possession of the throne in Jorvik and was confirmed in that position by Witan of Northumbria. My brother and I accompanied Ragnald. King Ragnald eventually died and was succeeded by his nephew, Sihtric. When AEthelstan became King of England he acknowledged Sihtric's reign and gave Sihtric his sister in marriage. Since then, however, AEthelstan has pursued constant warfare against not only Jorvik and Cumber, but also against Scotland. We all stood side by side at the Battle of Brunanburg in which the last of my brothers was killed. My grandson who sits here beside me is the only kin that I have left alive. And now AEthelstan's brother and successor has again invaded Jorvik and Scotland. He then forced the support of Scotland and invaded Cumbria.

"Throughout these twenty-seven years my sword, and those of my brothers, while they lived, have honoured their pledges to the King of Dublin and Jorvik and honoured the agreement with the kings of Cumbria who have ruled this country continuously since the Romans departed. How can we be called traitors? Whom have we betrayed? And if we have not been traitors, under the English laws, to which your king has sworn fealty, our land cannot be confiscated. We have come by our land through the legitimate laws of Cumbria. Your invasion, justifiable or otherwise, cannot be used to depose us of what is rightfully ours."

Applause thundered throughout the hall as Vidar returned to his seat.

* * *

The assembly, which was to begin this afternoon, and which had brought me and my new playmates to Carlisle, was to be attended by Duhb, the new king of Cumbria and

Strathclyde. He was here to explain to the people of this region just what impact his ascension to the ancient throne would have on them. I had travelled here with my grandfather so that Vidar could attend the assembly. The other boys had also come to Carlisle with parents or grandparents for the same purpose. Most had not known each other before this morning, however, left to their own devises, while their elders renewed acquaintances amongst the many attendees, we had devised our own amusement and by midday we were thick as thieves. But now our various guardians were beginning to gather us up in order to share in family lunches before the assembly commenced.

Vidar selected a secluded shaded area in which we could enjoy our lunch without disturbance. He had brought with him a retinue of servants. They had prepared a meal for us and now began to serve it.

Vidar was also accompanied by a wise old sage, named Stigandr. He was a very ancient man with pale blue eyes, the translucence of which, seemed to allow one to gaze directly into his soul. He had a slender build, from which his skin hung like soft, weathered leather several sizes too large for his frame. But he had a kindly smile which lit up his face as Vidar introduced him. "This is Stigandr. He is well named as his name means 'wanderer' and I doubt that there are very many places which he has not visited or sights which he has not seen. I have retained him to help me more fully comprehend the strangers with whom we must now deal so that we may prosper in this land. He is very learned, has studied with all of the best skalds and has even studied the works of the important Anglo-Saxon chroniclers such as Bede."

While we ate, he inquired, "Do you understand the purpose of this assembly?" While I was only seven years of age, I have always had a sharp mind and my grandfather always attempted to involve me in discussion regarding the social and political dynamics which could impact our future. I have always been curious about issues such as this and am an attentive student when Grandfather talks about the origins of our family and their travails.

To Grandfather's question I deferentially replied, "I know that the Saxons of Wessex and the Scots joined forces and defeated King Dunmail. I know that King Edmund gave King Malcolm of the Scots authority over Cumbria and Strathcylde and that Malcolm appointed his son, Scotland's Crown Prince, Duhb, to be our new king. And I certainly heard and understood what you said in the great hall yesterday. But please tell me, what it will mean for us, Grandfather?"

My grandfather was a fascinating man. While he was certainly every inch a sword Viking, unlike his comrades-in-arms, he sought out very possible opportunity to learn. While his fellows sought out taverns for drink and debauchery, more often than not, he sought the company of learned men who could tell him of their history and culture. As a result, he was a fountain of knowledge which probably was the reason that Ragnald and his successors had been quick to place him in positions of leadership. And he loved to share his knowledge with me. For my part, I was like a sponge, absorbing all of the knowledge which he would impart.

"In order to know the answer to your question you must know the history of our family here in Cumbria." I knew that while the Danish Kingdom of York and the Anglo-Saxon Kingdom of Wessex were contending for the domination of Britain, Vikings from Norway (Norsemen) were sailing around the north and down the western shores of Britain, seeking their own pillage and colonies. They established colonies on the far north coast and on the Hebrides Islands. Eventually they founded a colony in Ireland which grew to become the Norse Kingdom of Dublin. Some sailed much farther west, establishing a colony which would become the country of Iceland. *From there they sailed even farther west, establishing colonies on what would come to be known as North America. But that is a different story. Some of these Norsemen sailed further south from Dublin, founding a colony on continental Europe which would become Normandy. But that would not impact Britain for another century to come.* It was the history of the Kingdom of Ireland to which my grandfather was referring.

"By the year 900 AD Ivar ll had become the Norse king of Dublin. The Norse kings of Dublin had actively encouraged colonists from Norway to settle, not only in Ireland, but also in the Western shores of Britain, primarily in Cumbria and Strathclyde. Meanwhile, the Scots and the Picts united into a single kingdom of Scotland under the House of Alpin. They were intent on conquering Strathclyde and their raids came far south into Cumbria. Ivar had pledged Norse support to the King of Cumbria and as a result, Cumbria welcomed Norse settlers in exchange for a pledge of their swords against the Scottish invaders. Thousands responded to this invitation, my brothers and I was amongst them.

"As you know, my boy" the old man continued, "I moved to this land from my native land of Norway. Many of my countrymen had left before me. We left there because there was available land here. I was a young man then, recently married. I wanted land on which myself and my new wife could raise children in peace. King Ivar was offering land in exchange for the use of swords. My brothers and I were all sword warriors, and so, along with my four brothers and their families, we moved to this land of Cumbria. I was eighteen years of age and just married. Your grandmother was pregnant with our first child, your uncle."

Stigandr then picked up the tale. "When Vidar and his family migrated here, the land knew peace. But Ivar knew that peace would not last and he would be prepared when it ended. Alfred of Wessex and Guthred of York, who between them had held the peace together, both died in 899 as the Christians count the date. That was the year that Ivar put out his call for sword Vikings to migrate here from Norway."

Vidar then resumed, "me and my four brothers were each given small tracts of land. We came in peace. We did not seek the land already in use. We took unused and unbroken land and began to break it. Jointly we supported each other and assisted in defending against the plundering Scots. Your grandmother gave birth to your father, his two brothers and two sisters. We lost three others at birth or in their infancy".

Again it was Stigandr's turn. "While the Scots were still a largely disconnected number of clans, they did recognize a single king and they had a shared opinion of what they considered to be their collective land. When the Romans were here in Britain, the Roman emperor, Hadrian, had a wall build clear across the land in order to protect his northern border. You saw that wall as you travelled to Carlisle. It divides Cumbria from Strathclyde. While it has never been a border, even in Roman times, because the Romans stretched their empire hundreds of miles north of the wall, the Scots still tend to see that wall as their southern border and the Alpens who rule the Scots have all along been prepared to fight to make that a reality.

"In the year 905 the Scots launched a major attack against the Norse in Strathclyde They were successful and they killed King Ivar. Vidar's family was pledged to support Ivar and, as a result, was in the centre of the struggle."

Vidar continued, "We lost many men in that battle, including two of my brothers. Many of our women and children were slaughtered as the Scots pillaged northern Cumbria. One of my two surviving brothers Alv took his family and joined other Norse families who sailed south and established a new Norse community, now known as Normandy. The remains of our family became refugees in southern Cumbria.

"Emboldened by the Scots' defeat of the Dublin Norse in Strathclyde, the Celtic Irish took up arms against the stronghold in Dublin itself. In 910 they were successful in driving the Norse completely out of Ireland. The new Norse king, Ragnald, evacuated his army to Cumbria. From here he gathered both his Dublin and Cumbrian followers and, by 913, he had regained his Kingdom of Dublin. He then crossed the Irish Sea with a large army, recruited more when he landed here, and swept through Cumbria and Strathclyde, exacting vengeance. Your father, uncle and I all joined him. We then crossed Northumbria and attacked the Kingdom of York. We had great support from Danes and even many of the Anglo-Saxons in York who longed for a Northumberland independent from Wessex control. But the Bernicians and the Scots joined forces and defeated us.

"Ragnald retreated to Dublin, but in 918 he returned, and this time we overthrew the forces of York. Ragnald established himself as the King of both Dublin and York. In York he was received with open arms. In order to retain the support of the Danes, Ragnald refused to seize any Danish land holdings. Instead, he confiscated large tracts of land from a group of Christians, known as the Community of St. Cuthbert in Chester-le-Street. These lands he distributed to his warriors. I received a grant of some of this land. Under Ragnald's rule, the remnants of our family regrouped on our lands in Cumbria and for the next several years we enjoyed a relative peace in Cumbria." The old man paused, apparently lost momentarily in the remembrances of his younger days.

THE LEGEND OF STOR

* * *

Vidar fell quiet as we finished the remains of our lunch. Then he continued. "Ragnald kept Wessex at bay by recognizing their authority over York, but in virtually all matters, he maintained York's sovereignty. In 920 Ragnald died and was succeeded by his cousin, Sihtric, who, on his death was succeeded by his son Guthrith.

Stigandr then spoke, "In 924 Wessex appointed a strong leader, capable of restoring Alfred's legacy. This was Alfred's grandson, AEthelstan. He was aware of his tenuous hold on the north. In 927 he demanded a conference with his subordinate kings in the north so that they might renew their pledges to him. The Kings of the Scots, York, Strathclyde and the Earl of Bernicia were invited. All except King Guthrith attended and submitted to AEthelstan. AEthelstan interpreted Guthrith's absence as a repudiation of his loyalty and sent his army against him. We all fought in Guthrith's army, but we were unsuccessful. Guthrith was defeated and expelled from the throne of York, which AEthelstan then claimed as his own. Vidar's brother, one of your two remaining uncles, died in that battle.

"But AEthelstan was not content to simply subject York to Wessex. He was in pursuit of the dream of his grandfather, Alfred, to create a united Christian Kingdom of England. His first step was to make a pilgrimage to the shrine of St. Cuthbert at Chester-le-Street. While there, he reinstated to the Community of St. Cuthbert some of the land which Ragnald had seized. Some of that land belonged to your family. You still have some of that land, but only a fraction of what was originally granted by King Ragnald.

It was again Vidar's turn. "In 937 AEthelstan became suspicious of the loyalties of the Scottish king, Constantine l. This was partially because Guthrith's son, Ofla, married the daughter of Constantine. And so AEthelstan sent his army in to Scotland against Constantine. Ofla came to the support of Constantine and we joined Ofla in this battle. In 937 AEthelstan won a decisive battle against our combined forces of Scots and Norsemen. Ofla returned to Dublin and we again became fugitives in Northumbria. Your remaining uncle was killed in that battle.

"In 939 AEthelstan died. Ofla Guthrithson immediately returned from Dublin and claimed his father's throne of York. Again we fought beside Ofla and were successful in placing Olfa on the throne. However, in this battle your father was killed. You were only three years old at the time. I will speak more of this later.

"On Ofla's death, his brother, Blacair became the King of York.

"Last year Edmund, Athelstan's successor as King of England, decided to end Guthrithson control in Northumbria. First he invaded York and deposed Blacair. He then concluded a treaty with the new Scots king, Malcolm, who joined in his attack on the Norse and the Cumbrians here. As you know, they were successful. They defeated Dunmail and in exchange for his continuing pledge, Edmond granted King Malcolm client authority over Cumbria and Strathcylde. Malcolm, in turn, has made his son and heir, Duhb, our king.

"I tell you these things, Stor, because you must know of the responsibilities which will someday soon fall upon your shoulders. I came here with my family to acquire land. And we did that. But we did it at a terrible price. I am not bitter. These things happen. They are our fate. I was taught that three maidens are seated at the foot of the Tree of Life. They have been there since time began. They spend eternity weaving threads, each of which represents a human life. What they weave is our fate. When they choose to sever a thread, that life ends. You and I are the only members of my family left alive. I do not have many years remaining in my life. When I go, it will fall to you to hold our land and to raise a family that will benefit from it for generations to come. If this does not happen, we will have made these sacrifices for naught." His voice trailed off as he finished, his mind obviously lost in thought of past triumphs and tragedies while I struggled to comprehend the enormity of what I'd just been told.

"But I would be a warrior like you and my father. I have little aspiration to become a farmer," I complained.

Grandfather gave me a knowing frown. "I know that being a warrior sounds romantic and exciting to you, but if you follow that path it will be our undoing. Eventually we will all be killed. That is the fate of warriors. I am a rare exception. And the outcome of such folly will be the end of my line. You are now the only one left and if you are killed, my line will end. All that we have sacrificed for will die with you. It will all have been for naught. We may just as well have remained in Norway. No, my son, that way of life must end. I am far too old to become anything but a warrior. That is what I am. But you are young and so it falls to you to use our land and produce a family that will be able to hold it. That is the only way that our progeny may prosper."

I nodded my consent, but my heart was not in it.

"Come," his grandfather finally said, "they are assembling now. Let us go and hear what our new king has to say." Together we rose and walked towards the assembling crowd.

* * *

After the requisite fanfare and introductions, Duhb, surrounded by brightly garbed nobles and dour black robed clergy, rose to address the audience. He looked the part of royalty; standing erect, his eyes full of confidence beyond his youth. His sandy coloured hair was worn short and his beard neatly trimmed. "Greetings fellow citizens of Cumbria," he began. "As you are all aware, the old king, Dunmail, challenged the authority of our sovereign lord, King Edmund of England and allied himself with the Pagan Norsemen against us. With the help of my father, King Malcolm of Scotland, and our Lord Jesus Christ, we met the rebel in battle and defeated him."

A murmur swept through the crowd at this portrayal of King Dunmail and his actions. But Duhb moved on. "I am now your king. I have not come here today to dwell on the past, but rather to look to the future and how we may live in peace and harmony with each other. As you know, my own family, the House of Alpine, was originally Daldrian, we migrated here from Ireland. Long before that we lived on this island since before the memory of man. Now we are part of a united Scotland. Many of you are descendants of the old Kingdom of Rheged. Some of you are descendants of the Romans who once lived here. Others of your ancestors came here with the migration of Anglos and Saxons. Yet others of your ancestors are from Denmark and Norway. Most of you have the blood of many of these different peoples. But now we are one Christian kingdom and our kingdom is united with all of these other kingdoms of England under the overall protection of King Edmund from the House of Wessex, his laws and by our Holy Church. There is no longer any reason for us to war with each other. We can now live in peace and harmony as Christian brothers, as was ordained by our God.

"Dunmail is dead. There is no reason for further reprisals for his treason and therefore none shall be taken. With the exception of the personal estates of Dunmail, which are by right the property of the crown and shall remain property of the crown, along with the property of pagans, who have no claim to land in a Christian kingdom. All Christians who held land under the old regime shall continue to enjoy their ownership. Only land which is unoccupied or unclaimed by one of our Christian subjects shall become parts of our crown lands which shall be distributed at our pleasure." The audience warmed at this announcement. Relief was obvious on many faces in the congregation.

"We will live under the protection of my father, King Malcolm. He, in turn, will reign under the protection and the laws of King Edmund of Wessex. This island will enjoy peace and prosperity under a common set of laws. These laws will be based upon the written laws of England. My responsibility is to ensure that there is peace in this kingdom and to ensure transgressions of our laws are dealt with swiftly but justly. There will be no more trials by ordeal. Petitions before our court must be supported by evidence, not by witchcraft. Before I depart from here this week I will appoint a sheriff and a magistrate and mandate them accordingly. I will also hear outstanding grievances and ensure that they are dealt with equitably."

King Duhb continued on for an hour outlining the details of his intentions. But he had already won the support of the assembly. When he finished a single voice was joined by the multitude crying out, "God save the King." The days of an independent Cumbria were gone forever.

As the congregation was moving away, Vidar, obviously happy with the outcome of the assembly, said to me, "This session today raised some issues which require my immediate attention which I must attend to. I will meet you back here for our supper and advise you as to where things stand."

CHAPTER 2
THE MANDATE

After Vidar had departed to attend to his business, I spent the next several hours strolling through the ruins of the old Carlisle Castle and imagining, with wonderment, the events which had transpired there over the years of its majestic history. There were many pilgrims wandering through the ruins and I listened to local folk relate their knowledge of its history. I was soon well versed in both Cumbrian history and mythology and the castle, even in ruins, was the embodiment of both. The southern part of Cumbria was covered with pristine lakes surrounded by lush rolling fertile hills. It is known to this day as the Lakes District. But it was here in the rugged northern regions, with its windblown rocky crags and its fog enshrouded marshlands, that the most enduring mythology was born.

The island of Britain is cleaved on its western coast by Solway Firth which extends far inland. A line running from the eastern tip of the firth through to the North Sea marks the northern limits of the early Roman conquest of Britain. The Roman Emperor, Hadrian, ordered a wall to be constructed across the entirety of the island to protect his colony to the south from the fierce Celtic tribes of the north. While the Romans later were to extend their conquest far to the north, Hadrian's Wall has endured to this day and will play a continuous role in English/Scottish history. To garrison the western end of this line of defense, the Romans, on this site which I now stood, and which they called Luguvalium, constructed a mighty fortress. The Castle was magnificent in its size, its strength and its beauty. *It would dominate the landscape for centuries to come. Its magnificence was such, that later chroniclers and story tellers, would credit it as the inspiration for Camelot of Arthurian legend fame.*

After the withdrawal of the Romans from Britain, Luguvalium became the capital of the old Rheged Kingdom, which they named Caer Luel, later to become Carlisle. It was the site of many battles between the Cumber, the Celtic people of Rheged, and the Anglo invaders. *It remains unclear as to whether the Arthurian legends are based upon Romans defending themselves against various Celtic tribes, the Cumber defending against Anglo invaders or the Anglo-Saxon controlled Cumbria defending against Vikings, or a combination of all of these.* In all cases the invaders are portrayed as Godless pagans invading Arthur's Christian kingdom, defended by noble and chivalrous knights riding black horses which sound very like the Fell ponies for which Cumbria is famous. Grandfather and I had travelled to Carlisle on those same breed of Fell ponies.

Regardless, I would learn that over time, Luguvalium was breeched and sacked. The ruins, however, remained and on this afternoon, I was examining them and imagining their glory. Many of the old stories have been preserved in the songs of the writer Taliesin, a minstrel for the great Rheged king, Urien. Urien had led a united Celtic army to victory against the invading Anglo-Saxon forces before Rheged was eventually absorbed through marriage into the Kingdom of Northumbria. Taliesin's songs are preserved in a document called *The Red Book of Hergest*. I knew many of the songs of Taliesin and sung them to myself as I strolled through the ruins. My imagination soared as I recreated images of heroic adventure acted out on the magnificent sight of this now ruined fortress.

Today, some believe that even Tolkien used the myths and fables surrounding the old Rheged Kingdom to fashion Middle Earth in his monumental trilogy, Lord of the Rings. Tolkien attributed much of his legends of Middle Earth to origins in a book he called the Red Book of Westmarch, bearing a striking resemblance to the name of Taliesin's book.

* * *

On tiring of this adventure, I turned back towards the assembly place. On the route I noticed the Church of St. Cuthbert. It was a beautiful old stone structure with a façade which housed a number of imposing statues. I stopped to examine some of the fine art work incorporated into its construction. Intrigued by the exterior I decide to also explore inside. Inside I spotted a tall well groomed youth slightly older than myself. He heard me enter and turned to look in my direction. As our eyes met, I immediately felt a sense of recognition, but for the life of me, I could not remember ever having laid eyes on him before. As he approached, he surveyed me from head to toe. Eventually he asked, "what brings you to St. Cuthbert's Church?'

"I have been attending the assembly here," I replied. "Since it disbanded I have been sight- seeing in Carlisle. Did I not see you there amongst King Duhb's entourage?"

"Yes, I was there. My father is the king's arms bearer, Fairburne."

"You are a Scot then?" I inquired.

"No, my name is Ian mac Fairburne. My father's families are mostly Anglos from Bernicia. We are descended from the famous weapons maker, Aldwyn of Lindisfarne. Since him, most of my ancestors have all been smiths and weapons makers."

"I am Stor son of Eye. I live with my grandfather thirty miles east of here on the Eske River. We have just moved there from York to claim lands which were granted to my grandfather and his family for their support to Ragnald and Guthrithson."

As I spoke, I saw an expression of amazement spreading over the face of this young recent acquaintance. "What is it?" I quickly demand.

"Who was your mother?" he responds

"Jenz of Bernicia."

MacFairburne's amazement rapidly dissolved into a broad smile. Chuckling he said, "So you are little Stor. You are my cousin. Your mother and my father were sister and brother. Your mother died giving birth to you. My father often talks of your mother and you. He was very fond of her."

My head was swirling. I had not seen any of my mother's kin folk since my father was killed. And now, standing in front of me, was a relative, a cousin. The family resemblance was there, explaining the sense of familiarity when I first saw him. I was still tongue-tied as he spread his arms and embraced me. "It is so nice to meet you, my little cousin."

We chatted amicably for a long while about our respective families and shared relatives. During that time, Ian revealed that our common ancestor, Aldwyn, had lived at Lindisfarne when the Vikings had first attacked there. He told me about how St Cuthbert was from Lindisfarne and how the Community of St. Cuthbert had eventually fled from there. He told me how, years before, Cuthbert had travelled to Carlisle and had performed miracles right on the spot where we were standing and that was why the church was so named. I was fascinated as Ian explained his interest in St. Cuthbert based on Aldwyn's connection to Lindisfarne. He seemed to enjoy sharing his extensive knowledge of the acts of St Cuthbert and the many miracles attributed to him.

He told me about how the Community of St. Cuthbert was made up of the monks from Lindisfarne and was the custodians of the remains of Cuthbert. When the Vikings finally drove them from Lindisfarne they had wandered extensively throughout Northumbria, now Jorvik, seeking a new appropriate resting place for Cuthbert, where pilgrims could visit his remains. Many people claimed miraculous cures as a result of prayer before the holy man's remains.

He continued his story with enthusiasm. "When the Vikings conquered Northumbria and established their Kingdom of Jorvik they allowed Bernicia to remain a client kingdom under Anglo-Saxon rule. They sought a positive relationship with a passive Anglo-Saxon neighbor to their north, creating a buffer between themselves as their fierce Scottish enemies. As a result, the Earl of Bernicia and King Guthred of Jorvik created an independent homeland for the Community of St. Cuthbert between their respective borders. It is a very sacred place. Even King AEthelstan and King Edmund both made pilgrimages to pray before the shrine where St. Cuthbert's remains are resting.

While I had heard much of this story before, it had always been from priests who were trying to convince me of the superiority of their God over the Norse Gods of the Vikings. But this time it was coming from, not only a layperson, but a relative.

"So you must be a Christian?" I asked.

"Are you not?" he responded. Then, without waiting for a response, he plunged into a dissertation on the glory of the Christian God and his son, Jesus. How, through their love and mercy they had promised salvation to mankind from the fiery torments of an eternal damnation. It was the same dour forecast that I had heard from the joyless priests in York in which all things involving fun and enjoyment were sins and transgressions which would condemn us, but from which we could be saved by the Christian Church. But Ian was not dour like the priests. He was pleasant and refrained from preaching at me. He simply related his beliefs in a straightforward of manner, as though these truths were undeniably self-evident.

I finally blurted out that I too had been baptized by the Christian Church; however I certainly lacked his enthusiasm in this confession.

In spite of our divergent views on the issue of Christianity, I liked this boy and was pleased that he was my kinsman. Eventually, however, the sun began its descent in the skies and the dinner hour approached. We parted, wishing each other well, both aware that we both would be late for our evening meals.

* * *

When I was again reunited with my grandfather, all thoughts of the purpose of coming to Carlisle were eclipsed by my excitement of my meeting my Christian cousin. My description of our encounter pre-empted anything that Vidar may have had to say. When I finally completed my tale, Vidar simply smiled and said, "Well that is a good lead into what I am about to tell you. This morning while you played, I too was baptized as a Christian."

Nothing in my short life so far had ever shocked me as much as this declaration. "But Grandfather, you are a Viking. You have always relished the Norse gods. How can you even think about deserting them?"

"Relax my boy," he chuckled." I am not deserting anything. We Norse have many Gods. I am simply adding one more. But I am doing it for a reason and that is what I must talk to you about.

"The sun is setting on the Viking era in Britain. It is still far from being extinguished, but it is waning and we must be prepared for its final demise. We have come here from Denmark and Norway in the thousands. But there are no long term Scandinavian communities anywhere in Britain. We now speak their English language, dress and eat as they do, build the same kinds of house, marry their women, and most importantly, we worship their Christian God. Many of those who still recognize the Old Norse gods have also been baptized as Christians. Now all of Northumbria will come under Anglo-Saxon law. And it will be impossible to own land unless one is a Christian. That is what our new King Duhb declared today. Christians will be allowed to retain the land which they owned before the war with Dunmail. Pagans will not.

"That was the subject of the business from which I just returned. Stigandr and I were meeting with the new sheriff whom Duhb appointed. I am now the owner of all the lands granted to me, my brothers and all of their offspring, both here in Cumbria and in Dun Holm. As you are my sole heir and you are a baptized Christian, we will retain ownership of all of our land. Part of the deal depended on my becoming baptized as a Christian." And so I beat them to it." With that he winked and whispered to me, "Don't look so worried. I will continue to wear Thor's amulet around my neck, but I will hide it under my tunic. You, though, must promise to be with me when I die, in order to ensure that my sword is in my hand so that I will be welcomed when I arrive at Odin's banquet hall. And you must promise to send me on my way there in a blazing pier. I have no desire to have my old bones rot in the grounds of a Christian churchyard speculating upon some promised resurrection to some Christian heaven."

With that he rose and went off to prepare our evening meal, leaving his servants to ponder their role. While Vidar had brought a retinue of household servants along on this trip, he was still an old sword warrior, coveting his independence and therefore often preparing his own meals while his staff stood by uncomfortably watching but receiving no encouragement to join him. My eyes remained fixed to the ground pondering the words which he had just spoken. It worried me that Vidar was taking this baptism in such a cavalier manner. It was simply not true that the Christian God was just one more god which could be incorporated into a host of our ancient Norse gods. The beliefs attributed to them were diametrically opposed to the teachings of the Christian priests.

The Norse religion taught that there were many gods who spent their days feasting, drinking, debauching or warring with each other and thoroughly enjoying themselves in all of these pursuits. And the Gods had created men for their amusement. They expected men to carry out these same pursuits and laughed at human folly as we attempted to imitate these behaviours. At the foot of the Tree of Life sat the spinners, spinning a weave in which each strand represented the life of one person. Their life unfolded as the spinners guided the weave and it ended when the strand was broken. All was predetermined. All a man could hope for was that the gods would know his sword or his ax by the number of souls which it had dispatched to Valhalla and, if that man were lucky, and that sword or ax were clutched in his hand at the time of his death, he would be welcomed into Odin's banquet hall. There he would spend eternity feasting, drinking and debauching while he regaled friend and foe alike about his conquests and his follies while he was on earth. There was no purpose to a man's life; all was predetermined by the spinners' weave.

Already I had learnt that, for the Christians, it was all purpose. God created man for his own glory. He gave man a free will to follow him or to pursue earthly delights. All of the activities which gave meaning and joy to the life of a Norseman, or his gods, were considered sinful and the Christian God would hold him accountable at the end of his life. He would either be cast into an eternal fire with all other sinners or he would be welcomed to spend eternity with the souls of these dour, joyless priests. Given that choice, I believe that Vidar would probably choose the eternal fire.

For myself, I believe that, even at my young age at the time, I had decided to throw my lot with the Christians. In spite of the incredible attraction I find to the adventures of life as a Viking, I have considered that I and my Grandfather are all of our family who has survived this life of adventure. The price may have already been too high. I am not certain what the future will hold for my grandfather if he tries to straddle both of these divergent philosophies. However, like him, I still wear my Viking amulet on a chain beneath my tunic and I still fantasize about the joys and excitement of being a Viking warrior.

* * *

We ate supper in silence. When we were finished, Vidar and Stigandr picked up on our earlier discussion. "As I told you earlier, the English will eventually rule this island. I have watched these English since coming here and I have talked to many people who were here before me. They are an amazing people. I do not fully understand why they continue to exist. When Ivar the Boneless attacked this land, he swept across it like a fire in a strong wind. He was invincible. He reduced the Anglo-Saxon resistance to only a minute part of the tiny Kingdom of Wessex and outnumbered Wessex's army by tenfold. And so I ask myself, why was he unable to defeat them. And the only answer that I can find was in the Wessex king, Alfred. He turned the tide on Ivar and his brothers, Hubba and Halfdene, and drove them out of Wessex, East Anglia, Mercia and the low lands and eventually forced Halfdene himself to swear fealty to him even in York. How could he have done this? All I can attribute it to is that he was aided by his Christian God. He was a zealous follower of the Christian god. Their own church claims that the initial Danish victories here were the result of them deserting their God and their church.

"And then I look at the Norse victories after Alfred's death and along came his grandson, AEthelstan, also a fervent Christian who again drove back us Norsemen along with the Danes, Scots, Cumber and anyone else who failed to support him. Strong Gods these Wessex men pray to. Look at the miracles attributed to St. Cuthbert and the way he was able to bring this whole island into the fold of this Christian Church of Rome and how quickly after his death the Kingdom of Northumbria and even the Abbey at Lindisfarne fell into our hands when they deserted the teachings of their church. And what did AEthelstan do immediately after defeating us at York? He went directly to the shrine of St. Cuthbert; paid homage there and then reinstated much of the land that Ragnald had seized from the Community of St. Cuthbert. It is a powerful God that can make these things happen. Do not trivialize him, Stor."

Stigandr then spoke. "The English relationship to their church is a complicated one. At one time Christianity in Northumbria was accountable to the king of Northumbria. He appointed the bishops, and therefore could ultimately control the church. The Christian church, in the rest of

Europe was directed from Rome. There were other more minor differences in their teaching. It was decided to resolve these issues in a major conference held in the monastery at Whitby, away back in the year 664 by the Christian way of counting. Supporters of the Roman Church won out. Within a year a man named Wilfred, a supporter of Roman authority, was appointed Archbishop of Northumbria. He used his authority to challenge the king by unilaterally selecting his own bishops and parish priests. This led to a serious struggle between Bishop Wilfred and the king, whose name was Ecgrith. Despite strong support from their Pope in Rome, Wilfred was forced to withdraw.

"In Wilfred's place the famed Cuthbert was appointed Bishop of Lindisfarne. While the Pope selected Cuthbert it was Ecgrith himself who consecrated Cuthbert as Bishop. In short, a compromise was made that would ensure that neither the king nor the pope would act unilaterally in the selection of Bishops. In exchange, the Pope would be consulted in the selecting of any heir to the throne unless it was a succession of the royal born crown prince. And the church would consecrate the coronation of any new king. Cuthbert did not simply do his miracles. He sold this relationship to the Anglo-Saxons. Wessex inherited this church. Alfred converted the relationship into a partnership in which the English Christian Church is a partner in ruling England. And Alfred built upon that partnership. Not only did he appoint priests to his witan, they were also amongst his most prominent advisors.

"There is another very important thing that Alfred did. These Anglo-Saxons were not always one people. They had many different kingdoms here in Britain. Over time some grew while others waned. They all spoke the same basic language, *Englisc* but it was spoken in four very different dialects of which West Saxon (Wessex) was but one.

As Alfred expanded Wessex control he codified all law into one central set of laws which were written in West Saxon English. This forced everybody, under his regency, to speak English if they had land ownership, deeds or wills to record, to do so in English. Anyone with business before his courts had to speak English. Even his church, while retaining Latin, was required to be fluent in English, because they were the source of scribes and the source of literacy education. In many cases they also presided over the administration of the king's justice. All of this required English literacy. Alfred's successors continued his policy as they consolidated their control over more and more of Britain.

"Language is a strange and powerful thing. When translating from one language to another, many meanings are not translatable because they contain ideas and attitudes which are distinct to one language and foreign to the other. By enforcing English on all of Britain the Wessex kings have forced their views on all of their subjects. We may be Norse by birth but, more and more, we are coming to understand ourselves through our new English eyes. What we have seen in my lifetime, on this island, is a transformation of Britain into the nation of England, ruled by the Wessex kings. Regardless of who conquers this land in the future, this land will be England."

Vidar again picked up the discussion. "So it is in this country called England that our future exists. I have a plan that will ensure our survival, but I am old and soon there will be only you to implement this plan. So I must insure that you are ready to do so. You must learn to read and write in English and you will learn the ways of their religion and that sense of purpose that it imparts. These tools will serve you well."

THE LEGEND OF STOR

In response to this edict I was speechless. Long ago I had learned that when Grandfather took this tone, it was to be done and opposition would be futile.

Vidar rose and went off to his bed. I was left to contemplate the responsibility that was being thrust on my seven year old shoulders while I defended our land armed only with my quills and parchments of English writing and Christian religion.

* * *

After retiring to my bed, I found sleep elusive. Grandfather's words filled my mind. But finally I had fallen into a deep sleep and arose well rested.

Grandfather was already awake. A pot of oatmeal bubbled on the fire. Beside it a pot of strong brew steamed invitingly. "Good morning, young Stor," he addressed me. "Are you ready for a busy day?"

"What will we be doing?" I inquired.

"We will begin to put in place the plan which I told you of yesterday."

"I do not know if I will be capable of such an awesome responsibility. I had trouble finding sleep last night worrying that I was not up to it."

"Fear not, my boy. You are my grandson. And actually the plan is quite straight forward. You must build us a family and you must secure our land. You are still too young to start the first part but I would guess that, when the time comes, you will not require much assistance," he chuckled to himself. "As to securing the land, we will start immediately.

"As I told you last evening, we must look to the long term ownership of our land. While Dubh confirmed yesterday that our ownership will survive under his kingdom, we can be sure that there will be future battles between the different peoples who share this island or who come here in the future. And even if this were not to happen, we cannot trust the veracity of kings to seek our land to give to their friends and retainers. We must ensure that our land is fully occupied by people who are tied to our land and who are likewise tied to our family. In this manner, the people who actually work our land, and draw their sustenance from it, will regard us as the rightful owners regardless of what changes may come to this kingdom. Our tenants must owe their fealty to us. And they must believe that we rightly deserve it. Otherwise, they will eventually rise up against us.

"At present we own about one hundred hides of land." The English divide their land into what they call 'hundreds', or one hundred hides. A hide of land consisted of a sufficient amount of land to sustain a family and pay the lord of the manor his due. The actual size of a hide of land depends on the use to which the land is best suited and how productive the land could reasonably be expected to be. "So our one hundred hides are similar in size to an English 'hundred' or a Yorkish *wapentake*. However, only about a third of our land has been cleared and broken. When I and my brothers first took possession of this land it was all unbroken. Breaking it was much harder than it is today, because we now have metal plows that can be pulled by teams of horses. It took much longer before these innovations. Until it is all broken we will not be able to fully determine how many hides we actually will hold.

"The part that is already broken is settled mostly by people who fought under my command when we first came here. They are good people for the most part, and generally reliable to pay us our due for using our land. But they are free men. They are not slaves and we cannot compel them to stay on our land. Partially this is a good thing, because freemen are producing for themselves and therefore will produce a greater amount. As a result they will be able to pay us our due from the surplus of their labour. But as freemen, we cannot compel them to stay. They will stay because we benefit them to stay, that we are capable of defending them and because if they leave our land they will be forced to sell themselves into slavery or to sell their swords to others who will probably offer them a warrior's fate: death.

"The English have a system to gain both ways from this situation. They have their tenants enter into an agreement through which they are guaranteed tenancy by their lord and they in turn agree to work that land and not move elsewhere without the permission of their lord. The agreement also sets out the terms of their tenancy; how much of their goods and labour they will surrender to their lord and how much they will contribute to the military requirements of their lord. All of this is committed to a written agreement which can be adjudicated by a magistrate if one party believes that they have been grieved." With this, he described the system of feudalism which was largely in place in southern England and was now emerging in Cumbria.

We were just finishing our morning meal when a stranger approached us. I viewed him with trepidation. He was a fearsome looking brute, tall, muscular with wild, unkempt, long flowing blond hair and a beard to match. He was clad in a leather tunic with a large, dangerous looking sword girded in a scabbard on his back, the haft protruding well above his right shoulder. A sword thus worn gave its owner quick access to the weapon and I imagined that it had been withdrawn to taste blood on many occasions. A long, now-healed, deep scar bisected his face from above his left eye, across the bridge of his nose, and down his right cheek.

As he drew near his face lightened, a part smile, part sneer spreading across his lower face and a mischievous twinkle appeared in his pale blue eyes. "Yo, Vidar," he bellowed. "Who is this mighty warrior with you?"

"This is my grandson and future heir, Stor" Grandfather replied. "Come sit and share a cup of tea with us. I have much to discuss with you. Stor, this is Steinar, an able and trusted warrior who has served me in many battles."

Steinar reached across the table and grasped my hand, shaking it vigorously. "Well young Stori, you come of good breeding. I knew your father well. Both he and Vidar, here were unmatched in battle. No better men have I trusted with my life."

Slowly my fear subsided but I continued to watch the man warily.

After sipping tea and exchanging idle conversation, Grandfather turned the conversation to a more serious note. "Well Steinar, I have been told that you fought well for Dunmail. But he was defeated. That battle is over and that army disbanded. What do you plan to do with yourself now?"

"I'll be quite honest, Vidar," Steinar began, "I am beginning to weary of war. It is a young man's sport. If I could arrange it, I would like to settle down and raise a family if any wench would accept my ugly puss. But, alas, I do not know how I would be able to support a family. So I imagine I shall continue to shop around to see who might buy the use of my sword."

"This is as I had heard and this is why I have summoned you to meet with me. I have a proposition for you. As you know, I own almost one hundred hides of land along the Eske Valley." Vidar spread his arm and swept his hand across the landscape, as if thereby delineating the extent of his estate. A hundred hides was a very substantial estate.

"I have thirty-one hides broken to the plow and occupied by tenants. The tenants are good families for the most part. They are hardworking people and they pay me my rents. I plan to see the remainder of the land broken and settled. As this is done, we will be able to determine the total extent of the number of hides that the land will allow. I want you to oversee my land. I want you to be my sheriff and my bailiff. In return, I will give you three hides of land for your use. You can live on one hide and place tenants on the other two, which will provide you sufficient labour for a good livelihood, while you spend your time defending my land and my interests in it. Those three hides will be yours, and your family's, for as long as you, or your heirs, serve me in this capacity." This was a very generous offer.

Steinar sat speechless for several moments after Vidar finished. He finally blurted out, "My lord, you have saved my miserable life."

"Never mind the 'my Lord' business," Vidar scolded. "I am, and I always have been your captain. But I am still Vidar and you must still be my colleague, Steinar. And I have a reason to say this because I have one other task which you must agree to. I am becoming old. My years are not long. Stor is my only heir and he is only a boy. He will still be a boy when I die. He is very bright and learns quickly, but he has so much left to learn. You must swear to me, Steinar, that when I am gone, you will take this lad under your wing and ensure that my estates remain in his hand after my death. Any, and all, fealty which you owe to me you must also owe to my grandson."

"I would have it no other way, Vidar." Turning to me, he smiled and said, "You will be in good hands young Stor!" Back to Vidar he asked, "So when do I start?"

The old man asked' "Do you have something better to do this morning? If I'd wanted you tomorrow, I would have asked you tomorrow." We all laughed and the deal was done.

***

"So, where do we start?" Steinar was all business now.

"We have some matters to address immediately." Vidar replied. "First I want you, myself and Stor to tour the entire estate a make some initial plans for its division. Then we will return to Carlisle. Yesterday I arranged a meeting for two days hence with a priest from the Church of St. Cuthbert. He has a good command of the written language of both Rome and the Anglo-Saxons. He will help us draw up the contracts for our tenants. He will also arrange for you, Stor, to continue your education in reading and writing."

So Grandfather was serious about the statements which he made last evening. I could not contain my reactions. "How can that help me defend our lands" I exclaimed. "All that they will teach me is to read and write about their Christian sacraments. Am I to defend our land with a prayer and a sheaf of paper?"

"Patience, young Stor." Vidar counseled. "When you have mastered reading and writing English I will arranged for you to learn the art of the ax and the sword. You will need those too, but it will bode you well to also be able to read and write and possess a deeper knowledge of this Christian religion and English law."

"How can this help me? This is not our language or even the language of the Cumber amongst whom we will live. And it is not the religion of our ancestors. You, yourself still believe in our old gods and give sacrifices to them even though you are convinced to go through with this charade of baptism. If all around us will be swallowed up by the Christian English I don't know why we would even stay here."

"Stigandr will meet with you one day each week to teach you history and philosophy from a Norse perspective."

THE LEGEND OF STOR

The old man smiled patiently, then continued, "The land that I am from, the land that we called Norway, was but a dream. It was a narrow strip of rocks along the eastern coast of Scandinavia which could not support even me, much less a family. That is why we left it. It is not even a country. When I was a boy we had only just emerged as a kingdom, under the rule of King Harald Fairhair. When he died, Norway died with him. It no longer exists. I left there as a young man. Even if that country continued to exist, all of those whom I knew there have no doubt long since perished. There is no looking back there. We no longer belong. We are here and here is where we must build a future, or disappear from this earth forever in our funeral pyres. Forget our past, Stor. It is gone. It is up to us to build a new past for our descendants who are not yet born.

CHAPTER 3
STOREYE

Three mornings later we were on the road to Carlisle, Vidar, Stigandr, Steinar and I. It was clear and warm, the rain and gusts from the previous day having dissipated overnight. We were all in good spirits and laughed and joked with each other while we travelled. We had spent the past several days walking the estate and planning its future development. We had agreed that the land could be divided into 98 hides allowing for common lands, particularly around ponds and along creeks and the river. These lands would be used by all of the tenants for watering livestock. Steinar had selected the land which would comprise his three hides and Vidar had identified where the manor house would be built and which lands would be directly part of the manor. Now we would meet with the priest so that he could assist in drawing up agreements to which each tenant would affix his mark.

As we approached Carlisle I again became pensive and withdrawn. The previous evening my grandfather had advised me that I was to remain in Carlisle and immediately resume the studies that had been neglected completely since leaving York. It was not the studies that I so much minded, but the thought of being surrounded day in and day out by unsmiling, fun-hating priests who had little time to talk about the world around us, other than to admonish those who seemed bent on enjoying themselves. That reality was now sinking in, with a myriad of uncertainties about my immediate future. The nearer we drew to Carlisle, the more my good mood soured. Vidar and Steiner both teased me in an attempt to revive my earlier good spirits. For my part I smiled and feigned being cheered by them, but they both were aware of the misgivings that persisted. Still, Grandfather had spoken and there would be no questioning his decisions. I would be staying with the priests and mastering reading and writing in both English and Latin.

When we arrived in Carlisle Vidar led us to the Church of St. Cuthbert where Father Leo awaited. He was not what I had expected. He was a large somber man with a no nonsense countenance, but a twinkle in his eye betrayed a sense of humour behind his gruff demeanor. He ushered us into a small office in the church and bade us be seated. Vidar handled the introductions and then explained to Father Leo that he had asked me, Stigandr and Steinar to accompany him because he wanted to ensure that we also fully understood the contents of the agreements with his tenants and what would be expected of us. Father Leo, however, seemed more pleased with himself for having freshly dunked this old Viking barbarian into holy water and thereby saving his soul for Jesus.

The meeting with Father Leo went on for several hours. Vidar went into great detail regarding the security of tenancy of each of his present and future tenants. It would include their right of tenancy in return for upholding the obligations which they accepted in the agreement. Also included would be the right to will their tenancy to their heirs, the inheritance rights if they left no will and the agreement that the land would revert to the manor if a tenant died without leaving an heir. The agreements would also describe in detail the rents in coin, produce and labour and military service which would be delivered to the manor. The manor would receive a prescribed share of each crop of grain or bale of wool and an annual tariff on each head of livestock, poultry or pigs. Each tenant would contribute two days' labour to the lands of the manor each week and additional labour at spring planting and autumn harvest. Each tenant would supply the manor with armed manpower to support the peace of the manor or to ensure the safe keeping of the entire estate as required. The manor, in turn, would insure that each male member of each tenant's family received sufficient training in the art of warfare and the requisite weapons so that he might defend himself, his family and the estate as need should arise. Finally the agreements would include a commitment that, in times of emergency needs, each tenant and their families would provide whatever services were required to ensure the peaceful enjoyment of the manor by the lord and his heirs as well as their own.

As Vidar laid out his vision regarding these agreements, Steinar, Stigandr and Father Leo would interject to ensure that the meaning was clear and the agreements workable. When all of the details had been hammered out Father Leo promised to have his notes transcribed into legal documents upon which all concerned could put their mark. As he gathered his notes, he turned to Vidar and added, "If it is your intention to bind this land and these tenants to you, then you should give the estate a name by which men will know it."

Vidar smiled and turned to me. "I hope that I have made it clear, when I die this will all belong to Stor. It will be up to him to complete my dreams and so to him the land should be bound. What would you name the estate, my boy?"

By the swiftness of my response, it was clear that I had anticipated this request and had given it some thought. "Grandfather, you have been clear in your wishes that I rebuild our family on this land which has been paid for with the blood of our family. I will try my best to do so. I have given this issue much thought since we began this discussion several days ago. You have also pointed out to me that men who own land have started to take on a common second name that would give clarity of ownership one generation after the other, rather than identifying ourselves simply as our father's son whereby in each generation the name changes such as from Vidarson to Eyeson to Storson and so on.

"I have also noticed that many men take a second name from their trade, such as Olfa the Baker or Gudrun the Cook. " Struggling to keep a straight face, I went on, "But it seems to me that Stor the Viking Marauder would be a bad choice." All three mouths dropped open at this, and Vidar's and Steiner's faces turned cold as ice. The twinkle in my eye must have betrayed me because Grandfather let out a huge laugh and the others quickly joined him. So I went on. "I have also noticed that Norsemen often take the name of the town or village in which they were born. I wish to follow that tradition and therefore I would like to give my name to our land. I am Stor, son of Eye. I would like to call the estate Stor-Eye and I would like all of my decedents to be known as sons of StorEye for generations to come."

They all looked at me in amazement, but before they could interrupt I continued. "By naming the estate Stor-Eye I would not only be honouring my father, but I would be honoring all of our ancestors and the vast sea upon which you have travelled to come to this place. In our language of Norway, Stor, my name means "vast". Eye (pronounced *ee*) means "sea". In the Danish language it would mean "vast fields" which, of course, it is. And so I would name our estate StorEye and my children, and their children shall be forever known as the children of StorEye."

Vidar's smile announced his concurrence. Steinar said "It's a fine name but the two words together are pronounced Stori. I swear, when I address you, people will not know if I am talking to you or to a rock or a tree." He then broke into laughter at his own pun.

Vidar rose to leave. To me he said, "Your rationale in naming our estate gives me great confidence that you will face future dilemmas with much thought and wisdom. So, we will be leaving you here with Father Leo who will see to your keep and your education." He then turned to the priest and handed him several of King Edmond's newly minted coins. "This will defray your costs for the lad's keep. There will be more as it is needed. Stigandr will attend Stor one day each week to tutor him in Norse history, folklore, customs and philosophies. The two of you should consult frequently on his progress." He then turned to Steinar and commanded "Come. We will retire to the local tavern and have a drink to the day's accomplishments.

In the ale house, Steinar turned to Vidar and declared, "It truly is a fine choice for a name."

Vidar raised his glass in proud acknowledgement, "To StorEye."

As they drank their ales neither man would comprehend that, while the land would nourish the family and allow it to grow strong, it was the name itself that the children of StorEye would eventually carry to every corner of the Earth, where they would intermarry with every peoples of the world and the name would live on forever.

CARLISLE, 947

The priests at Carlisle lived up to my expectations appearing to have forsaken all fun, regarding it all as the work of the devil. They were, at all times, strict and serious, but they were attentive and effective teachers. I learned much about reading, writing, arithmetic, and astrology along with Christian dogma and philosophy. Soon I was competent in reading, writing and simple sums. A combination of my promises to my grandfather and a healthy fear of the wrath of my teachers motivated me to quickly master my studies. There was no room for sarcasm or childish pranks in my somber class rooms. Transgressions quickly met with ridicule or the stinging end of their rods. Early on I decided to accept their teachings in silent surrender. On the prescribed day each week, Stigandr would serve as a foil to my frustrations that arose from my Christian education. Through these discussions, I would come to realize that the importance for me was in the learning. I was not compelled to accept their conclusions.

Father Leo, on the other hand, was kind and considerate, inviting questions and debate. He had not come into the Church in his early life. He had been a warrior in his youth and, as such, he had joined his comrades in drink and debauchery. In his early thirties he had found his calling and took the path of preparing for a life in the service of his God. But he had not left either his sense of humour or his sympathy of human frailty behind him. He was as firm as his fellow clergy in his teaching but he lacked their unflinching intolerance of human weakness and folly. I came to like him considerably. As a result, it was Father Leo, as well as

Stigandr, to whom I could turn, when aspects of my education left me frustrated or angered. We spent countless hours debating Christian liturgy and philosophy.

I took considerable resistance to the idea that the Roman Empire was created by God as a vehicle to spread Christianity across the world. The Church taught that it was God's will, and part of his larger plan, to have Constantine convert to Christianity so as to merge the Roman Empire to God's Kingdom on Earth. They believed that, in the decline of Roman Empire and the coronation of Charlemagne, by the pope, as the Holy Roman Emperor, this was the culmination of the plan of God. Father Leo struggled valiantly to convince me of the truth of this dogma but my resistance did not falter. He finally conceded to me, "Stor, my job is to impart knowledge to you. I cannot force you to accept it. However, believe what you will, take care to whom you import your conflicting views. There are many who would see your views as heresy. Worse still, if your criticism includes a rejection of our belief that the divine right of kings flows from the infallible coronation of kings by the bishops of the church, then you could also be labeled a traitor and be subject to the lot that befalls a traitor.

CHAPTER 4
WAR AGAINST PAGANISM

One clear autumn morning, while the leaves still hung red and yellow upon the oak trees, Father Leo summoned me to his study. "What day is it today?" he demanded.

Without hesitation I responded, "It is All Hallows Eve"

"And what is the import of this day?" he continued.

"It is the day on which the Church recognizes and re-consecrates the soil which contains the remains of the holy saints, who lie in wait of the second coming of Jesus Christ and the resurrection of their bodies which He will reunite with their souls which are in heaven," I dutifully replied.

"Today we are going to journey into the forest to witness how some people, hiding behind a pseudo Christianity, use this holy day to celebrate their pagan religion."

We set out late in the afternoon as the sun fell in the heavens, walking purposefully towards the forest, with Leo providing the leadership. Once out of earshot of the village, Leo began his lecture. "I am well aware that while you have comprehended and absorbed all that I have taught you of Christian doctrine and, while professing acceptance of Christianity, your belief is superficial. Like your grandfather, you have been baptized into the Holy Christian Church, but neither of you have ever truly accepted the teachings of our church. Beneath this Christian veneer you both still cling to the false gods of your pagan forefathers, like Thor and Odin and a host of others."

I began to protest, but Father Leo simply raised his hand to silence me. "Hold your denials" he commanded. "I cannot determine what you choose to belief, but it is my responsibility to ensure that you comprehend where these beliefs can lead you. Vidar is old and set in his way. He cannot change. But you are young. You still have your whole life to live. I have a responsibility to ensure that you are aware of the dangers that your beliefs might cause you. I will not try to change you without your consent, but my tolerance is not shared by many of my fellow clerics. They do not share the concept of mercy and understanding with which I believe our Saviour has blessed us.

"It is not only you Norsemen who cling to your pagan beliefs while expediently pretending to accept the word of the true God and superficially accept baptism into his Holy Church. Many of our Celtic neighbours practice similar deceits. They cling to remains of the old Druid religion while publically proclaiming their conversion to the true Christ. It has been centuries since the Romans rounded up all of their known priests and executed them for participating in human sacrifices, but still their beliefs persist.

"I have explained to you already, that the disputes which existed between the old Ionian Christianity and our Roman Christianity were much more than a dispute over the dates on which Easter should be celebrated or even over whether or not the church should ultimately be accountable to our pope in Rome. In an attempt to attract Druid converts to the church, compromises were made with Druid belief. The Druids, like you Vikings, had many gods and goddesses. One of these Goddesses was Ester, their Goddess of Fertility. Every spring, on a date determined by their ancient calendar, they prayed to Ester to grant them a good year for growing crops and husbanding livestock. The Ionian priests compromised with these pagans by celebrating the miracle of Christ's death and triumph over death on the same days as these fertility rites had been celebrated. They even called the Christian celebration Easter. They believed that, seeing the former Druids joining in the celebration of Easter, they had rejected Ester and embraced Christian salvation. In truth the opposite had occurred. The Druids used the celebration of Easter to mask their continued celebration of Ester. One needs only to observe their supposed Easter celebration to see that it remains full of fertility symbols such as rabbits and eggs, all as part of the glorification of Ester. The dispute over the date to celebrate Easter was, in fact, a dispute as whether to use the date set by scripture to celebrate Christ's triumph over death or an appeasement to the Druid Goddess.

"These pagans treat all important Christian celebrations similarly. Behind the façade of celebrating the miracle of our saviour's birth, they are really celebrating their beliefs regarding the winter solstice. Today you will see for yourself how they celebrate All Hallows Eve."

Dusk was closing in on us when we arrived at a clearing in the woods. We hung back concealing ourselves by the forest while close enough to observe the happenings. The clearing was large and was adorned by a multitude of baskets of apples, pears, nuts, pumpkins and a wide variety of gourds in hues of pale yellows, greens and browns. Sheaves of various grains were placed artfully around the perimeter of the clearing. More than two hundred rough clad men and women were busying themselves with various tasks. Some were throwing grain in the air to separate the kernels from the chaff. Others tended fires over which large haunches of meat were slowly roasting, while yet others tended large boiling caldrons. Children were busy decorating the site by hanging streamers of brilliant colours from the surrounding trees and shrubs. Kegs of mead and ale were set about the clearing and some were already partaking of these libations. There were musicians playing an array of stringed and woodwind instruments to which people, having finished their tasks, were beginning to dance around the clearing in total abandon. A major celebration was obviously getting underway.

"While we are consecrating the final resting place of holy saints these people are busying themselves giving thanks to pagan deities whom they credit for bringing a good harvest."

The revelries intensified as more and more people finished their tasks. Then, just a huge full moon crested the tree tops, a hush fell across the clearing. From out of the forest emerged a lavish procession. It was led by a tall attractive woman dressed in a simple, but elegant gown. Her long dark hair, with only a few strands of grey, fell loosely down her shoulders and was garnished with arrays of flowers. "That is their Goddess." Leo whispered. "She is a witch. She has a great knowledge of the black arts which she practices extensively."

The goddess was followed by four younger women, similarly, but less elegantly dressed. "They are her apprentices. They are learning the black arts," Leo continued his discourse.

Next was a man dressed in furs, his face and head covered by a mask which depicted the head of a goat. "He is the consort of the Goddess. You will recall that the scriptures describe the Devil as having horns and cloven hooves. For these people that Goat is the representative of the Devil himself. He is the consort of the Goddess." The goat was followed by about two score of people dressed and masked to portray a variety of animals. "They also believe that laws of nature, rather than those of God, determine man's fate.

They believe that men and animals are all equally related and that some can transform themselves from human to animal. The masks depict that transformation."

Once the procession reached center of the clearing the Goddess began an incantation, joined sporadically by the entire congregation. When she finished, the music again flared and the entire assembly threw themselves into frenzied dancing.

"Eventually the goat will select one of those young apprentices and they will slink off into the forest to rut like animals," Leo went on. "Then the rest of them will couple up and follow his lead. An orgy will ensue."

As promised, the goat eventually rose from where he had been seated quaffing ale. He made his way to the circle in which the maiden acolytes were seated and beckoned one of them to join him. She rose with a demure hesitation and, taking her hand, he led her towards the forest edge.

They had only taken a few steps when the forest surrounding the clearing erupted into chaos. From the forest scores of burly, darkly garbed, and heavily armed, men emerged from the cover of the trees. They all carried raised axes or swords which glimmered in the moonlight. Alarmed, the revelers leapt to their feet and, in panic, began running in all directions, attempting to avoid the intruders. But the intruders were many and soon had forced the revelers into a tight circle. Few had managed to escape. Once the intruders had their prisoners under control, several dark robed priests strode forward and one declared, "You are all under arrest on a charge of heresy in the name of the True God's Holy Church."

Alarmed, Father Leo motioned me to silently retreat from our hiding spot and slink back into the forest. Once away from the fringe of the clearing, Leo beckoned me to run. However we had just moved a few paces when a sharp voice ordered us to halt. The burly, dangerous looking owner of this voice, axe in hand, blocked our retreat. In a flash, Leo's sword was in his hand. "Stand aside," he snarled, "or I will run my blade through your innards and impale you on that tree."

The intruder hesitated, a flash, first of surprise, and then of fear, crossed his face. He reluctantly lowered his weapon and stepped aside. Leo grasped my shoulder and impelled me past this brute. Once past him and beyond his view, we broke into a run.

"I am sorry, Stor," Leo gasped. "I wanted you to witness the pagan ceremony by people who publicly declare themselves Christians, but I had not anticipated the attendance of those blackhearts who intruded on their festivities."

Once we had placed a good distance between ourselves and the melee in the clearing we slowed to a walk. I turned to Leo and asked, "What will become of those people?"

"I am not sure," Leo replied. "This would not have been allowed to happen when King Dunmail ruled this land. His was a reign of religious tolerance. To my knowledge this is the first time since his overthrow that my Christian brothers have been so emboldened to carry out such a mass arrest for heresy. I suspect that the peasants and villagers will be given the opportunity to recant their pagan practices and beliefs. If they do so they will be absolved and given a penance. For the goddess and her entourage I have great fear. Many of my fellow clerics are overly zealous and unmerciful in their pursuit of Christian purity when faced with heretics."

* * *

My question was answered several days later. I went out into the village square in front of the church. A crowd was gathering at the entrance to an alley which extended between two single storey stone buildings. In the alley a crude gallows had been erected by placing a long large pole from one roof top to one on opposite sides of the alley. Twelve nooses dangled from the pole. Each of the loose end of the ropes was held by two strong men. Eventually, from a doorway, towards the far end of the alley, twelve of the male revelers, still garbed in their ceremonial costumes, now torn and tattered, were escorted towards the gallows. Their progress was slowed by a number who were being dragged or pulled to their fearful destination. Each man had his hands bound behind his back. The goat was amongst them.

Their captors brought them to a halt beneath the gallows. Each captive was forced to stand on a plank which rested about a foot off of the ground on two short stools. The nooses were placed around the necks of each captive while the loose ends of the ropes were pulled taunt and tied in place to pegs which had been pounded into the earth for this purpose. While a priest intoned a chant, at a pre-determined signal, the guards kicked the stools free, leaving the hapless prisoners to dangle helplessly from the pole. They kicked wildly and struggled to capture air in their lungs, but those breaths were not to be. Eventually the struggling became mere twitches as the dance of death reached its conclusion. The crowd began to wander away in order to take in the next spectacle which the priests had prepared for them.

In the center of the square two large sturdy stakes had been driven into the ground. They protruded about four feet into the air. Around each stake were piles of firewood stacked high against the stakes. The goddess and her apprentices were herded into the square and led to the stakes. Sobbing and wailing with terror, the first three apprentices were manacled together to the first stake. The remaining two women approached their fate more stoically. The goddess herself obscured the events with a sneer of contempt, while her companion revealed a much greater fear as she approached death with a determined resolution. The two were manacled to the second stake.

While the presiding prelate resumed his incantations, torches set the biers ablaze. The flames surrounding the goddess and her companion crackled and quickly climbed up their gowns. The other fire was much slower to blaze. It instead issued great bilious clouds of smoke. Those watching discussed the proceedings with an analytical eye which betrayed an obvious history of watching these types of events. One knowledgably explained, "The three young ones obviously confessed and recanted their evils and, as a result, received divine mercy by being burned on a fire of green wood. They will succumb to the smoke before the flames ravage their bodies. The other two will suffer the full effect of the inferno." All, however, were now shrieking in pain and terror as the fires consumed them. I was revolted by the entire spectacle. While most of the congregation stood transfixed by the grotesque display of cruelty and punishment demanded by these priests, I and several others turned and quietly walked back to our homes, carefully concealing our disgust at what we had witnessed.

**

"That was an outrage," I ranted in my next meeting with Father Leo. "How can a Christian Church, not just permit, but preside over such atrocities?"

"I share your feelings when my fellow churchmen act so callously," Leo responded. "But you cannot hold Christ's Holy Church responsible for the misdeeds of a few of its servants. Besides, you must remember that our scripture teaches that the wicked shall be cast into the flames. While I have deep regrets about the lack of mercy shown the pagans,

I regret even further that I caused you to witness it. But I also believe that it is fortunate that you now know the importance of not revealing any attachments that you, as a baptized Christian, may still harbour towards your grandfather's Old Norse gods."

For many months I harboured a strong resentment of Leo's apologetic attitude to the most negative behavior of his church regardless of his respectful and kindly behavior towards me. My sympathy towards Christianity was badly shaken. But, in my broodings, Stigandr reminded me that my own predecessors carried out equally callous behavior towards those who had unsuccessfully opposed their military ambitions. That behavior included the *blood eagle*. Which involved staking a defeated opponent to the ground, ripping open his spleen, tearing out his lungs and tossing them over his shoulders like bloodied wings, while the victim still writhed in his death throws.

I will admit that the whole experience left me quite confused. Not only did my young mind have to wrestle the beliefs of the Norse and Christian gods, but I now also felt a respect and fellowship with those simple Celtic people who embraced the natural world that sustained them and bravely faced the ensuing persecution. In my confusion I plunged myself into my own joyless studies while longing for my eventual return to StorEye.

CHAPTER 5
VALHALLA

ESKE RIVER VALLEY, 949

It was a blustery day in early spring when my studies were interrupted by a harried Steinar who burst into the church dormitory where I was studying. "Pack your things young Stori. We are returning to StorEye. Vidar is ailing and his time is short." To lighten his message he added, "You have loafed around Carlisle too long already. It is time to go home."

I rapidly assembled the few belongings which I had accumulated while living in Carlisle and after bidding Father Leo an emotional good bye, I set off with Steinar. While the sun shone brightly above us, the wind bit cruelly into every seam of our clothing and left us chilled in spite of the heavy blankets we wore wrapped around our bodies. Steinar was solemn, no trace of his normal boisterous mood.

I inquired, "How bad is he?"

"Not good" Steinar replied. "The years have caught up to him. He will not live through the summer. He wants you with him during his final days."

We rode on in silence. I was content to keep to my own thoughts. My mind wandered through reminiscences of that old lion who had been my grandfather. I dwelt on the many good times that we had spent together and how much wisdom had been imparted to me by my aging patriarch and how much I would miss his wise counsel. Over the past years Steinar had grown to be a trusted friend and I felt great affection for him. But Grandfather had been my rock; the foundation of my formative years. I was unsure how I would fare without him.

I had not been scheduled to leave Carlisle for several months but I had done well in my studies and now excelled at both spoken and written English and Latin. While Father Leo had turned out to be a pleasant surprise, I had not yet fully forgiven him for being an apologist for the atrocities of his church. However, unlike the humourless priests whom I had encountered in the past, he was a tough but fair task master. And under his stern exterior he possessed a sense of humour and a passion for life. He had striven to convince me that I should become a man of the Church. I had rebuked his every effort, reminding him of the task which Vidar had given me. I would consider no other course for my life. I remained silent about the frailty of my faith in Christianity.

But, for all of his proselytizing, Leo accepted my decision. Before taking to the cloth, he had been very much a worldly creature. He had been a warrior and had fought many battles and had the scars to prove it. He joined in the imbibing and debauching that generally was practiced by soldiers enjoying their victories. While he had put this all behind him when, as he claimed, the Christian God had called him, he still enjoyed good spirits and his eye would keenly follow the buttocks of a passing wench. Neither had he lost his talents with a sword. He travelled well-armed and constantly prepared to defend himself.

The reality of Steinar's announcement now shook my thoughts back to the reality that lay ahead. It had come as no surprise that my grandfather's health was failing. During my years at Carlisle, I had made many trips home to StorEye. On each trip I would ride out with Grandfather and survey the progress of our developing estate. I had watched the land being broken and tenanted. I had met and talked with every retainer on the estate and was familiar with all of their families. I had watched Grandfather administer the estate, deal with grievances and settle disputes amongst tenants. I had witnessed how the old man had tempered his rigid sense of justice with a compassion that made men love and respect him and, when necessary, fight and die for him. While I had complete faith in Steinar, it was hard for me to imagine StorEye without my grandfather's guiding hand. I had also witnessed Vidar's health regress as age took its toll. I knew in my heart that Grandfather's days were running out. And so it was with mixed emotions that I relished the thought of spending those last days with him.

On the fourth day after my arrival Vidar called me to his side. I could tell by his tone that this was to be a serious conversation. "Kings are not usually precocious. They are motivated by a need for power and they will do what they must to obtain, protect and extend that power. Some might have noble goals for which they will use that power, like Ragnald's desire to ensure land for our countrymen, but their first goal is the power. They are a necessary evil, but they are not to be trusted. In the long run, strong families provided the greatest protection. Sometimes family members may turn rabid against their own, but generally the bonds of kinship provide the greatest source of trust. Our family is now weak. The two of us are all that are left. But we are strong in that there is no basis of dissent between us.

"When I die you will be on your own, but you will not be alone. First, you can trust Steinar with your life. But I have ensured an even more stable environment for you. To understand it, I must tell you the details of your father's death.

"Your father died on a shield wall. It should not have happened but we were betrayed. Our right flank was being protected by a Scottish noble named Cuillen who is the son of our King Duhb. He was a young man who was appointed to this position on account of his rank, not his ability and certainly not on account of his courage. He was a coward. During the heat of the battle he deserted and pulled his forces off the shield wall. Our right flank began to falter and our shield wall lost some of its cohesion. In the following confusion, an opening occurred in the wall giving one of our foes a clear path to wield his axe at my comrade, Torald. Your father was beside Torald and he threw himself into the gap. He was off-balance and the axe struck his shield in such a manner that it caused him to stumble forward. Unprotected, a spear found the space in his armour between his mail and his helmet. It drove deep into Eye's neck, killing him instantly. He died so that Torald could live.

"After the battle was over, Torald immediately acknowledged his debt which he owed to your father. He swore to me that he would undertake whatever I requested of him in gratitude for your father's sacrifice. I knew that you had become an orphan and that I was your only living kin. I also knew that I would probably not live long enough to see you to adulthood. At my request, Torald swore that, in the event of my death, he would accept you into his family and protect you as if you were his own.

The old man paused again before delivering his most shocking piece of news. "There is only one way for our family to grow, and that is for you to produce children. You are no longer a child. You are twelve years of age and well on your way to becoming a man. With this in mind I have also arranged your betrothal. When you are both of age, you will marry Eyja, a daughter of my great friend, Torald, the Earl of Deira. Torald is the head of a large and powerful family and Eyja, while only ten years of age, shows promise of becoming a healthy, attractive lass. Torald is a friend of our family and well known to me. Your betrothal cements the oath that Torald has sworn to me." He then paused again while I absorbed this information.

I was not so shocked by Grandfather's revelation. Arranged marriages were the common method by which the children of propertied families determined spouses. These arrangements were often concluded while the children involved were quite young, so it came as no surprise to me that Grandfather had concluded this responsibility. While I had some vicarious knowledge of the pleasures that existed between men and women, I had not yet reached full maturation and, only weeks earlier, had the experience of spilling of my seed in my sleep and awakening to pangs of embarrassment. I therefore could not yet fully fathom the incredible experiences that awaited me. I also had experienced very little contact with young women and so, had only limited knowledge of how to behave in their presence. As a result, the reality that jolted me came more from the fact that this betrothal actually involved me and would eventually lead to this young girl becoming by wife. My imagination raced with the possibilities that this might entail. My reaction was more one of curiosity about who this new family was and the kind of girl to whom I was now betrothed.

Realizing this, Vidar continued. "I have asked that Eyja's dowry be in the form of gold. Torald offered land, but you will have more land than you need. You will need gold to ensure that you become well established on your land." As he continued it became apparent to him that I was lost in thought, my mind wandering elsewhere.

The sun had risen when I awoke the next morning. I had lain awake for hours after retiring the previous evening, my head swimming with Grandfather's revelations. While I had often contemplated a future with wife and children, giving my future wife a name brought a reality to the fore in a manner which I had not previously experienced. Fear and anticipation contended with my imagination as hundreds of potential scenarios, some wonderful, some terrifying, raced through my mind. But finally I had fallen into a deep sleep, dreamed a lifetime of dreams but arose well rested.

* * *

I will always remember that summer day that Grandfather last summoned me to his side. I had been back from Carlyle for almost three months. During that time, the summer days had been majestic and the land had responded to the hot sun's caress by bringing forth an abundance of produce. The sheep had fattened and the grain crops were already standing tall. When I was not at Vidar's side, I spent days roaming StorEye with Steinar. I was never at a loss for questions, whether addressed to Steinar or to a tenant whom we happened upon. I was insatiable with my appetite for knowledge. Why was this crop being grown on this particular piece of land? How was it planted? How was it tended? How would its harvest time be determined? How would the harvesting be carried out? How would the harvest be processed? How would it be stored? I asked the same questions about each crop and about all of the livestock. I went on and on trying to gather every remote detail as to how the land produced its bounty and how that bounty was distributed and how it might be expanded upon.

However, most of my hours were spent sitting and talking to Grandfather. Vidar had arranged to have a special lounge built for him. It was fashioned from leather which was strapped with thongs to a wooden frame which allowed Vidar to sit with his feet up and his head raised so that he could view his surroundings. The lounge was generally placed outdoors where Vidar could enjoy the warming rays of the sun. I was shocked when I first returned home by how Grandfather's strength had deserted him leaving him confined to his lounge or his bed. The old man's beard and mane were now completely white and his skin well wrinkled. His mind was as sharp as ever and his eyes still twinkled in recognition whenever I approached. He always had more knowledge to share. He did not confine his discussions to our land and how I should nurture and protect it. He also kept me fully apprised of the political developments of all of Northumbria and how it might impact us.

He spent hours explaining to me about how, throughout the centuries before the Danish invasion of Britain, the old Kingdom of Northumbria had dominated the financial wealth of Britain and how Britain was the wealthiest land west of Rome. Traders from Scandinavia, Germany, France, as far away as Spain and the Mediterranean Sea had brought wealth to the eastern ports of Northumbria from Jarrow to as far north as Edinburg. Of all of these ports, York had been, by far, second only to London, as the benefactor of this trade. The ports of Wessex had been small backwaters at that time. This was why the Danes had concentrated on first dominating York and making it their capital.

Stigandr often joined us. He reiterated time and again how Alfred of Wessex knew that if his dream of a great Anglo- Saxon England was to become a reality, then York must be dominated by Wessex and that the English language must become the language of all of England. He had established a code of laws and those codes were written in English and imposed wherever his authority extended. As a result, a premium existed for literacy in the English language. In this effort he had a great ally in the Christian church. Between Alfred's court and the church they began a process of creating education centers which would teach the English language, both written and spoken, along with their teaching the Christian religion. Wherever Wessex authority was established, these centers would follow.

He also talked about the long term military strategy which would ensure England's survival. For Vikings, conquest and plunder was the required motivating fuel which kept their armies strong. A defensive army cannot live on plunder in order to maintain the loyalty of its warriors. However, a king could call out a large following of peasant farmers in times of attack. If the invader could maintain stealth and mobility the battle would be over before opposition could be amassed. Even if the defenders did arrive in time, they were usually untrained, undisciplined and armed only with staves and pitch forks. They made easy targets for experienced Viking sword warriors. So Alfred, in his day, had begun building and garrisoning settlements, which became known as burhs. Each burh was fortified, sometimes drawing on existing Roman ruins, more often using mainly the surrounding geography, accompanied by earth works supported by logs. Each burh had a barracks to house a local company of trained soldiers who could maintain the peace and enforce the law. These burhs were located so that no Anglo-Saxon lived further than a day's ride from a well-trained and well-armed burh garrison.

Viking raiders generally held superiority if a defending army faced them in the field in a shield wall. But the Vikings had a more formidable task in attempting to over-run a well-defended fortification. Neither could they maintain a siege, as over time the English could call on reinforcements. So the

Viking attackers would simply wander off in search of more immediate plunder.

But Alfred's brilliance went further. Each burh also had a church, a hall and a magistrate or reeve to administer the king's justice and a tax collector to ensure the financial support required for the burh, its garrison and its administration functions. Alfred's son, Edward, and Edward's son, AEthelstan expanded the construction of burhs in conjunction with their expanded territorial influence. Now a network of burhs covered all of southern England and was beginning to be seen in York. Since these burhs had a locally supported tax base and a local administration capable of defending its citizenry, the people began to see themselves paying taxes and fighting to protect, not just the king's realm, but their own family, their own village and, by extension, their own country.

Vidar had told me, "I have instructed Steinar to start planning for the building of StorEyeburh."

***

But this day Vidar's strength had declined much further; his voice barely a whisper and the gleam in his eyes were beginning to fade. The old man beckoned me closer so that he could make himself heard. "My time has come" he whispered," but there are still some things which I must tell you." I began to protest this extreme diagnosis, but the old man waved his hand to silence me. "There is not time. I must tell you these things."

"First" he began," while I still hold some awe at the powers of this Christian God, I am an old Norseman at heart. When I die, I wish to be sent to Valhalla in the style of my ancestors. Second, when I die you must ensure that my estate is settled in your name. I expect no problems in that regard but you must make sure.

Then, I have arranged for you to go to York and stay with the family of your future kinsman, Torald, and become his squire. I wish for you to remain there until you and Eyja marry, then you will return here to raise your family on our land. Torald will ensure that you learn the ways of war so that you can defend our land as need be. He will also make sure that you have the opportunity to learn the ways of the city dwellers of York and particularly the merchants. They are a shrewd lot who will rob you blind if you allow them to do so. You are a smart lad and will learn quickly. Torald will also give you the opportunity to learn of the royal court. Watch them closely. They have even less scruples than the merchants.

While you are there you will meet those who would recruit you into a life of daring-do, promising glory in exchange for your sword. You have nothing to prove to them and nothing to prove to yourself. Your task is simply to learn and then return here to protect your land and raise your family. Right now our family is weak. When I go, there will be just you left. It is your duty and my sincere request that you devote your life to nurturing our family back to strength. And Stor, I know that you can do it. You have my blessing. Now, get me my sword and ensure that it is firmly grasped in my hand. Tie it there if you must."

The old man then went silent. We sat there feeling the warmth of the sun, me holding his grizzled old hand which firmly held his sword.

Three days later Vidar was dead. I oversaw the lighting of his funeral pyre and watched the ship blaze out into Solway Firth, taking Vidar to keep his appointment with Odin in Valhalla. Beneath my breath, I said my goodbye to my grandfather along with a Christian prayer for his soul.

CHAPTER 6
ROUGH JUSTICE

INTERLUDE

Only a year after his decisive victory over Northumbria, King Edmund died. His son, Eadred, succeeded him. Eadred had summoned the Northumbrian witan, under the leadership of Wulfstan, Archbishop of York, to affirm their submission to Wessex. The witan, an ancient Anglo-Saxon structure provided a forum through which the leading nobles and clergy could have input into the decisions of the royal court. They were particularly active if the succession to the throne was unclear. This structure was well established in York and its composition reflected the origins and religions of all of the people. Wulfstan's attitudes well reflected his constituents of York.

While they pledged their allegiance to Eadred, they chafed at Wessex reign over them and were already plotting to invite a fiercely independent Norse Viking, Eric Bloodaxe, to become the new King of York. To Eadred's chagrin, Bloodaxe gladly accepted and arrived in York to assume the throne in early 948.

Eadred, furious with the betrayal by the witan, assembled his army and marched on York. He struck first at the town of Ripon, the educational and cultural centre of York. In an act of pure terrorism; Eadred sacked the town and leveled it to the ground, including its sacred cathedral. Under the threat of similar treatment for the City of York, the witan surrendered, promising to expel Bloodaxe from the throne and appoint a more mutually agreeable candidate, Anlaf Sihtricson, brother of Olfa.

Believing that he had succeeded, Eadred turned his army to march back to Wessex. But Bloodaxe had not yet left the country. He laid an ambush for Eadred's rear guard and massacred them in the first military defeat for the House of Wessex since 902. Eadred turned his army back to York, only to find that Bloodaxe and his army had taken to their boats and were long gone. Anlaf Sihtricson became the King of York.

STOREYE, 951 AD

We had not left StorEye as planned, immediately after Vidar passed away. It was far too dangerous to travel to York. While I was still residing in Carlisle, King Edmund had died and had been succeeded by his son Eadred. The turmoil created over the struggle between Wessex and York, while not impacting western Northumbria, which remained under Duhb's Kingdom of Cumbria and Strathclyde, had totally destabilized the east. Then, no sooner than Eadred had forced the witan in York to back down, the Scots broke their truce and invaded Bernicia. Eadred sent his army against them but had not subdued them until earlier this year.

Dubh had tried to keep Cumbria and Strathclyde neutral in this conflict, but with his father, Malcolm, leading the Scottish army into Bernicia, some renegade Scots clans felt licensed to make their own forays into Cumbria. This gave me my first taste of real combat.

Approximately seven months after Grandfather's death I was meeting with Steinar and Father Leo at StorEye. Leo came there often after Vidar's death to enquire about my well-being and to review routine documents which he had prepared for us. The day was clear but cold and the winter's snow still covered the ground. The crisp air was suddenly shattered by a cry, "Raiders, raiders!" We rushed outside to see one of our tenants racing towards us while pointing back over his shoulder, obviously indicating the source of his agitation.

Grabbing our swords we quickly mounted our horses and raced off in the direction of the raid. As we crested the rise, the scene of the raid spread out before us. Three people were on the ground, obviously wounded or dead. The house and outbuildings were all aflame. There were about thirty raiders who were just beginning to flee the scene, herding several dozen head of sheep before them. From all directions our tenants were racing towards the homestead to assist their besieged neighbor. The raiders numbered about thirty, all armed with spears, shields or swords. In the distance more help was coming to fend off the attack, but they were still far away.

Instead of dashing directly into the raiders, Steinar halted us and quickly surveyed the situation. He then led us at a gallop, skirting the raiders and into a ravine directly in the path of their retreat. He yelled and motioned for the other tenants to follow. Once there, we quickly dismounted as other tenants joined us. I had my sword in hand and was ready to do battle. But Steinar handed me the reins of his and Leo's mounts and ordered me to stay where I was and mind the horses. He then led our small throng on foot towards the raiders.

The raiders were all mounted, and seeing our small numbers, all on foot, left the stolen sheep and organized themselves for an attack. Steinar's training of our peasantry soon became obvious. In mere moments he had them organized into a shield wall, men with shields in the front rank standing shield to shield. Behind them, the men with spears and swords formed a second rank, their spears in hand and their swords sheathed. He then ordered them forward in unison into the face of the charging raiders. They stopped just as the raiders were upon them. As the shield bearers braced themselves for the onslaught, the second rank thrust their spears at the charging horses. Half of the attackers' horses were killed instantly. In their death throws they created mayhem at the feet of the shield bearers. The swords of the second rank were instantly unsheathed and, over the shoulders of their shield-bearing comrades they rained vicious blows on the disarray of fallen horses and their riders. The raiders quickly, but far too late, realized how badly they had misjudged their opposition. Those left standing fled the battle in a disorganized retreat with our peasantry in blood-thirsty pursuit.

As I stood there with the horses, brooding at my exclusion from the fight, Leo yelled, "Stor, look out." I instinctively dropped to the ground just as a sword whistled past my head. One of the raiders had slipped around our horses and saw an opportunity to escape on horse-back, dispatching me as he fled. The force of his swing carried him fully around so that his back was to me. On falling, I rolled on my back, sword still in hand. With all the force I could muster, I slashed at the raider's leg. My blow was good and sank into the bone just below his knee. He bellowed in pain as he sank to the ground, a look of complete disbelief spread across his face. I was on my feet in an instant, my sword thrusting at the centre of his chest. My aim was bad and my sword plunged directly into his throat. I saw his eyes catch mine and he knew as he died that I had killed him.

I stood there in shock. I did not even see the battle end. When I gathered my wits, our troop was gathered around five survivors from amongst the raiders. They were seated on the ground looking quite forlorn. I assumed that the rest of them were dead. Many corpses littered the site of our battle.

Our side suffered nothing worse than minor injuries. Steinar and Father Leo had led the carnage.

The young man, who had raised the hue and cry, was sobbing. "That was my father, my mother and my sister whom they killed."

Steinar glared at the five survivors. They were a sullen looking lot, dressed in dirty, stained garments with filthy unkempt hair and beards. All had suffered fearsome wounds, but none would be immediately fatal. One of them stood out from the rest. His face was not covered by a beard. He appeared to be not more than a few years older than myself at most. "What is a mangy cur like you doing amongst this lot?" Steinar growled. The boy appeared struck silent by fear.

"He's my son." One of the older men replied.

"How old are you, cur?" Steinar snapped.

Finding his tongue, the boy replied, "Thirteen years my lord."

"I am not your lord." Steinar growled. "So how many of my people did you butcher today, pup?"

Again the father replied. "The lad did no killing. He was only armed with a stave."

Steinar slapped the man across the head with his mail covered hand, leaving him sprawling in the dirt. "When I want an answer from you, dog, I will ask. Now, boy, is what he said true?"

The boy nodded in acknowledgement.

"Fetch a wagon and some rope," Steinar ordered. "I will spare the boy, but the rest will pay for those whom they slew." Turning to the boy he said, "You shall be free to return to your home, if you have one. But you will leave here with a brand on your cheek so that all men will know you as the outlaw that you are, and feel free to kill you if you cause them displeasure. When we send you back home, you can tell your kinfolk what happens to those who disturb the peace at StorEye

"Before you go," Steinar continued, "You will witness the hangings. I will remove your bonds and you will be free to throw your weight on the legs of whichever one you choose and aid him to a swifter and more merciful death."

When the men returned with rope and wagon the prisoners were led to a sturdy oak tree and ropes, with nooses, were thrown over stout branches. The men were hoisted onto the wagon, their hands bound at their backs. When all was ready, the wagon was pulled from under them, leaving them to kick and squirm in the air as the nooses began to choke off their lives. The boy, while obviously terror stricken, wasted only a moment before he leapt to his feet and, with tears streaming from his eyes, grabbed his father's ankles and let his weight fall to the ground.

The other three outlaws were still doing their macabre dance as Steinar lead me away. "It was important that you witnessed the fate of murderers," he said softly. "Someday the role of dispensing justice will fall to you."

As we were gathering our horses I heard the blood curdling scream of the young lad as the brand seared his flesh. We did not look back.

I could feel my body shaking. The look in the eyes of that man, who I had killed, and those of his companions whom we dispatched, visited me in my dreams for many weeks to come.

* * *

I found myself filled with mixed emotions as we rode back to StorEye after dispatching the raiders. On the one hand I was filled with an exhilaration which surprised me. I had experienced my first battle and had killed a man. On the other hand the act of slaying the man and witnessing the grotesque execution of his companions left a sickening feeling in me. I rationalized the whole episode by reminding myself of the stricken anguish of the lad whose family had been murdered. The raiders had received the justice which they deserved. Regardless of the horror we had created dispatching them, we had done what was required.

We arrived back at StorEye to a barrage of questions about what had transpired. I avoided this inquisition by tending to my horse, ensuring the he had food and water after brushing him down.

When I finally entered the manor house our house servants gasped at my appearance. The sweat and dirt which covered me was mixed with blood. It was mostly the blood of the raider which I had dispatched, but some was my own. I had sustained several minor scratches from my dive into the dirt to avoid the sword thrust which had been delivered at me. One of those wounds was a minor scrape to my forehead. It had bled freely, giving the appearance of a wound well beyond its gravity.

One of our serving girls rushed to my side. Her name was Keela. I had spoken to her occasionally in line with her duties. "My Lord, You're injured," she exclaimed, her face all drawn up in concern."

"Fear not," I declare. "My wounds are only superficial."

"I will fix you a bath in your quarters and tend to your repair'," she responded demurely. With that she scurried away to prepare my bath.

A few moments later she returned to announce that all was in readiness, beckoning me to follow her up the stairs to my chamber. As I followed her dutifully, I could not help but notice the enticing curves of her lithe young buttocks. She was a couple of years older than me, with a pixie like face which was pleasant to look upon. Her smile was radiant, framed by flaming curly locks, her complexion smooth with a healthy tan.

I entered my chamber to find a steaming tub awaiting me. Keela stood beside the tub. She stepped towards me and gently began to disrobe me. As I moved towards the tub she stopped me and quickly removed my small cloth, causing me momentary embarrassment. She then held my hand and guided me into the waiting tub.

As I settled, her hands began carefully washing my face and examining my wounds. "You were lucky here, my Lord," she murmured. "This is indeed only a surface cut." She then proceeded to gentle cleanly around the scrape, ensuring that she caused me no extra pain.

Once she had finished with my face her hands directed themselves to the sweat and grime on the rest of my body. Her touch was light and gentle but I was beginning to find it quite arousing. I am fourteen years old and have reached puberty, but I had not yet known a woman. Even so, I found myself engaging in erotic fantasies as her fingers sought out areas of my lower torso which she must have considered in need cleansing. I began to feel an embarrassment as her ministrations caused my member to stiffen under her gentle caress. Without further warning I felt her hand encircle me and I realized that our activities were about to lead to a certain conclusion.

When she had finished cleaning and caressing absolutely every inch of my body, she rose and beckoned me to step out of the tub. She was waiting with toweling to dry me off, her gentle fingers never waning in their exploration. When she had completed drying me she took a step backwards and quickly disrobed, leaving her clothing in a heap at her feet. She then grasped my hand and led me to my sleeping platform. After a few moments of allowing my fingers to explore her naked body, I could resist no longer, so I awkwardly mounted her, attempting to portray carnal knowledge much greater than I possessed. I think that she suspected my virginity and seemed to revel in it.

After a few moments of erotic bliss, we lay spent and exhausted while my mind reviewed every thrilling second of my seduction. But within a very short interval, our fingers were again gently exploring each other and we were at it again. The evening continued this way until hunger finally drove us to don some clothing and go in search of food.

CHAPTER 7
JORVIK

YORK, 951

"Look young Stori, you can see the spires of the churches in York." Steinar exclaimed.

Sure enough, in the distance the tops of the highest structures were visible through the mist, protruding as if to welcome the weary travelers. York was the second largest city in Britain with a population of about 30,000 people of Danish, Norse, Anglo-Saxon and Celtic origin all sharing a common culture which was that of Northumbrian Anglo-Saxon. The city was built on the sight of the original Roman capital of the north and its Roman character, with its high stone arches could clearly be seen even at this distance. It was originally a walled city. The high walls still stood, but the city had spilt well outside its confines. The old Kingdom of Northumbria was ruled from this city. When it fell to the Danish Vikings they renamed it and made it the capital of their Kingdom of Jorvik, now called York.

I felt a stir of excitement. I was eager to get to the city about which I had heard so much. Certainly, I had lived there as an infant. But now, as a lad of fourteen years of age, the city held promises of whole new adventures.

Steinar had insisted on accompanying me, along with a large retainer of seasoned warriors. Our journey had taken us through Ripon on the way to York. There we had witnessed first-hand the extent of Eadred's ravaging and the extent of the blood-letting in Bloodaxe's counter attack. Ripon had been a small town of about 200 people. Small as it was, it had housed the greatest library of Northumbrian writing, which, along with its noted clerics, made it a highly respected centre of learning for all of Britain. Its greatest fame, however, was the magnificent Church of St. Wilfred's Ministry. Now, its masonry majesty lay in ruins. Eadred had even allowed the sacred remains of St. Wilfred to taken and be hauled back to Wessex.

The entire country had been ravaged for the past half century in the wars between Wessex and the Scandinavian rulers of the Kingdom of York. But none of that scorched earth warfare compared to the ravaging of Ripon. Every building within twenty miles of Ripon had been put to the torch. The town itself had fared no better, with only rubble strewn around the ruins of the once glorious church of St. Wilfred. The rest of the town had been leveled. Resentment towards Eadred was wide spread but fear of his vengeance forced those resentments to fester rather than spilling out in open rebellion. Eadred had accomplished his mission. He was feared more than he was hated by these northerners. As we were leaving the city, I heard Steinar mutter, "That surly Saxon dog."

* * *

The city of York was a different matter. Sixteen churches dominated its skyline. The streets bustled with commerce as merchants and customers all scurried through the streets in search of money making exchanges. In most of

THE LEGEND OF STOR

Northumbria, barter was still the medium of exchange but in the City of York coin had long been in common usage. One of the central issues between Wessex and York had been the minting of coins and who would collect the tax on those coins. The city extended to the river Foss. At its wharves numerous ships' crews were busy unloading goods from all over Europe and loading their outgoing cargos of slaves, metal goods, wool and wool products for sale on the continent and even as far as North Africa. This section of the city lay outside the walls and housed the Danish population. As that was our destination, we skirted the main approach and entered the Danish section directly. We passed through a commercial area near the docks; the stench of manufacturing assaulted our noses, but failed to dampen my excitement at the hustle and bustle of the busy population. We made our way through these noisy throngs and eventually arrived at the great town home of Torald, the Earl of Deira.

We had sent news of our impending arrival ahead, so that we were expected. As we approached, the great iron gates were thrown open to bid us welcome. The quarters were immense. They were situated within a courtyard enclosed by a high, well-fortified, stone wall. Inside, the buildings were also of stone construction and many of the windows were replete with stain glass characterizations of either flowers or images of both pagan and Christian significance. A troupe of household staff awaited us, some of whom led us to our quarters, while others escorted our horses and the remainder of our entourage to stables where men and horses alike would be fed and bedded down.

* * *

I found myself in a large bedchamber with a high beamed ceiling. There was an amazing bed, raised off the floor, and covered by soft inviting fur pelts. The mattress was filled with a soft fluffy material which I later learned was goose down. I had never slept on anything other than straw filled mats, spread on the floor. This promised a very new experience. There were several large padded chairs and small wooden tables. Light streamed in through several large stained glass windows, similar to the ones that had been visible from the exterior of the house.

A small rap on the door revealed a household servant bearing a large bowl of warm water. "His Lordship thought that you might wish to wash up after your journey," he announced. Stepping back he inquired, "Will you be needing anything else?"

When I acknowledge that this would be fine, the servant advised me that Lord Torald would be waiting to receive me in the main hall as soon as I had removed my coat of mail, bathed and changed my garments from the dusty tunic in which I had been travelling. I was amazed at the welcome which I was receiving and much of my apprehension about meeting my future in-laws dissipated. As soon as the servant closed the door on his departure, I leaped on the bed and stretched out all of my limbs. What luxury. I had never experienced such a comfortable place to sleep.

I readied myself for the waiting reception, dressing in the finest tunic in my possession, carefully leaving my sword and scabbard in the room. With the exception of household guards, weapons were forbidden in the reception and dining halls. The Vikings had long ago recognized that weapons and strong drink did not mix well.

As I dressed in my finery my thoughts were scrambling. I had long anticipated this coming encounter with my future family, but I was torn by fears as to what type of fiancée awaited me. Grandfather had promised that she was attractive, but his priority was that I produce a family. I feared that if he could have achieved his goal by marrying me to a brood sow, he would have done so.

As I finalized making myself ready, Steinar appeared in the doorway, announcing that he too was ready. We walked to the dining hall; me with the trepidation of a convicted felon going to his execution. Together we entered the grand hall. I was almost overwhelmed by its magnificence. The stone wall soared at least twenty feet above us and there met the large arched beams which supported the oak roof boards. From the ceilings, heavy chains held gigantic chandeliers. Each of them held dozens of sparkling candles which fully illuminated the large hall. Further candles shone from holders on the walls. These were interspersed with hanging tapestries imported from far away exotic places. The central piece of furniture was a massive oak dining table which sat on a raised platform. Benches along each side of the table provided seating for at least two dozen diners. Smaller tables extended out from the platform to provided seating for several hundred additional guests.

Directly in the center of the room stood a giant of a man with a long, rich, flowing robe and a huge well-groomed head of brown hair and beard, neither of which had begun to grey. Jewels sparkled from a large belt encompassing his girth. His arms were adorned with numerous elaborately carved bracelets of silver and gold. He had a firmly chiseled face which marked him as a man not to be trifled with, but his blue eyes gleamed with warmth, which I found disarming. My eyes nervously scanned the room, looking for a glimpse of my bride-to-be.

As we entered, he spread his long arms and proclaimed, "Welcome young Stor. I am Torald, your host and guardian for the next several years." His arms clutched me into an embrace in which I momentarily feared that I might be smothered or crushed to death, or both. As I stammered for a response, Torald turned to embrace Steinar with the same enthusiasm, however, Steinar's size was comparable to Torald's and he therefore did not look as endangered as I had felt. Releasing Steinar, Torald turned again to me and declared, "Steinar here is a fine man. He has saved my hide many times. Vidar selected a solid guardian to ensure your well-being."

Without further discussion, Torald's long arm encircled my narrow shoulder as he led me towards small throng of people standing off to one side. "Come Stor, let me introduce you to my family." I was introduced, first to his wife and then to his brothers, sisters, sons and daughters. When he came to a well-built attractive young man, he said, "this is Ulphus, my oldest son and heir. He and his lovely new wife live at my manor, Toraldesbi in Deira. You will be accompanying Ulph to Toraldesbi, where he will see to your education as a warrior. Ulphus is already a skilled warrior and has fought in a shield wall. He will teach you well. He is also your future brother-in-law, so he has a stake in keeping you alive." Next he introduced me to a younger son, Byrniulf who would also join us a Toraldesbi.

During these introductions, I had noticed a plump, young, homely looking girl, far younger than I had anticipated, standing towards the far end of the gathering. She appeared to ignore me and shyly gazed instead at the floor before her, her long golden hair hanging like straw well past her shoulders. Was this to be my future wife?

I went through the introduction fighting my sense of distress at what was, I was sure, to come. But when we got to her, Torald said, "And this is my youngest daughter, Kari." I could scarcely believe my ears. She was the last for me to meet. Relief flooded over me. But where was Eyja? I stammered a greeting to my future sister-in-law, but my eyes were darting about looking for clues as to the identity of the girl to whom I was betrothed. My search was in vain and so I passively allowed myself to be directed to where I was to be seated.

Torald was seated beside me. He was animatedly attempting to engage me in conversation but, to his amusement, I remained distracted. About forty people were standing or sitting around the hall. I examined every one of them, quickly assessing each female for clues as to whether she might be the one. My eyes suddenly stopped on a young girl who had just entered the hall. She was gorgeous. Her long dark curls framed a face of pure beauty. Large green eyes. Soft red lips. A short upturned nose. A long pale blue tunic fell over her lithe, young, well-formed body. Suddenly she picked up a large carved pitcher from which she began pouring ale for the guests. My heart plummeted as I realized that she was merely one of Torald's servers. As she came closer, I realized that this was not the body of a girl as young as Eyja.

I had almost abandon my search and was about to inquire of my host regarding her whereabouts when I saw her. I think that I audibly gasped because I heard Torald chuckle beside me. My throat went dry and my mind numbed. There was no doubt. This was her and she was everything that I could have hoped for. I silently begged Vidar's forgiveness for having doubted his concerns for me.

She was a slender slip of a thing at the early stage of blossoming into womanhood. By any account, she would have been attractive, but to me she was radiant. Her hair fell in long golden curls around the face of an angel. Her limbs were long and sleek and her beginning stages of womanhood caused her garments to fall tantalizingly to her ankles. I hardly dared to guess her identity when Torald turned his attention to her. "This is my daughter, Eyja, your betrothed."

My world stood still. I was enchanted, my tongue frozen speechless.

At this stage of my young life I was still awkward with young women. Since my first carnal encounter with Keela I had engaged her on a number of similar encounters and had known several other young women. But this was different. To this date I do not know if it was her incredible beauty, her regal bearing or simply that she was my betrothed, but I found her so overwhelming that my stomach did flip flops while my mouth seemed to fill with stones and my tongue swelled to thrice its normal size.

Eyja raise her head and looked me squarely in the face, her large blue eyes beaming. She finally broke the silence. "I am pleased to meet you and I will serve you faithfully." I remained speechless, barely managing to stutter "Hello," and feeling like a fool, before Torald rescued me by continuing the introductions.

When the introductions were complete, with crimson cheeks, I turned to Steinar and whispered, "Well I made a complete fool of myself there. She must think that I am some kind of idiot."

Steinar, seeing my dismay, mischievously chuckled and replied' "Well, my lord…" letting the words trail off and grinning at me like the idiot who I felt myself to be.

The tables laid out for the feast were weighed down with huge platters heaped with mounds of food. There were platters stacked with beef, mutton, pork and a variety of fish and poultry. There were steaming bowls of vegetables and there were huge jugs of wine. I was seated at the place of honour, immediately beside Torald's wife. Steinar, while also a guest at the table of honour, was seated at the far end. The rest of this elevated table sat the various members of Torald's large family. Far down the table, on the opposite side from me, was Eyja. Other guests were seated at the lower tables.

The serving staff worked at trying to ensure that everyone at the raised table ate too much food and drank too much wine. Dancers and jugglers entertained the revelers throughout the meal.

Conversation abounded and laughter was loud and boisterous. But I kept largely to myself, speaking only enough so as to not offend anyone who directed remarks my way. My thoughts raced from embarrassment over my awkward silence upon meeting Eyja to absolute wonderment that this shy young beauty was to become my wife.

I was further awestruck as I realized that this sumptuous banquet was being held in my honour. Torald had received me as if I were royalty. After the meal was over, I summoned the courage to ask Torald's son, Ulphus, the cause of this honour.

Ulphus was Torald's eldest son. He was thirteen years older than I and was already a warrior of some renown. He looked the part. He was a big man in both height and breadth but his body showed no signs of softness. He had a light brown mane which covered his head and most of his face. Though it was long, it was well groomed. He had soft green eyes which revealed inner warmth which seemed to welcome my approach.

Ulph looked at me in disbelief. "You really don't know?" he roared. "My father owes his life to your father and to your grandfather. He fought beside your father in a shield wall, and, in that battle your father took the sword blow that was meant for my father. Your father died so that mine could live. In another battle, my father was captured and would surely have been executed but it was Steinar and your grandfather, along with a handful of others, who snuck into the Wessex camp and rescued him. Torald often speaks of his debt to your family. He will show you favour even over me, his first born son. We all are indebted to your family and we will all insure that you are treated as one of ours. Torald insisted that Vidar, upon his death, send you to us so that we could begin to repay our debt. And we will. So enjoy yourself, Stor. You are part of our family even now before your wedding to my young sister."

Steinar approached and, on catching my attention, beckoned to me. "I am leaving you safely in Lord Torald's hands. I must return to StorEye in the morning. We have left it unattended too long already. Your safety here is assured. Now I must retire so that I can rise and leave at daybreak. Farewell young master. Rest confident that StorEye is in good hands and anxiously awaiting your return." We embraced and Steinar took his leave.

I wandered through the great hall seeking Eyja, hoping to find her unattended and speak to her. Maybe I could say something that would help repair the terrible image that I was sure I had created. But every time I spotted her she was surrounded by friends or relatives and engaged in animated conversation. Finally I spotted her standing alone on the far side of the hall. She was looking directly at me, as if studying me from a distance, probable assessing the idiot to whom she was betrothed. She saw me as I looked her way, smiled demurely and disappeared behind a large column. I hurried across the room to where she had been standing, but, when I reached the column and looked around, she was gone. I did not see her again that evening. Finally, after searching fruitlessly, I gave up the hunt and, after bidding my respects to my host, retired to my room.

I lay in the wondrous bed for many hours but, in spite of its comfort, sleep evaded me. My thoughts swirled between thoughts of the lovely and gracious Eyja and the rest of her family who were to become mine. Torald was every inch the patriarch and played that role well. His wife, Madellena was a striking woman, with only hints of silver in her golden mane. She also dressed well for her role as family matriarch. She had greeted me pleasantly and was generous with her attention to me. In spite of her warmth I suspected that she was a strong woman who held a tight rein on Torald's excesses. As I came to know her better, this observation proved itself true.

Disease and warfare had not been kind to Torald and Madellena's sons. Ulph and his younger brother, Byrniulf were the only ones still living. Ulph was to become my mentor. I felt both awe and fear towards him but that was offset by a strong sense of safety in being his responsibility. I would come to love him as the father of whom I had no recollection. Ulph's wife, Torete, while somewhat plain of face, exhibited an incredible pleasantness and a love for Ulph and her children which knew no bounds. She had assured me that I would come under her protection as much as any of her offspring.

Byrniulf was considerably younger than Ulph, more my age. He was a strong young lad who already was quite adept with a sword and an axe. Ulph's tutelage was very apparent. But where I lacked in fighting skills, I far surpassed him in my academic training. In spite of these differences, we would quickly become close friends. We both shared the same curiosity about the world around us and would quickly gain fame for avoiding any and all of the restrictions which Ulph and Torete would place on our explorations.

Ulph and Torete had two sons. Norman was the oldest. Achile was their youngest. Both were considerably younger than me but I often entertained myself playing with them. While Kari was Eyja's sister, she was closer in age to her nephews and watched over them like a mother hen. Three years separated Kari and me, but I think that she quickly developed a crush on me and would follow me like a puppy whenever she could do so.

FRED STOREY

* * *

The following morning I arose, after an incredibly comfortable, if late arriving, sleep, and dressed myself for the day. I was escorted into a small room off the main hall. Torald, Ulphus and their wives were seated at a small table. Torald stood and beckoned me to join them. "I trust you slept well," Madellena inquired. With a nod I joined the family for breakfast.

The conversation remained light while they ate, but as the table was being cleared and the ladies took their leave, Torald asked seriously. "So, how was your trip to York? Did you come by Ripon?"

"People were starting to rebuild, but Ripon remains in ruins," I replied. "The entire city was razed to the ground and destruction spread for miles around it. The people there are terrified of Eadred, but this does not temper their hatred of him."

"The House of Wessex has always been hated and mistrusted across all of Northumbria," Torald said bitterly. "They bleed us dry then send their black robed, joyless priests to preach to us the blessings of suffering and self-denial."

"But are you not a supporter of Bishop Wulfstan?" I asked guardedly. I was well aware that Torald was a member of the Witan and had stood side by side with Wulfstan in opposition to English rule of Northumbria. Wulfstan was the Anglo-Saxon Archbishop of York and therefore the ranking prelate in the north.

"Wulfstan is a different matter. Like most of the church in the north, the priests here understand Northumbria and, like us, they oppose our exploitation and oppression at the hand of Wessex. For example, they know that our wealth is based on commerce, and so, unlike Wessex priests, they waive the Sunday observances to allow merchants to move goods. They preach to us of a life of peace, love and forgiveness. Not the virtues of pain, suffering and martyrdom which Wessex's priests seem to thrive on. Our church in York understands Northumbrians and they represent our interests. They are not here to spy on us and connive ways to extract the last penny out of Northumbria and into the coffers in Wessex."

"But what of King Anlaf? Does he not shield York against these very offences?" I inquired cautiously.

"Ha!" Torald snorted. "That puppet of Wessex. Old Ragnald's seed must have been wearing thin when that cur was spawned. His predecessors were brave and honourable warriors. But he does not have the courage to relieve his bowels without Eadred's permission. Do you know that he pays Wessex for the pleasure of minting Wessex coins? What kind of king is that?"

"But I have seen Anlaf's coins. They bear his likeness," I protested.

"Look on the reverse side," Torald replied. "They bear the mark of a Wessex moneyer and Wessex receives a license fee to have them produced for us."

Torald went on in this vein for some while before his son, Ulphus inquired, "So how were things in Cumbria before you left?"

"We have not had many dealings with Wessex since Edmund and his Scottish supporters conquered King Dunmail five years ago. Dubh ruled Cumbria fairly and we were mostly left in peace by him," I replied. After retelling the story of our skirmish with the highland renegades, I went on, "Even when Malcolm broke his peace with Eadred, last year, there was little fighting in Cumbria. However, in reprisal, Eadred extended his direct rule into southern Cumbria, but he seems to have little interest in the affairs of northern Cumbria. We remain under Malcolm's rule;

however, Duhb's kingdom has been reduced to Strathclyde. Scotland has a new client king in Carlisle whose name is also Malcolm. He calls himself Mael Culem Dunmailson and claims a relationship to old King Dunmail. However, most people in Cumbria do not believe this. Dunmail is simply another pronunciation of the name Donald which is a very common name in both Cumbria and Strathclyde. Regardless of his name, he is loyal to Eadred of Wessex."

"And is he also loyal to our Anlaf?" Torald asked.

"Anlaf is not well known in Cumbria. And, like the kings of Wessex, he seems content to ignore us. We do not have the same rich land and wealth that you enjoy in York and therefore it is not so highly coveted. But to answer your question, Anlaf's ancestors, Ragnald, Guthric and Sihtric are all revered by many in Cumbria, and based on that, Anlaf could draw support from there. But even my grandfather, Vidar, with his sword pledged to Ragnald and his successors saw inevitability in Wessex rule eventually extending to Cumbria."

Torald thought about this for some time and then his mood seemed to lighten dramatically. "In a few days you will be going to Toraldesbi with Ulph and Byrniulf. Before you leave I have a present for you." He waved and a servant entered cradling a long bundle wrapped in cloth. Torald handed the bundle reverently to me. As I opened it and gazed at its content Torald spoke. "This is your father's sword. I kept it for you. Your father carried two swords into battle; one short and one long. He has gone to Odin's banquet hall gripping the short one in his hand, but this one I kept for you. Since you have now spilt blood, it is time for you to wear it." I was awe struck. The very thought that this beautifully crafted weapon, with its jewel studded handle actually belonged to my father and was used by him in battle, was overwhelming. But Torald was not finished. He handed me three jeweled golden arm bracelets. "These also belonged to your father. But I would not wear them too openly. Eadred's priests will see them and believe you to be a pagan." Such bracelets were worn as badges of honour by Viking warriors.

When I regained my composure I blurted out, "But you proudly display your bracelets."

Torald chuckled, "Priests like good Wulfstan understand the pride that we old Vikings take in our heritage. But the sight of these drives the dour priest of Wessex into frenzies."

I spent the next several pleasant days at Torald's home in York. I was treated warmly, as one of the family. In time I would come to think of him as a grandfather, but I would also come to think of Ulph as the father that I never knew and Byrniulf as my brother. But that gets me ahead of my story.

On several occasions my stay brought me in contact with Eyja, but at each of these, I became tongue tied and ended up hanging my head in embarrassment. She, on the other hand was always cheerful and inviting of engagement with me. My own reaction thwarted those efforts and left me frustrated. However, I did manage some snippets of guarded conversation. Finally the time came for me to leave, with Ulph and Byrni, for the manor in Deira.

CHAPTER 8
STRANGER IN PARADISE

SILVER COIN FROM YORK
ERIC BLOODAXE
948 A.D.

TORALDESBI, 951

Stigandr had taught me well the history of York and before it the history of the Kingdom of Northumbria and he had spoken at length about Torald and his family. Torald's grandfather had come to York with Halfdene as a captain in his army. When Halfdene had established his Danish

Kingdom of York, Torald's forbearer had been appointed Earl of Deira, an honour now held by Torald himself. Deira had been the name of the ancient Anglo kingdom which had merged with the Kingdom of Bernica to form what had become the Anglo-Saxon kingdom known as Northumbria. It had spanned the breadth of Britain from sea to sea and from Edinburgh in the north to the Thames in the south. By the time of the first Viking invasions it had shrunk to a mere fraction of its earlier glory. None the less, Toraldesbi was still an impressive estate. These days Torald fully engaged himself in the commerce and politics of York, and as result, he spent most of his time at the house in the city. But he was the Earl of Deira and, as such, he held extensive lands in old Deira and that is where he had built his manor.

Toraldesbi Manor was even more magnificent than his house in York. The great stone manor house was surrounded by lush green rolling hills and small copses of forest. All of the land, as far as I could see, in any direction, was part of Torald's estate. But life was not the luxury of York and I was back to sleeping on the floor with only a pallet of straw between me and the cold ground. And I was not here for its comforts. I was here to learn how to fight and how to kill.

Ulph was a tough task master. He told me that it was his duty to make me a warrior and that if he failed, and as a result, I was killed in battle, Torald would probably disown him. So Ulph pushed me to my limits to learn the arts of war. I learned how to fight with a sword, with an axe and with a spear. I learned how to use a bow and arrow. I learned how to fight on foot and when mounted. I learned how to fight in single hand-to-hand combat and how to fight in a shield wall. I practiced and practiced and when I thought that I would drop to the ground from exhaustion, I practiced even more. While our weapons were made only of wood, unlike the finely honed steel which would be used in real battle, they still raised welts and bruises.

When the Vikings had first begun their incursions in Britain, they brought with them their dreaded shield wall. This involved warriors lining up several men deep with the warriors in the front rank overlapping their shields with that of the warrior next to them. From this formation they would engage the enemy. Once a shield wall collided with the enemy line what ensued was practiced team work amongst surrounding chaos. Many strategies were employed by the individual warriors. Often one warrior would hook his war axe on the shield of the man opposite so that, as his shield was pulled down, his comrade beside or behind him could bring sword or axe crashing into the head of the opponent. If his comrade failed to strike, he would be left defenseless and slain himself. Another favorite tactic was for one warrior to use a short flexible sword and crouch down to thrust a wounding blow beneath his opponent's shield and into the legs or crotch, causing the opponent to falter and drop his shield so as the warrior facing him to the right or to the left could dispatch him. However if the warrior behind or beside failed to shield his comrade's head when he dropped into his crouch, an opponent would deliver him a killing blow before he could strike. A man in a shield wall had to stake his life on the skill and discipline of those beside and behind him.

When fighting in a shield wall, as several of the enemy fell, the wall itself would fall back one pace so as to cause the opponents to stumble over their own dead or wounded, and then the attackers would catch them off balance with killing blows of axe and sword. The whole wall had to fight as a unit and collectively sense when to step forward and when to step back. The initial successes of the Viking invasion could be attributed to this skill. However, over the years, the

Anglo-Saxons had learned to master this method of fighting and in many cases excelled over the skills of their enemies.

Horses were used sparingly in these battles. A horse will shy as it closes on a shield wall, leaving the opponent the opportunity to kill or maim the beast, thereby dismounting its rider to be quickly dispatched. Mounted troops were usually reserved either to assist flanking an opposing wall or to pursue the opponents once their shield wall had been breached and they were fleeing in panic. As a result, mounted riders were not the noble knights of legend. They were simply warriors who could fight well mounted.

And so I practiced, mainly on foot, fighting in shield walls. I was not the only student. My education was amongst a group of several dozen youth who were the children of retainers of the manor. Nor was Ulph their main teacher. This was provided by a handful of seasoned warriors, all of whom had survived shield wall encounters. These hard men would line their students in opposing walls which would spend hours each day attacking each other with wooden weapons until the tactics of a shield wall fight became our second nature. Ulph was the overseer who ensured that these practices continued until each of the youth wished to curse his existence. As our skills grew and our pride in accomplishment began to soar, our love and respect for Ulph and his training crew grew. In time we would become a formidable fighting force.

Meanwhile, I much enjoyed the company of Byrniulf who was only a few years my senior, but far and away my superior in martial skills. Norman and little Achill also comprised part of our sessions but they practiced amongst younger children closer to their age and size. Byrniulf was also vastly more skilled in armed fighting than I. This was not only due to our age difference, but he had been under Ulph's tutelage since he could first walk. Ulph often paired me with Byrniulf to practice against his skills. At first I was discouraged by my gross inferiority in the face of his skills. After he had defeated and disarmed me in dozens of subsequent skirmishes I expressed my dismay. "Is Ulph simply using me as fodder for your skills?" I asked.

He laughed and proclaimed, "My brother believes that you will only learn if you face a superior foe. When I was younger he had me face the same challenge which you face today. It made me so angry but I eventually gained sufficient skill that I could put up a reasonable defense."

In time his words proved true and I could at least avoid absolute embarrassment when sparring with Bryni.

During these sessions I saw another side of Ulph. Not only did I receive special attention from him in the form of praise, when I had earned it, and chastising when I deserved it. Ulph would take the time to sit and talk with me and Byrniulf about all manners of things unconnected to our training. We discussed crops, livestock and many issues of land management. We discussed the activities of merchants, manufacturers and tradesmen. We discussed human nature, including the mysteries of women's behaviour. We even, on occasion discussed religion and politics; however, we generally left those discussions until Torald was present. Over time I came to respect, and even love Ulph. Although he was only twelve years my senior he was a fountain of knowledge. And he seemed committed to using his knowledge to teach me. He was like the father which I had never known. On the other hand, Bryni became my soul brother. We were inseparable and together we engaged in all forms of mayhem which occurred to our young minds. Boredom seldom visited us.

But if Bryni was my friend, and Ulph my mentor, Torald was my benefactor. Torald and his family would also spend considerable time at Toraldesbi manor. On these occasions, Torald would often engage me in endless discussion.

Torald loved to argue the politics of the royal courts in York and Wessex and even of Carlisle and Edinburgh and of the bishops' palaces throughout the land. He would discuss the economic policies which he always described as Wessex plots to deprive Northumbrians of their wealth. I was fascinated with these subjects and always ready to participate or debate when Torald, good naturedly, goaded me into it. And goad me he would.

***

Often, during these visits I would encounter Eyja. It seemed to me that with each encounter she became more enchanting. In time I had learned to engage her in extensive discussions of trivial matters but if the conversation became serious or personal, I again was struck mute or stammered like an idiot, babbling nonsense. Finally one day she challenged me. "You seem to avoid talking seriously with me," she said challengingly. "If you really do not like me and do not wish to marry me, I am sure that I can persuade my father to release you from the bethroval pledges which Vidar made on your behalf."

I was stunned. I could feel the panic rage through my body. This time, however, instead of striking me mute, I blurted, "But I adore you. It is only my adoration of you that leaves me without words because words cannot describe how much I want you. From the first time I laid eyes on you, I have adored you."

"Oh you silly boy! I adore you too. So I had better marry you quickly and bear you many children before you can escape me." With this she leaned forward and kissed me gently on the lips. Our arms immediately embraced. As I embraced her I felt, with embarrassment, my manhood harden against her. But I only held her closer, thinking what a fool I had been not to have said these things to her months ago.

After that encounter my lessons became easier. The sword and the axe were lighter and my movements with them grew smooth and fluid. Practices became almost dancelike as I floated through the exercises smiting opponents with ease. While I never could surpass Byrni's skills, in time I could hold my ground and occasionally even defeat him. Other lads began jostling each other to avoid standing opposite me. Our weapons were only made of wood but they could raise welts and draw blood when they connected with flesh. With time, I became proficient in the use of swords, axes, knives and bows and arrows, both while standing on the ground and when mounted.

Between my incessant practices with weaponry I would seek out Eyja, if she was here in Deira. We would take long walks together, arm in arm, fantasizing our future together. These were the happiest moments of my young life. Marriage in these days was not a matter of romance and it was not a matter of choice. Guardians arranged marriage for as much practical advantage as their ward could bring. Children complied with those wishes. And, if possible, they bore and raised children of their own. On one of our walks, Eyja gently pulled me to a stop. I turned to her and drew her into my arms, playfully kissing her and receiving her kisses in return as we now did so often. Gazing into my eyes she said,"Torald is my guardian. I would have felt obliged to marry whoever he chose for me regardless of my feelings for that man. I am so happy that Torald chose you for me. I know that I will be happy for the rest of my life." My heart soared and I told her that I would be also.

Ulph often travelled back to the City of York and on many of these occasions he brought me and some of my fellow future warriors with him. Together we would enjoy the hospitality of Ulph's father and family. On other occasions Ulph would drag Bryni and me with him through the streets of the city, where we could explore the wealth that the city offered. This city had been the center of power during the heyday of old Northumbria. The Danes had made it their first target of conquest and had continued to use the city of York as the capital of their new Kingdom. When Ragnald had swept across Britain from his Kingdom of Dublin he made York his capital. For centuries the wealth of Europe and the Mediterranean had unloaded at the wharfs of this city.

When we eventually escape Ulph's supervision of us, Bryni would suggest that we seek out the company of willing young women. My adoration of Eyja, and its accompanying fidelity would result in my declining his invitation and he would tease me merciless for my infatuation with his sister.

The city was divided into many sections, some inside the wall, some without. My favourite was the Danish section outside of the wall. It sprawled from the wharves where the ships' crews loaded and unloaded wares destined for, or coming from, all over the world. The Danish houses were made from large wooden planks built parallel to the ground to an elevation of seven feet. Their roofs were thatched with straw and daubed with tar. We would visit butchers and watch them wade through offal and feces as they plied there trade. The stench was unbearable, but was rivaled by the smells from the tanners and leather workers as they fashioned beautiful saddles, belts, shoes and all other manner of leather goods. There were jewelers who fashioned gold and silver with inlaid gems of every colour and size. And the din was incredible as all strata of York society scrambled to carry out their respective business or carry on their shopping. And, as with any other city, at any other time, when dusk fell, it drew out the prostitutes to flog their favours near the exits of the neighbourhood taverns.

In my wonderment, I would question every tradesman, shop keeper or merchant that we encountered. I was like a sponge, taking in every detail that I could about how each business carried out its affairs. No question was too mundane to be asked, and no answer was too obvious not to be savoured. Ulph also toured me through all of the ale houses and taverns in the city where I learnt what the citizens of York really thought and what things that they would kill or die for.

Inside the walls of the city were the churches; magnificent stone structures with spires stretching into the sky as if competing with each other as to which one could actually reach to heaven. Each church was adorned with massive statues which, on close inspection revealed the Northumbrian union of Scandinavian pagans and Anglo-Saxon Christianity. Common were statues of Norse Gods posed in intimate discussion with Christian saints or of Viking nobility dressed in their finery juxtaposed to the crucified Christ.

YORK, 952

I was now fourteen years of age. I had reached my full height. My frame was filling out and taking on new muscle. Eyja was a year younger, and her bosom and buttocks were blossoming into those of a young woman. And chaos was about to erupt in York. Agitation against King Anlaf's reign as Wessex's puppet was growing daily. It was all that Torald could talk about. It was winter, early in the year of our lord, 952.

This morning we were with Torald in Deira. We had just finished our morning meal when he exclaimed, "We should never have let Eric leave. He was a real king of Northumbria."

It was Torald's custom to goad me into arguments so that he could insure that his case would withstand a thorough critique. But on occasion I would cheekily reverse our roles, demanding that Torald defend his beliefs and actions. This was one of those days.

"So why did you and your fellow members of the Witan cave in to Eadred and vote to drive Eric off of the throne? Why did you not mobilize the armies of Northumbria behind Bloodaxe and drive the Wessex cur back where they belong?" I asked.

Instead of the outburst that I had anticipated, and had attempted to provoke, "We were wrong, but I never supported that decision." He said sadly. "Wulfstan did not support deposing Bloodaxe either. But the Witan were divided. Oswulf, the High Reeve of Bamburgh and Earl of Bernicia opposed us. He managed to convince other members of the Witan that we could not successfully oppose Eadred of Wessex and that Eadred would level York in the same manner as he had leveled Ripon. He may well have been right. Unless Northumbria was united we could not withstand an invasion by England. Only Wulfstan, Orm and I stood solidly behind our king. In the face of those divisions in the Witan, Wulfstan capitulated and we agreed to make his decision unanimous."

He paused, and then continued, " But things have changed. Eadred's *wergeld* is driving us all to ruin."

THE LEGEND OF STOR

The *wergeld* was an amount of money a man could forfeit to save his life in exchange for having taken the life of another. Eadred had charged York *a wergeld* for every man in his army who had died as a result of Eric Bloodaxe's ambush following the razing of Ripon. Part of the capitulation by the Witan of York in order to save their city included their agreement to the payment of the *wergeld*.

His next words brought stunned silence to our small gathering. "But Anlaf has now been deposed. Oswulf of Bamburgh is now on his own in support of Anlaf. The rest of us are prepared to stand up to Wessex and we have invited Eric Bloodaxe to return and again take the throne of York. We have sent messengers to locate him and pledge our support. Wulfstan is already travelling south to ensure that we remain aware of Wessex's plans should Eric agree to return."

No one was sure of the location of Eric Bloodaxe since he fled York four years earlier. After leaving York in 948, he had been reported to have made plundering raids in Ireland and Wales. Persistent reports abounded that he was involved in slave trading as far away as Spain and North Africa. While these rumours could not be confirmed, there is little doubt that Eric and his fleet travelled widely and engaged in looting and violence. But the trade routes between York and the entire coast of Europe were widely travelled. It would only be a matter of a short time before Eric Bloodaxe would hear messages that he would be welcome back in York.

Only a few weeks later, however, it was not news of Eric that we received, but of Wulfstan. The news was not good. The government in Wessex had arrested Archbishop Wulfstan, that tower of support for an independent Northumbria, and had incarcerated him in a dungeon on the remote shores of East Anglia. The witan were leaderless and close to panic.

Then, as things seemed most bleak, the news came: Eric Bloodaxe, our deposed king, was on his way back to York to reclaim his throne.

* * *

Eric's arrival in York was a reason for us to leave Toraldesbi and return to the city. Torald wanted his entire family there to witness Eric's triumph. It was a grand event. We were joined by almost the entire citizenry of York at the city's wharfs to watch the fleet of Eric Bloodaxe sail into the harbour. The colourful shields of the Viking warriors girded the gunwales of their sleek war ships and shining swords glistened as they were waved in the sun. They looked just as fearsome as their predecessors had when they first appeared off Britain's coast. The only difference was that now, the fearsome animal carvings that always graced the bow of Viking warships, had been removed as a sign that they came in peace.

A great cheer went up from the crowd when Eric disembarked. Citizens lined the streets, singing his praise and waving colourful banners, as Eric led a procession all the way to reclaim his Royal Hall.

Bloodaxe wasted little time once he was reinstated as our king. His first act was to cancel the payments of the *wergeld* to Wessex. Within weeks he issued his own coins. On one side was his likeness and the inscription *Eric rex*. On the reverse was a sword and, in an obvious show of contempt for Wessex, the inscription 919, commemorating the date when King Ragnald had first consolidated Norse authority over the Kingdom of York.

THE LEGEND OF STOR

* * *

Spring was just beginning to unveil its first new greenery when Torald summoned Ulph and me to York. When we arrived, he announced, "We are going to meet our new king."

Our audience had been arranged for the following day. For the occasion I was dressed in my finest apparel. I wore an ankle length woolen garment with a fine fur collar fastened with a carved and polished silver brooch. On a leather strap from my neck hung a jeweled hunting horn which I had received as a present from Torald. On my right arm I had proudly clasped two of my father's bracelets. The third bracelet I wore on my left arm. Thus clad we were ushered into King Eric's royal hall.

I gasped in amazement when I saw the hall. Vidar had often told me of Odin's Banquet Hall and I had imagined how it would appear. To me it seemed that it was there that we were now entering. The highly polished wooden walls supported a plank ceiling which towered above us. Massive chandeliers hung down, where multitudes of candles cast a soft glow on all of the intricate carved ornamentation decorating the walls. The furnishings were all of heavy polished planking, built to withstand the rowdy celebrations of men of war. Warriors, adorned with heavy, glittering jewelry sprawled on sturdy benches. Tables were stacked with food and drink of every description.

In the center of the room, sitting on as massive oak throne, was King Eric. He was a big, muscular man with a long flowing brown mane and a matching beard. He was well groomed and looked very much the king. He had a handsome face that looked as if it could portray anger, cruelty or kindness as required. Around him were lower benches to accommodate audiences with his subjects. To the side sat poets and chroniclers ready to glorify and revere his every word. Around the hall, his armed guards kept a watchful eye on his well-being.

We sat patiently while Eric concluded a discussion which was underway when we had arrived. The conversation suddenly seemed to turn ugly. One of Eric's men had made some reference to sending an army to Norway to unseat their king, Haakon and subject him to the blood eagle. Eric had succeeded his father as the King of Norway but, with the help of Wessex, his older half-brother, Haakon, had unseated him and driven him out of Norway. I did not see Eric draw his sword. It appeared in his hand as if by magic and struck with neither mercy nor hesitation. The man's head flew from his shoulders and rolled into a bloody mess several yards away. Eric stood there a moment and then, composed, he sat back down and smiled, "Haakon is my brother. I, and I alone, may threaten him."

Then he rose again acting as if the incident had not occurred. Looking directly at us he loudly proclaimed, "This is Torald, noble Earl of Deira. He has supported us well both in our earlier reign and upon our return. He is worthy of my gratitude and I give it freely. Come Torald, bring your sons and talk with me," motioning us to the now vacant seats by his throne.

Our discussion was cordial and direct, interspersed with expression of Eric's gratitude to Torald for his loyalty. The man appeared guileless, saying what he thought and not worrying himself about the consequences. He left no room for pettiness or indecisiveness. I found myself liking the man, regardless of his reputation as a vicious brigand and a pirate. To me he was very much what I thought a king should be.

One of Eric's visions of being a king was that of being a giver of gold. The chronicles will account for this generosity time and again. As our audience was winding down, he ladened us with so many gold and jeweled presents that we were required to summons help to take it all home. But before dismissing us he turned to me and said, "So you are young StorEyeson. I have heard of the deeds of your predecessors. They were men who command respect.

"I will be having trouble with Bamburgh. He will raise an army against me. But I will go to meet him before he can do so. I know Torald will send men-in arms to support me. I would like you, Stor, to join me." I could not believe my ears. Somehow I managed to respond, "I will consult with my guardian, Torald, and make arrangements accordingly."

* * *

When we had returned to Torald's home, he summoned the entire family to gather around the table in his great hall. After recounting the events of the audience with King Eric, giving emphasis to Eric's request that I join his campaign against Bamburgh, he paused to give everyone a chance to absorb this news.

Kari giggled, "I cannot believe that you turned down the king."

"He did not turn him down. He deferred his answer to me. After all, he is my squire and I am his guardian. He did what was right." Torald sharply replied.

"But he may be killed," Eyja sobbed.

"Ulphus has trained me well. I am a warrior and I can take care of myself," I retorted.

"You may be well trained, but you are not yet a warrior. Until you have actually been in a battle, you are untested and you cannot know your capacity. Plus you are only fourteen years of age," said Torald calmly. "And besides, Eric does not want you as a warrior. You are a Norseman. And your mother was an Anglo from Bernicia. You can read and write in English, Danish and Latin. Eric wants your abilities to aid him in the negotiation of a peace once he has defeated Bernicia.

"I have sworn an oath to your Grandfather to protect you. And you have become like a son to me. But you are almost a man now Stor and should know your own mind," he continued. "What do you wish to do?"

I could feel my mind battling between the sense of adventure and the chance to prove myself in battle and Vidar imploring me not to cast my sword and my life in other men's quarrels. Vidar's predictions of an eventual Wessex triumph over all of England played loudly in my deliberations. But I believe that it was my young man's sense of adventure that sealed the decision. Finally I said, "I will do what the king bids me to do."

I could hear Eyja's sobs intensify. But it was Ulph's words that settled the discussion. "If Stor joins Eric's campaign in Bernicia, Bryni and I will go with him and we will bring him home safely."

When our discussion had ended and I had retired to Torald's sumptuous guest room and was readying myself for bed, I heard a gentle rap on my door. When I opened it, there stood Eyja, tears continuing to mar her beautiful face. "I am so afraid for you, my beloved," she whispered.

"I can take care of myself. Also, I will have Ulph and Bryni there with me."

My words seemed not to comfort her. "You may be killed and I will never have known you"

'I will survive and I will be back to marry you before you even have time to miss me"

Her beautiful eyes seemed to fill with purpose. "That is not a chance that I am prepared to take." Gently she took my hand and led me to the down filled mattress on its raised platform where, that night, I was to experience the greatest paradise that I would ever know.

CHAPTER 9
FOR OTHER MEN'S GLORY

It was a warm, sunny day in late summer when Eric's force took to the field. It was a magnificent array, some seven thousand strong. Most of our men were on foot, but we had with us trains of horse-drawn carts which carried our supplies, our armour and our weapons so that our men would not be overburdened. I was on horse along with Ulph, Byrniulf and the rest of Eric's nobility. Our banners proudly announced our advance. I chatted gaily to Ulph, Bryni and other members of our party, deliberately disguising both my excitement and my apprehension as we headed to war.

My thoughts wandered back to my bittersweet parting with Eyja. Amongst sobs and hugs she had given me a small silver Christian cross which she had hung around my neck with a delicate silver chain. It now hung beneath my tunic beside a metal pagan amulet which I had worn since I was a young child.

We had been marching for about three weeks, moving directly towards Bamburgh Castle from which the High Reeve of Bamburgh, Oswulf, ruled the ancient kingdom of Bernicia. We had scouts travelling far ahead of our army and reporting back regularly on the whereabouts of the enemy. We would be facing an army of about nine thousand, for Oswulf had drawn large support from Wessex, Cumbria and Scotland to swell the ranks of his northern Anglo army. While Anlaf had not been seen in the area, we knew he would not be far afield, awaiting Bamburgh's victory. While his name had drawn considerable Cumbrian support, Eric was not without allies from that region. Many of my neighbours from the valley of the Eske River were amongst our host.

Word came late in the afternoon that we were closing quickly on the Bamburgh forces. Eric was a fine general. Once he knew the approximate point at which our armies would meet, he moved our columns in such a manner that we would be approaching Bamburgh's forces from the east, the morning sun at our backs. His scouts found level terrain that would give us a slight downhill advantage. Then we moved at a pace that would insure that we arrived at the potential battlefield ahead of the enemy so as to guarantee our positions. Once there, we struck camp and carried out our final preparations for fight. Late that afternoon Bamburgh's forces came into view. They too established their camp. Tomorrow we would meet them in battle.

As dawn broke the following morning the opposing armies were forming shield walls on their respective sides of the field of battle. I sat astride my horse, clad in gleaming mail and a highly polished helmet, both of which Torald had given me before we left York. My father's sword was sheathed across my back, its hilt protruding over my right shoulder to provide easy access. Ulph had given me a short sword which, like my father's sword, was honed to a sharpness that only fine steel can hold. It hung in a sheath from my belt.

I had been kept out of the shield wall. My assignment, along with a company of mounted warriors, was to ready myself on a hill overlooking the scene of the battle. If the enemy attempted to flank our wall, our job was to charge into their flankers and disrupt their efforts. In the event that the enemy line broke our task would be to chase them down while they fled and inflict as much damage as we could before they could escape. Otherwise I was part of a reserve force, held in waiting

Suddenly the air was shattered by thousands of swords and spears, from both sides, clashing against shields while their bearers screamed insults at the opposing army. Then the walls began to move towards each other. Their progress was slow but the din was reaching deafening levels. Finally the lines met. The crash of their collision could be heard for miles.

When shield walls collide it is a terrible sight, but initially it is not as deadly as it appears. It is a lot of pushing and shoving and cursing and sweating as each side attempts to force a chink in their opponent's wall. When that happens then the blood really begins to spill. The pushing and shoving went on and on as the day progressed, with neither side giving more than a few yards at a time and neither side breaking. At various points along the line, one side would force a small wedge into the opposing wall and then swords would take their deadly tolls. But in today's battle, exhaustion was carrying the day. The sun was high in the heavens. Strength and endurance were waning.

Eric called his captains together to assess the situation. It was determined that the enemy had suffered greater losses than us. This was probably because of our superior position and our ranks were more motivated. We were fighting to rid the land of the oppression by Wessex and to avenge Edmund's slaughter at Ripon. The enemy ranks were more mercenary in their motivation which gave us the upper hand. Although we had cut into their numbers, all we had really accomplished was to neutralize the superior numbers which with they had started the day.

Eric finally spoke, "This battle will be decided today and it will be decided by the shield wall. Our troops are exhausted and so we must provide them with all possible reinforcement. If we cannot defeat Bamburgh's army today then they will retreat and regroup and we will simply have to chase them and fight them elsewhere. But that is to their advantage. We are farther from home than they and the summer is wearing on. Our supplies will not allow us to chase them into the autumn. We must defeat them here.

When we dispersed, I met with Ulph and Byrniulf, and together we raced toward the battle. "Stor, Bryni," Ulph said, "We must now join the shield wall. Stay close in front of me. You will use your shields to protect us while I deal death over your shoulder. Remember what I taught you. Keep your shield up. They will try to hook the top with their axes and pull it down. If they are successful, then we will die. And watch carefully that the man opposing you does not crouch down to plunge his sword up under your shield. You two will be fighting side by side. Protect each other"

Entering a shield wall is a terrifying experience. Sheer horror competed with the fear that coursed through my entire body. I was afraid that my fear might paralyze me. Once engaged in the wall, all thoughts evaporate and my attention concentrated onto the foe before me. If you lose that concentration, you die. I had spotted a weak spot in our wall, and Byrniulf and I rushed to fill it: Ulph on our heels. The months and months of practice now paid off. I smacked my shield against that of my opponent and leaned into it. My arm was fresh and his was tired. His shield faltered and Ulph's sword sang its terrible rhapsody. We repeated this again and again with deadly success. Several times I was able to deal a disabling jab beneath my shield, causing the foe to stagger back, to be felled by Ulph's or Byrni's sword.

We continued in this manner for what seemed like hours. My arm was wracked with the pain of the exertion. I was beginning to falter and I was wondering how long I could continue without succumbing to the onslaught. Then suddenly there was a space in front of me. We charged in to fill the void, continuing to deal death as we proceeded. We were now stumbling over our fallen foe and slipping in their split blood and innards. But we kept up our incursion with more and more of our comrades joining us in the breach. Then, just as suddenly, their wall broke. I did not know at the time that there were many such breaches all along the wall. But now the enemy was in full retreat and we were on them like hounds. My long sword was out now and as we chased them I was mowing them down like a man cutting his crops. Energy coursed through my body. I cast aside fear and reason. Mindlessly, we killed and we killed. Finally I stopped and fell to my knees in exhaustion. King Eric had won the day.

I slowly rose to my feet and surveyed the carnage. Dead and dying, in the thousands, from both sides were strewn across the field of battle. Some men were dispatching the mortally wounded. Others were looting the dead, carrying off armloads of armour, weapons, jewelry, and even shoes and leather tunics. I had no appetite to join them. I felt sickened by the carnage.

As the enormity of the scene set in, I did not see just corpses. These men had left behind widows and orphans. They may have been the enemies of Bloodaxe or Bamburgh but they had not been my enemies. I shuddered as Vidar's words came back to me. "Do not exchange your sword for promises of glory." There was no glory here. I did not wish to meet these men again in Odin's Banquet Hall. I wanted them to miraculously rise again from this dreadful place and return home to their families.

In my short life until now, I had bade Vidar's wishes and embraced the Christian Jesus. My faith stemmed from my loyalty to Vidar's instructions. But as I did so, in the back of my mind and of my heart I had clung to the Gods of my father and grandfather. However, now, as I looked around me, I could see no sign of glory as the fallen were welcomed into Odin's Banquet Hall. Nor could I accept the idea that these men had met the fate spun for them by the weavers at the Tree of Life. This was carnage and we had done it. The thought sickened me.

As Ulph led us back to our camp, I reached beneath my tunic and tugged the amulet from my neck and let it fall from my hand to rest amongst the carnage that we had done.

* * *

BAMBURGH CASTLE

After thoroughly defeating Bamburgh, Bloodaxe led his army all the way into Bernicia to Bamburgh Castle. It was a huge rock monolith towering on a cliff and looking out over the ocean. With only one approach by land, it would have been easily defended against attack. But Bamburgh's forces had been so devastated in our battle that the fortress put up no resistance. While we were still a long distance away, the High Reeve sent his emissaries to discuss Bernicia's submission to Eric, the King of York. While Bloodaxe had shown no mercy following the battle, his anger had now cooled and he was prepared to be generous so long as Bamburgh and his nobles swore absolute fealty to his Throne of York.

As we rode into the castle, an old woman in the crowd shouted at Eric, "May the Lord strike you dead, you filthy pagan." As several of our host moved quickly to strike her dead, Eric merely gave her a curious smile and waved them off.

"We do not need their love, only their submission", he retorted.

Bamburgh's submission involved an elaborate ceremony which left no doubt who was now in charge.

"I am Oswulf, the Christian High Reeve of Bernicia. On behalf of the people of Bernicia I surrender my sword to you, King Eric of York", and with that he rose and handed his sword, hilt first, to Eric. He then fell to one knee and raise the cuff of Eric's robe to his lips and kissed it. "You have dealt a resounding blow to my armies, and while this act is now being done with great difficulty, I submit to you as my sovereign."

He then rose and sat back on his throne, beckoning Eric to sit at a similar throne beside him. He spoke entirely in English and I dutifully translated his words to Eric's native Danish language. He quickly continued, "Before you decide on my fate, and that of my people, I beg that you will allow me to speak."

"So speak" Eric snarled.

"I am the direct descendant and heir of Ida Flamebearer, King and founder of the Kingdom of Northumbria," Oswulf continued. This was not completely true. The royal family of Northumbria, in the last decades of its existence, had been rife with fratricide in their struggles to succeed each other. It is doubtful that any direct descendant had survived. While I was aware of this history, I held my tongue. "After Ivar the Boneless conquered Northumbria, he murdered my ancestor, Aella, the last king of Northumbria." Again I knew the truth; Ivar had executed Aella, by the feared and gruesome blood eagle, as punishment because Aella had slain Ragnor Lodbrook, a Norse war hero, by having him thrown into a pit of vipers. And again I held my tongue.

"When Ivar's brother, Halfdene, succeeded to the throne of York, he invited my grandfather, Egbert, to succeed to the position of High Reeve of Bamburgh." Halfdene knew well that a barrier between York and the savage Scots would serve his interest and would appease many of his Anglo-Saxon and Christian subjects.

This arrangement proved so successful that Halfdene's son, Guthred, entered into an arrangement with Eagburt, to create a further buffer zone between Danes and Scots, and Christians and pagans. They both donated tracts of land in the region of Chester-Le-Street to serve as a home for the Community of St. Cuthbert which became known as *Haliwerfolkland*, the home of the holy man's people. Today, nothing is unchanged. Your kingdom will be well served by both the St. Cuthbert buffer and the existence of a loyal Christian Bernicia ally."

While considering Oswulf's proposal, Eric's mood moved from contempt to a growing interest. After working out the details of the proposal, Eric accented to it. "Your earldom and your position shall be continued but many of my men have died in this struggle. You will pay York a *wergeld* to compensate our losses for having had to come here."

When Eric was done, Oswulf's eldest son and heir, Waltheof, rose, approached and knelt before Eric. "I affirm my father's pledge to you," he said.

When it was over, we accepted Bamburgh's hospitality with a great feast which he held in Eric's honour. During supper his acknowledgement of Eric's superiority was accentuated by his accepting a seat beside Eric while Eric himself occupied the throne, the seat of honour which had always before been occupied by the High Reeve of Bamburgh.

During the entertainment, Oswulf's son, Waltheof, approached me and beckoned me to accompany him. He led me to a corner of the hall so that we might speak privately. He was a man of about thirty five years. He was tall and had his father's bearings but he lacked Oswulf's attractive feature. His eyes were closely placed, giving him a furtive appearance. His hair and beard were unkempt, detracting from the imposing physique which his body provided him. He spoke to me in a low, but pleasant tone. "So you are Stor son of Eye. I understand that you are a Christian and that your mother was an Anglo Bernician. You are obviously intelligent and well educated, so I am curious as to why you serve Eric," he said, more as a question than a statement.

Without betraying any emotion, I simply replied, "Eric is my King."

"He will not serve you well," Waltheof replied. "Under the rule of Wessex, we enjoy the rule of law. Eric is a frivolous despot, who rules as it pleases him and varies with his whims. He is bound by no constraints and will act upon any fancy which might visit him. You are only safe if you please him and that may change at any moment."

"You should explain that to the people of Ripon and advise them why the Anglo-Saxon Christian Eadred of

Wessex chose to obliterate the greatest center of English learning in the world and put all of its inhabitants to the sword," I responded coolly.

Waltheof initially shuttered at the directness of my response, but quickly recovered and his smile returned. "We might be opponents today but you will eventually see the error of your loyalties and we will become allies. Who knows, we may even become friends."

I ignored the pomposity of his remarks and turned the discussion to a meaningless commentary about the quality of the entertainment which his father had provided.

After the feast had been consumed and we were enjoying the entertainment supplied by Oswulf and the reveling of the commanders of the army of York, King Eric motioned me to join him. "Tell me Stor," he started, "You are a Christian. I know that these Christians hate me, but that old hag on the street earlier has me wondering. What is it about these people that they are so prepared to die for their Christian God?"

I think Eric realized that I was conflicted between the beliefs of by forbearers and those of the Church of Rome. I thought for a moment before replying. I had no desire to confess my turmoil over gods and their purposes to Eric Bloodaxe or to reveal my earlier conversation with Waltheof. Instead I replied, "Christians believe that their God creates great miracles on their behalf. They believe that for one to benefit from these miracles, they must accept their God as the one and only true God. They regard belief in the old Norse Gods as an affront to their God."

"They did not see any miracles when they met us in battle," Eric snorted.

"But that does not mean that they never see miracles, "I replied. "Their holy island of Lindisfarne is just down the road. St. Cuthbert, who was the Bishop there hundreds

THE LEGEND OF STOR

of years ago, is said to have performed many miracles. They say that he could converse with animals and that by a simple touch of his hand he could heal peoples' afflictions. He has been reported to have calmed the sea during ferocious storms, saving the lives of men who were out in boats fishing"

"How can they cling to rumours of the actions of a man who has been dead for hundreds of years?"

"They claim that the miracles continued long after his death. Pilgrims went to Lindisfarne to pray at the site where his coffin lay and their prayers were answered. This is supposed to have continued until the monks at Lindisfarne were forced to evacuate that site because of their fear that his remains would be destroyed in one of the continuous Viking attacks there." I went on to tell him about the *Haliwerfolkland* and their forced flight, until they finally found refuge at Chester-Le-Street. And I told him that when they had opened Cuthbert's coffin to facilitate moving his remains, it was reported that his body bore no signs of decomposition.

He thought for several minutes, and then asked, "So, is that why AEthelstan and Edmund and even Eadred all made pilgrimages to Chester-Le-Street?" I acknowledged that all three English kings had made the pilgrimage and paid homage to St. Cuthbert. He astonished me by replying, "Well, I am now the king. So we too shall go to visit St. Cuthbert."

* * *

Before leaving Bamburgh Castle, with Waltheof serving as our guide, we made the short trip up the road to see the ruins of Lindisfarne. Eric told me that he would have marched his whole army north as far as Edinburgh, so that all of Bernicia could view his power, but it was now autumn and the idea of a long march south, and then back to York, in the winter, with his whole army, was not practical. So, retaining only a reasonable bodyguard, he dispatched the army directly back to York. In doing so he instructed his captains," Take whatever plunder as you find in this miserable country. And take as many healthy young men and attractive young women as you find. They will bring a good return in the slave markets of Spain and Morocco."

I looked at Eric aghast. "But they are now your subjects. Oswulf bent the knee to you," I blurted out.

"Now they will remember me and they will fear me. That is how a king rules."

With that we mounted and made our way to Chester-Le-Street and our appointment with St. Cuthbert. Along the way Eric talked continuously about his aspirations of uniting all of the people of Northumbria under his leadership. The more he pursued this topic, the more that I suspected that our pilgrimage to the shrine of St. Cuthbert was but a ploy to convince his Christian subjects that he would make a good king for them as well as for the pagans. But Eric turned out to be not the straight-forward kind of person that I had thought him to be. So he was to surprise me again at Chester-Le-Street.

Bishop Aldred served both as the Bishop of Lindisfarne (now in exile) and the secular head of the Community of St. Cuthbert. He welcomed us and we toured the shrine, Aldred providing historical antidotes as we proceeded. At last we came to the coffin which housed the saint's remains. Eric inquired of the bishop as to whether the coffin could be opened so that he could look upon the relics directly. The Bishop complied and arranged for the lid of the coffin to be raised. When the lid was lifted a gasp was uttered throughout the room. We had expected to see only a pile of bones. But the legend was true. Instead, what we were seeing was the corpse of St Cuthbert. The flesh was dried and wrinkled and appeared very old. But it was not decomposed. It was intact.

When we had regained our composure, Eric inquired about a small book which had been placed in Cuthbert's withered hand. Aldred explained that he had been told that the book was a Gospel which had been placed there by King AEthelstan when he had made this pilgrimage.

Eric then asked Aldred if he could have a few moments alone with St. Cuthbert so that he could pray. The sincerity of his request drew an immediate agreement. As the bishop and his retinue withdrew and closed the door, leaving only Eric and I with the saint, Eric fell to his knee before the coffin. And it was then that he left me in absolute shock. He reached into his pouch and withdrew a glimmering Viking war bracelet. He then gently took the saint's arm and placed the bracelet around it. After pulling the remnants of the saint's garment down so as to conceal his act, he motioned to me to advise the bishop that he should return to our presence.

* * *

The journey back to York was long and cold. But we made good time being unencumbered by the presence of the army. I spoke to Eric often along the way, but never once did the topic of St. Cuthbert arise. I will never know the reasons for Eric's strange behaviour. But that is the nature of kings. They do not feel obliged to explain themselves.

King Eric did, however, offer me a position in his royal court. I told him that I was engaged to be married and that I was obliged, by my oath to Vidar, to return to StorEye and raise a family. He responded with a simple smile and wished me the protection of the gods, whoever my God may be.

CHAPTER 10
HEIR TO STOREYE

TORALDESBI, 953

The first signs of spring were just beginning to show when I finally arrived back at Toraldesby. My reception was overwhelming, as I was embraced by every member of the family and all of the servants. I was truly the prodigal son returning and Torald held back on nothing to celebrate my safe return. Eyja looked lovelier than ever, having developed fully into her womanhood in my absence. The moment I dismounted she threw her arms around me with such passion that I found myself questioning why I had ever left. Through sobs of joy we affirmed our love and commitment to each other.

In my absence, our wedding day had been set for early in the coming summer. Eyja, Madellena, Torete and Kari had the wedding planning in full swing. After spending the first week of my return in the constant presence of Eyja as we clamored to make up for the time lost by my absence, I began to realize that I was mostly getting in the way of the wedding planning.

With all of the commotion brought about our wedding plans, Ulph decided that he should escape to the city for a short respite. He invited me and Bryni to join him. As the weather was warming, the trip would be pleasant and so we accepted. After we arrived in York, we parted company and I went off to once again explore the wonders of the markets in the Danish section of the city. Ulph had business to attend to and I suspect that Bryni went off wenching.

I had wandered up to a stall which housed a jeweler who fashioned small rings and bracelets out of silver and gold. My eye caught an intricate gold band fashioned in the shape of a bird. The creature had a long curved neck and long, very thin legs which circled around to touch the back of its head, thus completing the ring. I inquired of its origin. The goldsmith explained that the bird was called a stork. He said that it was a creature long revered in Europe and that as far back as ancient Greece; a man named Aristotle had made it a crime to kill them. He went on to say that when he was a child, living in Denmark, his grandmother had told him that storks were considered symbols of fertility and that whenever there were many storks, many babies were born. I thought that the ring would make a perfect bridal gift for Eyja and so I purchased it immediately.

When I returned to Deira and presented my gift to my betrothed and explained its origin, she smiled broadly. "It must work its spell very well. It is good that we are getting married very soon. We will be starting our new family sooner than you might have planned." I was thunderstruck and found myself demanding that she clarify her meaning. As the reality set in, I felt a thrill which I had never before experienced. StorEye will have an heir.

We were married the following month. With the exception of a slight enlargement of her breasts, Eyja did not yet show signs that she was with child and we refrained from sharing this news until after the wedding. When Torald heard, he was ecstatic. He told me afterwards, "Now we truly are family."

The wedding itself was a magnificent affair. I am sure that Torald invited the entire population of his earldom to witness the event. We were showered with gifts and well wishes, but I was admonished by Eyja's mother that we were not to leave for StorEye as planned, but must wait until after our child was born. Our reward however was to be elevated from our coarse straw pallet to the luxury of a feather bed much like the one that I had enjoyed when I first arrived in York.

* * *

Since returning from Bernicia, I had given much thought to how I felt about King Eric. I liked him. He was an old scoundrel, approaching life with his sword in his hand prepared to take what he wanted by whatever force it required. He reminded me a lot of the stereotypical image of my ancestors, but he was mercurial in his mood swings. At one moment he was kind and generous and full of mirth. Then, in a moment, he could become a cruel and merciless tyrant dealing death as his whims dictated.

One day I raised my thought with Torald. Normally it was he who started our discussions by evoking a political response from me. On this occasion, however, I took the initiative. "I think I now understand why my grandfather believed that Wessex will prevail and will eventually rule all of England," I stated.

Torald reacted immediately, "That's madness. How could you make such a statement?"

I related to him my thoughts about King Eric. He responded by unequivocally declaring that Eric was acting within his authority. Kings had the right to be capricious at their pleasure. 'Why else would a man become king other than to exercise his will however he chose. As long as he supports Northumbria in its struggles against Wessex, he will have my support."

"But kings like Eric will not survive. He rules through fear and well-distributed booty. But his subjects do not love him. Many would kill him in a moment if they felt that they could do so without reprisal. Throughout history kings have been slain by their own subjects, often by their own family members, in their struggle to succeed. When they are deposed, their successor simply applies his whims to the task of governing. Wessex is different.

"It is not just their language and their religion which they teach all over the land which they control. It is their system of written laws. The king's ability to be capricious is limited by those laws. They, and their nobles, cannot simply execute a man at a whim. They must give him a trial in which his guilt must be demonstrated. With the exception of traitors, if he is a Christian, they cannot seize a man's land from either him or his estate. It provides a sense of security which does not exist under kings like Eric.

"They also have a great advantage through their system of fortified burhs. Not only do the burhs provide a line of defense against invaders, but the town's people view the garrison as their own troops rather than those of the king. As a result they support the garrison, and by extension they support the king. Tyrants, like Eric, would never trust the existence of such garrisons which were not under their eye and watchful control." I paused. Torald gave me a look of skepticism so I dropped the subject.

CHAPTER 11
THE LAST KING OF YORK

INTERLUDE

Eric Bloodaxe, apparently named after his skills with, and willingness to freely use his massive war axe to achieve his objectives, was a direct offspring of Harald Finehair. Harald had forged the first Kingdom of Norway. After his death the kingdom had crumbled for the lack of a successor capable of keeping it together. Eric was one of several brothers who had fought with each other in an attempt to reestablish the kingdom under their respective leaderships. Several brothers had been slain in this endeavor, probably at the hand of Bloodaxe. For a short time Eric had prevailed but his brother Haakon had succeeded him. But Haakon had also failed and the kingdom had again crumbled. Eric had taken to the seas, eventually landing in York. Haakon had fled to southern England and had found favour with the House of Wessex.

TORALDESBI, 954

Spring arrived early this year in Deira. We had spent the winter huddled indoors against a stormy season. But in spite of the weather, Eyja and I enjoyed our first year together, waiting for the birth of our first child. Eyja looked radiant in her early pregnancy, and even as her body hung heavily in the later months, she was strong and healthy and bore the child well. Finally, as winter blew its last gasps of cold air, our first son was born.

The birth did not occur without trauma. Eyja bore her pregnancy without complaint, but, particularly in the latter stage, she looked drawn and tired. I, on the other hand, spent the days running from fear to panic trying to attend her every need. I am sure that I nearly drove her to distraction with my over-attentiveness. She often laid down the law and chased me out of the room, declaring the she needed rest which was impossible with me present.

The labour was even more traumatic. Eyja was a very slender young woman and her labour was long and painful. Her pains went on unremitting for two full days. Midwifes and serving women joined Torete and Madellena, rushing in and out, gathering boiling water, swaddling and over-all mysterious things which are needed for assisting a labour. I was banned from the birthing room and consigned to pacing the entire manor, stricken with worry and despair. I cried and I prayed and I came to an accommodation with the Christian God, pledging eternal fidelity in return for Eyja's wellbeing. And he listened. Eventually Eyja's anguished screams were replaced by the sound of our son's cries as he gasped for his first breaths.

As soon as I was allowed into the birthing chamber, I pulled back the swaddling clothes in which he was wrapped and examined every inch of his body, counted all of his fingers and toes. He was complete and he was perfect. I paused momentarily to silently thank Vidar for the task that he had assigned me and the woman through whom he had arranged for me to fulfill it. I turned to Eyja. She looked spent and disheveled and I knew that I had never loved her more than I did at that moment.

We named him Boandi. While Eyja struggled to nurse him and regain her own full strength, I strutted around the manor proclaiming the existence of Boandi of StorEye. Mothering seemed to come naturally to Eyja but, in truth, she had spent much of her early life assisting Madellena in the care of her younger siblings. Madellena was there as much as Eyja would permit, and was never unprepared to show Eyja all of the aspects of child care that she already knew. Eyja was constantly ordering her from the room so that she could care for our son herself.

Ulph, on the other hand, found every possible opportunity to raise a toast to his new nephew and to brag of all accomplishments, real or imagined, of me, his new son. While Eyja and I knew that their love motivated her family's behaviour, we were soon looking forward to escaping their attention in our return to StorEye.

As the weather warmed, we began making our arrangements to travel to the Eske Valley. Eyja's excitement at the prospect of being the lady of our own manor was only slightly dampened by my attempts to convince her that StorEye would not provide the comforts to which she was accustomed. She would simply laugh and tell me that she was looking forward to being the wife of a poor country farmer. Her youngest sister, Kari, begged to come with us, promising that she would be needed to help Eyja with the care of Boandi. She had proved very useful in that role since our son was born. But her mother adamantly refused, pointing out that Kari was now betrothed to a young man from York and it would not do well to have here traipsing off to Cumbria. Her mother, therefore, assigned one of her household servants to travel with us and help with the baby's care.

***

The wars that had ranged across Northumbria had left many people destitute. Many of these men had become outlaws and made their way by robbing, and often slaying, travelers. The Kingdom of York was not a safe place to travel. Local ordinances forbade travel more than six miles without permission of a cleric in Eric's court. We, therefore, were required to apply for a permit. Our voyage was to take us into the City of York, where we would spend several days with Torald and the whole family. Steinar would meet us in York and provide a considerable armed escort to accompany us to Cumbria.

Our visit to York would have been memorable in itself. Torald threw a great feast and we were showered with gifts, both for ourselves and for Boandi. Torald renewed his oath to fulfill his obligation to Vidar by ensuring that no harm might ever befall me and reminded me that, as his son-in-law I could always call upon him. Ulph was even more demonstrative, reminding me that I was his adopted son and that I would always hold that place in his heart. I laughed and reminded him that he already had two sons to worry over, but he would not be put off by my levity. And so we embraced and swore each other our fidelity.

Torald also delivered to me the dowry which he had promised Vidar. It was all in bags of newly minted gold coins bearing the name, *Eric Rex*. Along with the gifts and personal goods, we were leaving York with quite a fortune and we would require a considerable armed guard to accompany us.

But my real surprise came the following morning by way of a summons to Eric's royal hall. I had made many visits to the royal hall before, when we were visiting Torald in York, but it had always been as part of the company of Torald. This was the first time that I had been personally summons and invited to bring Eyja with me. As we proceeded to the hall, my mind raced with the possibilities of what might lie in store for us. I had questioned Torald persistently before leaving his house, but he seemed to have no more indication than I as to the king's purpose.

Eric saw us almost as soon as we entered the hall. This was not the usual scene of feasting and drinking that I was accustom to in the royal hall. The mood today was all business. King Eric motioned us to join him immediately. He greeted us warmly, and after I had introduced Eyja, he exclaimed, "So this is the beautiful Eyja that our young Stor has kept hidden away in Deira."

Eyja was unfazed by his comment, and demurely replied, "My lord, you can hardly call it hiding me away. I was quite busy with the task of producing a family, which is what my husband promised his grandfather we would do."

Eric roared with laughter, "Well I am told that you are off to a very good start." He then turned very serious and asked, "We received your application for a travel permit. So you are really planning to return to that backwater called Cumbria and deprive my kingdom of your talents and your wife's beauty."

"My lord, you have long known that those were our plans." I replied.

"Then I will not attempt to further dissuade you. But travel will be dangerous and so I am proposing that you make an alteration to your plans." I started to protest, but he cut me off. "I am taking an expedition west towards Cumbria. We will be travelling as far as Stainmore, which is on your way. So you should join me as far as Stainmore. There, I will be turning south and so you can arrange to meet your escort from Cumbria at that point and continue on your own way. By then you will be well past the main dangers that threaten the rural area closer to York.

"I am presently arranging a small army of less than one thousand men, as I do not expect conflict. We will be ready to leave within three days and, with that small a force, we will be able to travel much faster than if I was taking a large army. I urge you to delay your departure for several days and then join me on the road."

I looked to Eyja who simply added, "It is a good idea. Boandi will be much safer travelling in the company of our king and his forces than if we were to go with only our own small retainer to protect us."

"Then it is done," Eric stated jubilantly.

* * *

True to his word, three days later Eric had his troops assembled and we were ready to travel. We had spent the previous day finalizing our own preparations and saying final goodbyes and were ready to go. It was a grand summer morning, with the sun beaming merrily in a cloudless sky. It was a good decision to travel with the king. Our small entourage consisted of three horse-drawn carriages and a few outriders. We were located in the centre of Eric's army, with troops spread out both before and after us. We closely followed Eric's own carriage and so we were in the most protected part of the entire procession.

Bryni accompanied us for several miles. My anticipation of our return to StorEye was only dampened by the knowledge that Bryni would remain in York. During my stay in York he had become my greatest friend and I knew that our separation would be painful. When it was time for him to turn back to York, we stopped and embraced, affirming a friendship that would never be undone.

Aside from the safety afforded by Eric's army, I was looking forward to travelling with him. In spite of the fact that he had all of the appearances of the pirate and brigand that he was, I had come to like him. He was grandiose in everything that he did. I imagined that he was not all that different from my own forbearers except on a much larger scale. And, while Eric was quick to anger and merciless when crossed, he was generally pleasant and almost always generous. And today was one of those days.

While Eyja, Boandi and their maids rode by carriage, I was mounted, as was Eric. He drew his horse in beside me and began an animated conversation. Apparently, Eric's brother, Haakon had accepted the fact that Eric was now the King of York. In an attempt to repair the damages from their disputes over Norway, Haakon had made arrangements with a number of lesser nobles from Gwynedd and Powys, quasi-neutral, predominately Celtic regions on the western edge of Wessex-controlled country, to ship goods through York rather than via the Irish Sea. What was needed to finalize this arrangement was Eric's demonstration that he could ensure greater safety of passage to the markets in York than the dangerous sea route to the west. The purpose of the trip was for Eric to meet with these nobles and attempt to persuade them that such a guarantee was possible. The meeting had been set at Stainmore, which was a virtual no-man's-land between Wessex and York.

Eric explained to me that he had taken this large a force with him, not so much for his own protection, but as a demonstration to these nobles that he could readily raise such a force and thereby could provide the safe passage, which was their concern.

He chuckled as he told me, "But I don't completely trust my brother, Haakon. We have warred against each other. So, I will arrive at Stainmore two nights in advance of the proposed assembly and I will scout out a location to camp my troops that will guarantee me the greatest protection from duplicity during this meeting."

"So do you plan to just sit around that lonely moor for two days while you wait for this delegation to arrive?" I asked.

"This is the best wild boar hunting country in all of Britain," he claimed. "I will spend several days hunting, and then, like kings of old, I will serve a feast provided by my own hand, to conclude our meeting."

Eric's good cheer remained all the way to Stainmore. There we were met by Steinar and a company of men that he had conscripted to secure our safety for the short trip that would take us to StorEye. While I had been living in York, Steinar had visited me at least once a year in order to keep me apprised of all of the developments at StorEye. In this time I had come to love and trust this man to whom my grandfather had given the guardianship of my future. At the sight of him, therefore, I leapt from my mount and rushed to embrace him. Seeing him caused our home at StorEye to seem much closer and I now chafed to get my new wife there so that I could show it to her.

We spent that last evening in Eric's camp, and in the morning set out on the final leg of our trip home, leaving Eric still in good spirits and preparing for his hunt.

CHAPTER 12
THE STORK

STOREYE, 954

The morning of our departure from Stainmore, I spent my time mounted, riding beside Steinar as he brought me up to date on the affairs of StorEye and the progress on completing our manor house and building our burh. Steinar, himself, had taken a wife, a widow with two children. They now had a third child which was born from their union. Steiner seemed quite content in this relationship, but I was surprised by how much he had aged. His body still appeared strong and erect but his graying temples and his facial wrinkles gave proof to the fact that he was no longer a young man.

By midday, clouds had drifted in and a stiff breeze now assaulted us. I gave up on my mount and retreated to the shelter in which Eyja and Boandi were travelling. We huddled together under heavy woolen blankets, well protected from the elements and intimately discussing the life which now lay ahead of us. I spent much of the time attempting to describe our new home in ways that Eyja could picture it before it actually came into view.

Steiner and I had spent many hours planning the construction of our manor house. While I had not yet seen the house, I could well imagine its appearance. It was a round brick and stone structure which rose up three stories from the ground. The ground floor was large and open, with a two large oak doors, which, when open, gave a feeling of actually being outside. This area was used for storage of tools, weapons, fire wood, straw, hay and other animal feed. It could also house a substantial herd of livestock if, in fact, they were threatened by a ferocious storm or an armed attack. The second floor provided the means for cooking and relaxing. It was our great hall. The third floor contained the sleeping quarters, and, while now it was one large open room, it was built with a view to dividing it as the need might arise.

The house was built with its defenses as the overriding feature of its design. The ground floor doors were constructed of thick oak planks which could be tightly barred against unwanted entrance. There were small window with internally locking shutters. When open, the upper floor windows would allow the occupants to rain down a barrage of missiles on anyone on the ground trying to force an entry. The upper floors were accessible by way of an internal staircase that wound around the inside of the exterior walls, from left to right so that a person attempting to wield a sword or an ax in their right hand, while climbing upwards, would be hampered in each blow by the exterior wall. Anyone fighting to repel such an attack would have a clear field to swing a weapon in their right hand out over the open spaces of the interior of the house. At several landings above the stair well there were "murder holes". These involved a solid trap door which, when raised, could facilitate pouring boiling water or oil down upon any intruder attempting to access the upper floors.

The roof was planked with wood, supported by large oak beams. The exterior of the roof was covered by large clumps of sod so as to provide a greater degree of fireproofing than the more common thatch roofing. Steinar had assured me that, while not being able to stop an army bent on our destruction, a small group of people could keep a fairly large group of raiders at bay.

The house was built to protect us from attack or inclement weather, and to provide for our necessities. It was not built for luxury. However I had made one major concession to our comfort. On the third floor Steinar had allowed for the construction of a sleeping platform with a thick down-filled mattress and comforter where I could escape with Eyja for sleep and pleasure.

***

The weather had mellowed as we finally reached StorEye. Light, fluffy clouds danced in the sky and the sun cast its warmth on the ground. As we mounted a rise, the distant tower, which was our house, came into view and when I drew Eyja's attention to it she became delighted. "It looks wonderful," she whispered.

This was not the rich lush soil of Deira, but its rolling hills and rocky outcrops were interspersed amongst thinner crops of oats and barley which were now high and green and swaying gently in the soft summer breeze. The fields thrived with hundreds of grazing sheep. Our tenants' houses dotted the landscape and most of their yards and fields were fenced with long intercrossed split logs which zigzagged their way across the land. Herds of fattening sheep were well on their way to recovering their thick woolen coats which had been shorn many months ago. Some fields held herds of rusty brown long- haired cattle. Tenants were busy all over the place carrying out their various chores.

As we approached the manor, I could see men busy building a fortification around the manor itself. This would form part of the fortification of our burh. The work was far from finished, but sturdy stone structures soared about eight feet in the air, framing what would obviously become the main gate. A beam had been laid on top of these structures, completing the frame of the gate. Attached to the cross beam, and standing above it was a large metal rod which had been twisted to form the letter "S", an obvious reference to StorEye. When Eyja saw it she gasped in amazement. "Look Stor," she exclaimed, holding up her delicate hand so that I could see her ring. She held her hand in such a manner that the stork on her ring was upright, with its long legs wrapped out of sight behind her hand. Pointing to the "S" she continued, "It's my stork."

Sure enough, the curvature of the "S" was elongated so that it did very much resemble her stork with its long curved neck bending into a long beak. "Well, it is a fertility symbol, and we will need its help to build a family." I chuckled. As I thought on it, I decided that I would arrange to have an actual likeness of a stork crafted out of metal. The stork would replace the "S" over the gate as a symbol of our home.

* * *

We had been back at StorEye for only a few days. While Eyja was still organizing our household, I only had time to meet a few of our tenants when a messenger arrived from York. King Eric was dead. I could not believe what I was hearing. While a servant ran to fetch Steinar, Eyja and I plied the young messenger with questions. "How could this have happened? Where did it happen?" It was as if we could not get information fast enough.

As it turned out, there were no answers to many of our questions. From what was known, Eric had left his encampment at Stainmore, and with only a small handful of retainers accompanying him, he had set out to hunt wild boar. He had been ambushed and murdered. But it turned out that the whole affair was an ambush. There were no nobles and there was no meeting. Haakon, his brother, had betrayed him and lured him out to this lonely place where an ambush was waiting. Nobody believed that Haakon had acted on his own. It was strongly suspected that he had been acting as part of a conspiracy involving both Eadred of Wessex and Oswulf, of Bamburgh. Maccus, the self-styled king of the Isle of Mann and a son of Anlaf Sihtricson, had been seen in Stainmore several days before Eric arrived. Many suspected that he might have been the actual murderer. Though Anlaf was suspected of having a hand in it, there was no definitive evidence and, in light of the power of the alleged conspirators, there was no one to avenge poor Eric. We could not know at the time, but Eric Bloodaxe was to be the last King of York.

* * *

YORK, 954 AD

On the day after King Eric Bloodaxe died, Torald's family had spent a quiet evening at the townhouse in York. They were just preparing to retire for the night when they were alerted to a commotion outside of their outer gate. Servants appeared in the great hall and advised them that a large contingent of armed men were at the gate and were demanding admittance. Torald rushed to an upper floor window, threw open a shutter, and looking down at the men at the gate, demanded, "What is the meaning of this disturbance?"

"I am here on the authority of Oswulf, High Earl of Northumbria at the pleasure of Eadred, King of all England and Guardian of the King's Peace. I possess a warrant which demands that you open your gate and permit me admittance and advise me why you should not be arrested and a charge of treason laid against you."

"Are you mad?" Torald replied. "Our lawful King is Eric of York."

"Eric is dead," the ruffian advised.

"I do not believe you," Torald shouted down.

Some scuffling took place. From the back of the gathering a man was dragged to where the gate light shone upon him, revealing his identity. "Lord Torald," the man cried. "It is me, Harak, clerk of the witan." Torald recognized him immediately and demanded, "Harak, what is the meaning of this?"

"It is true," Harak wailed. "The King has been killed, Oswulf's men occupy the city and most of the witan have been arrested."

After some arguing and yelling, Torald recognized the truth of the situation and permitted the intruders to march him, Ulphus and Byrniulf across town, under guard, to what had been Eric's great hall. Several days later Torald and Ulph were released but Byrniulf was detained to be sent, along with thirty other sons of York, to Wessex where they would serve a hostage against good behaviour of their families towards Oswulf's and Eadred's rule.

* * *

A month had passed since we had received the news of Eric's murder but we had heard nothing further. His murder had dampened our move to StorEye. Both Eyja and I had known a kindness towards Eric and both of us feared the consequences that his death would bring to the family in York. But we had resolved to continue forward and enjoy our new home. Once we had gotten the house in a livable condition, I had thrown a small feast and we had invited Steinar and his family and several other families, whose male family head had fought for Vidar, to join us. Our land was completely tenanted and I had been around to meet all of our tenants and their families. I had overseen a number of disputes and had heard a number of grievances, but, all in all, the estate was running smoothly. Eyja had accompanied me on several trips to the market in Carlisle and on one of those trips I had renewed my acquaintance and introduced Eyja to Father Leo. We had been warmly received by the good father who promised to visit StorEye often and keep a close watch on our souls.

Finally, not just news came from York, but Ulph himself appeared at our home. We welcomed him warmly, but we were impatient to get news of what the aftermath of Eric's death had wrought. We did not have to push hard. "Eadred has abolished the Kingdom of York and the witan," Ulph told us. "He has replaced the kingdom with an earldom and he has named Oswulf of Bamburgh as Earl of Northumbria." Oswulf is seeking vengeance against those who supported Eric when his army crushed the forces of Bernicia. While we are all in some danger of his vengeance, we believe that Eadred has demanded our cooperation and has charged Oswulf to secure it. He has demanded hostages to live in Wessex against our good behaviour. Our brother, Bryni, has become such a hostage."

Fear for Byrni's safety overwhelmed any other reaction to Ulph's news. However he quickly assured me that Bryni would be safe so long as Torald did not take up arms against Wessex or Bamburgh.

Ulph paused to allow us to absorb what had been spoken. Then he continued, "But I don't think his reach is far enough to concern you here in Cumbria. Father has closed his home in the city and has retreated to Deira. His title as Earl of Deira remains unchallenged but it no longer commands its previous authority. I do not think that Oswulf will pursue him further. But most of the nobility of Northumbria is outraged that Eric's murder should be so openly flaunted by Oswulf and Eadred. Eadred has allowed Oswulf to force damages from his subjects to offset the damages done to him in the war with Eric. The trouble is far from over."

"What of the witan of York?" I inquired

"It has been disbanded and its members scattered like my father. Bishop Wulfstan has been released from prison but the church has forbidden him from returning to York," Ulph replied. "The only good sign is that Eadred and Archbishop Oda have appointed Bishop Oskytel, a fellow Northumbrian, as Bishop of York."

We talked on and on into the night about all that was happening. The one over-riding message that Ulph had brought us, he kept repeating throughout the evening. "Do not leave Cumbria unless Torald sends for you. On this, trust nobody. You are safe here but elsewhere in England you will be in grave danger." We even established a code word so that if we were summoned we would know the legitimacy of the request, "The stork is needed"

* * *

True to Ulph's words, the events that swirled around Northern England did not impact us here in Cumbria. No armies appeared at our door. At StorEye we prospered. Eyja again became pregnant and I settled into the job of managing a substantial estate. I am also now a thane in Cumbria. A thane is a person who owned five, or more, hides of land and has the responsibility of raising the tax on his land. Having such a large land holding, I was often called on to provide counsel to our King, Mael Culem.

But other events were unfolding. To our north, King Malcolm of Scotland was murdered. He was succeeded by his cousin, Indulf. Indulf immediately reinforced his army and began a campaign against the Danes in Edinburgh and the Lothian. It was clear, however, that it was Indulf's goal to seize all of Bernicia. Oswulf's work would be cut out for him.

CHAPTER 13
THE HOSTAGE OF WESSEX

GLASTONBURY, 954

Our worries for Byrni's safety and well-being were constant, but he corresponded with me on a regular basis, apprising us of his situation. Upon reaching Wessex, the hostages had been separated and sent to different locations. Byrniulf was escorted to the small town of Glastonbury. Glastonbury was built on the site of an old Roman ruin, but the occupancy of the site extended back a millennium before the Romans came to Britain. The town had been revitalized as one of Alfred's burhs and was fortified with a stone wall. The town was built around a church and chapel which was the home of the famed Father AEthelwold and, until recently, had been the home of Dunstan, *who was to become one of the most beloved saints in England.* It was also the nearest burh to the splendid castle belonging to AEthelstan Halfking (not to be confused with his illustrious forbearer whose name he shared) and his wife AElfwynn. AEthelstan was part of the senior Wessex nobility, being Ealdorman of East Anglia and being the brother of the Ealdorman of part of Mercia. His wife was closely related to the nobility of Mercia. While AEthelstan and AElfwynn spent much of their time in East

Anglia, they maintained their castle in Glastonbury and it was there that Byrniulf was sent to live as a hostage.

Being a member of a noble family, and being held as a hostage, was not necessarily an uncomfortable existence. While a death sentence was always a potential reality should the hostage's parents rebel or war against the hostage holder, the hostages themselves were generally treated as visitors deserving of the hospitality afforded to their station. This was the case with Byrniulf. While he was neither allowed to carry arms nor to leave the estate unaccompanied, he was otherwise treated as one of the family.

And what a fascinating family it was. AEthelwold was, along with Dunstan, one of the foremost scholars in Wessex. Both of them had studied with the monks of Iona. Their studies not only covered contemporary Christianity, but also grammar, metric and patristics. Dunstan had lived as a hermit in a small room which he had constructed off the side of the church. He remained there until King Eadred enticed him to join the King's cabinet. Still, he returned to Glastonbury often. When AEthelstan Halfking and AElfwynn were in residence so was their court along with a continuous parade of nobility from East Anglia, Mercia and Wessex, many of whom included family of the lord or lady. These also included the children of the hosts, of which their oldest son, AEethelwine, would become a close companion of Byrniulf. Their youngest daughter, the beautiful AEthelfleda resided there also.

But the most fascinating person at the table was Prince Edgar. Edgar was the son of Elfgiva who had died within a year of his birth. His father, the late King Edmund had been murdered three years later, leaving Edgar and his older, half-brother, EAdwig, orphaned. As both boys were in their minority, Edmund's brother, Eadred, was crowned king. It had been arranged for AEthelstan and AElfwynn to adopt the young prince. Edgar's brother EAdwig, being older, was therefore not the subject of adoption. Edgar was now residing at Glastonbury as a full time student of the scholar, AEthelwold.

***

The three young men were laughing and teasing each other. More particularly, the older two boys were teasing the younger. "Bryni, we never should have let him come with us," AEethelwine said. "He's too young. He won't even know what to do with it."

Byrniulf laughed, "He knows what to do with it. He's like a dog in heat around women."

"But he is only just turned fourteen years of age," AEethelwine protested.

"I'm old enough to thrill all of the girls," Edgar announced. "I've done it often enough."

"He's right," Bryni declared. "I've seen him sneaking around your little sister, AEthelfleda. He can barely keep his hands off of her."

"You bed my little sister and, prince or not, I'll have your hide. She's still a baby," AEethelwine sputtered.

"She's only a year my junior, but relax. She is still a maiden." Edi jibed, watching AEethelwine redden with anger.

Edi laughed and said, "Anyway, we are not talking about little sisters tonight. Tonight we're here for real wenches and the treat is on me." And with that the three of them strode into the tavern, AEethelwine, the heir to Glastonbury, Bryni, the hostage and Edgar the prince who was second in line to succeed the King of England. Their object here was the tavern wenches.

Once seated comfortably inside, jugs of mead were served to them. The mead was followed quickly by three comely ladies with sharp wits, shapely bodies and pretty faces. They were immediately drawn into the banter, much of which was centered on whether or not the prince could do what they had come here for. He simply smiled and told the ladies that they would not be disappointed with his performance, at which one of them slipped a hand under his tunic, smiled and proclaimed, "No, I don't suppose I will be."

Then, drinks in one hand and a lady in the other, they all rose and moved towards other rooms where beds or couches were provided.

* * *

Byrniulf had now been living at Glastonbury for three months. He felt quite comfortable as he took his place at the grand table. His earlier discomfort and unease at being a hostage had all but disappeared as his hosts had gone out of their way to make him feel at home. Around this table there was a far reaching feel of sympathy and political accord. While none of them would support secession from England by Northumbria, they did believe that greater autonomy for the North and fairer treatment from Winchester would not be a bad thing.

Tonight's dinner party included Halfking at the head of the table beside his wife. They were joined by the clergymen, AEthelwold and Dunstan and two other couples of a similar age, AEthelfric and his wife and Wulfheag and his wife. The two men, Aelfric and Wulfheag both were Mercian cousins of the hostess, AElfwynn. At the far end of the table sat Prince Edgar, AEethelwine, AEthelfleda and Bryni. Edgar was fourteen years of age, AEethelwine, nineteen, AEthelfleda, thirteen and Bryni, twenty. As they were all now students of AEthelwold, they were considered to be "the children" in spite of the maturity of AEthelwine and Byrniulf. Dinner had been eaten and AEthelstan Halfking rose for a toast. He was short in stature but the sureness of his voice implied nothing but authority.

As he raised his glass we all came to our feet. "A toast to the success of the rebirth of the teachings of St. Benedict," he declared. All those present assented enthusiastically, raising their own glasses and, in unison, declaring "St. Benedict."

Over the years, since most of England had come to embrace Christianity, the Church had become incredibly wealthy. In an attempt to control church politics, while at the same time, buy their way into heaven, the nobility had erected fabulous cathedrals on their estates and given the church extensive tracts of revenue producing land. This, coupled with the huge revenues from tithing their parishioners and charging exorbitant fees for administering the sacraments, saying masses for the souls in purgatory and selling dispensations to the living, had made the wealth of the church second only to that of the crown. But that wealth was not shared equally within the church. The church hierarchy, the bishops and archbishops lived like princes while the village priests and monks, who did most of the real work of the church, could barely feed themselves. Celibacy by the parish clergy was encouraged by the church hierarchy, but not for religious reasons. It was to avoid supporting the parish priests in a manner in which they could afford a wife and family.

In reaction to this disparity there was now a growing movement to force the church to adopt the modest life which their Savior had exemplified. St. Benedict had developed, through both writing and example, a code by which the church should abide. It emphasized poverty, piety and service to God's flock. Dunstan and Æthelwold were amongst the leading proponents of this Benedictine reform and they schooled their students accordingly.

"So how are things going at court?" Æthelwold directed his question at Dunstan.

"Eadred claims his support for monastic renewal, but he does little to support it. Unfortunately he also does little to curb the antagonisms of our opponents."

"Are you still safe there, Dunstan?" Æthelstan inquired.

"As long as Eadred is on the throne I am physically safe. They might hate me and besmirch me, but they will not harm me. The king would not stand for it. Much as he drags his feet on the issue of monastic reforms, he values my advice on so many other issues that I am under his protection."

Everyone at the table understood what lay behind this discussion. When Eadred's brother, Edmund, had been King of England, Dunstan had been a fixture at court. He had been a leading advocate for monastic reform of the church. The need for reform arose out of the unhealthy relationship between the church and the nobility. This conflict was not confined to England, but existed across northern Europe. Many churches, monasteries and even major cathedrals had been built on land belonging to the nobility and were financed through the largesse of the nobility. As a result, many churches had no independence from the nobility and they were staffed by lay ministry, many of whom were appointed by the nobility itself. The reformers wanted to see an expansion of independent, self-sufficient monasteries, staffed by Benedictine monks who would follow the rules of chastity, poverty and full time attention to exploring the will of God as had been proscribed and practiced by St. Benedict. There was considerable resistance to this reform.

Dunstan, as the leading advocate of monastic reform had earned many enemies, and attempts had been made on his life. Dunstan became so troublesome that Edmund had been prepared to exile him. Before he could do so, however, King Edmund suffered a near-death hunting incident and gave God credit for his survival. As penance, he granted Dunstan leave to remain in Wessex and had made him abbot of the monastery at Glastonbury. On ascending to the throne, Eadred, while also lukewarm on monastic reform, had extended his brother's tolerance of Dunstan and had even invited him back to court as a member of his council. Regardless of the king's protection, Dunstan still had many enemies who did not wish him well.

After dinner was through the young people gathered to follow up on the dinner conversation amongst each other. They all had heard the discussion before, both at the dinner table and in their classes with Abbot AEthelwold. He was, after all, both a friend and disciple of Dunstan.

Bryni again expressed his skepticism, "I still do not understand what this church reform issue is all about. Why are people willing to risk their lives over it?"

AEethelwine was quick to jibe his friend, responding, "Bryni, you Viking barbarians are all alike. You only converted to Christianity because you believed that our God was more powerful and more likely to lead you to victory over us Christians."

"We converted to Christianity so that you English barbarians would not slaughter us and steal our land," Bryni was quick to retort, but then smilingly asked, "Seriously, what is this all about?"

Edgar replied, "The church is corrupt. Most churches are built on land donated to them by us nobility. The nobility, through its largess, keeps the Church obligated to it. They have the Church in their pocket and the clergy will do their bidding. This completely contradicts the teachings of Christ."

"Maybe so, but why do you care? Isn't it better to have priests who will do your bidding?" Bryni persisted.

"Certainly, if you have no interest in getting to heaven. Jesus taught that a life of simplicity and purity of spirit was the only way to get your soul to heaven. It is a priest's job to get you to heaven. How can he accomplish this if he himself is corrupted by strong liquor and debauchery? God will ignore him. You need a pious priest to get you to heaven."

"Well you are going to need a very pious priest, Edi," AEthelfleda added. "You are always trying to get your hands under my skirts."

"Yeah," AEethelwine added, "We cannot keep you under control when we go down to the tavern wenching. You're like a dog in heat chasing all the trollops. And here you are, not even old enough to know what to do if you catch one."

They all laughed at Edgar's expense, but he only smiled in agreement. "But that is why I need very pious priests, so that they can save me from myself."

On and on they went, half serious, half joking as they probed the issues that so perplexed the older generation. However, they were all aware of the depth of the issue. Between the nobility and the church they together owned virtually all of the wealth of England and they had little interest in changing the system which supported their privilege. Centuries earlier, to set an example, St Benedict had demonstrated a truly Christian life, by forsaking his worldly possessions and entering into a monastery which encouraged chastity, simplicity, moderation and dedication to the word of God.

WINCHESTER 955

The following year EAdred died leaving no direct heir. Next in line for succession was Edmond's son, EAdwig. EAdwig was despised in Northumbria. He had long stated his preference for levying heavy taxes in York to encourage trade to flow through London rather than York. He continued minting coins in Wessex and selling the coins to Northumbria at a substantial mark-up. He supported unequal taxation of rich and poor alike if they resided north of the Humber. And he supported the continued *wergeld* against York for the deaths attributed to Eric Bloodaxe. EAdwig was also opposed to reform of the current church structure.

Edgar, his younger brother, presented a much more accommodating approach to Northumbria. The nobility of York had lobbied the Wessex witan to select Edgar to be king, but their voice was ignored. Anger at Northumbria was still fresh in the minds of the Wessex witan and so they selected the more punitive EAdwig to be their king. Northumbria was further outraged.

***

The coronation of EAdwig was planned as the grandest event ever to be witnessed in the whole of England. All of the Anglo-Saxon, and much of the Scandinavian, nobility had been invited to attend. A carnival atmosphere surrounded the palace at Winchester. Musicians, jugglers, dancers and all other forms of entertainers jostled each other for space for their performances. The fairgrounds had swelled far beyond its capacity.

The coronation ceremony had proceeded smoothly and Archbishop Oda had placed the crown of England on EAdwig's head and proclaimed him king. The nobility from all over the kingdom, decked out in all of their finery had witnessed the event and the Wessex contingency had cheered loudly as EAdwig became the crowned the king of all England, without any other king openly claiming a part of the dominion. Now they were all sitting at their places in the great hall of the palace awaiting the new king's entrance so that the banquet could begin.

As the appointed hour for the feast arrived and passed, nervous tittering and shuffling could be heard throughout the hall. Alarmed, Dunstan rose and strode out of the hall towards EAdwig's private chamber. When he reached the doorway, he pushed aside the guard whom he caught unaware and who put up little resistance. Dunstan threw open the door, took one determined step inside the chamber and stopped dead in his tracks, his face frozen behind a mask of disbelief. There on the bed were three bodies completely disrobed. EAdwig was in the process of mounting his cousin, AElgifu while her mother AEthelgifu, sat beside them caressing EAdwig's back and shoulders.

"What is the meaning of this?" Dunstan screamed as he strode towards the bed.

The trio scrambled to grab up bedding to hide their nakedness, but only EAdwig spoke. Assuming a royal authority, he leapt from the bed and rushed towards the Bishop, arms raised in a posture of attack, screaming, "How dare you enter my chamber uninvited?" as he moved to strike at Dunstan. Dunstan, in a surprising move for a man his age, deftly sidestepped the king's attack , extended a foot as EAdwig hurtled past him, and sent His Highness sprawling in a heap on the floor.

"You have struck the king." EAdwig bellowed. "I will see you hanged."

Ignoring him, Dunstan ordered the women to help the king dress himself and get him to the banquet hall. Without awaiting a response, the Bishop wheeled about and stormed out of the chamber.

Upon entering the banquet hall, Dunstan announced, "The King will be joining us presently. In the meanwhile, let the feast begin."

Dunstan returned to the table and took his seat. But as his sense of outrage subsided, he began to consider the potential ramifications of what had occurred. EAdwig had constantly opposed Dunstan's reforms and probably harboured him little love. This incident might have pushed things over the edge. Rising, he proceeded rapidly to the outer entrance, and once out of sight he broke into a run.

Moments later EAdwig stormed into the hall, rage blazing in his eyes. "Where is that priest? "He screamed."

Realizing that he was referring to Dunstan someone offered, "He rushed outside."

"He assaulted me. Mount a guard and bring that felon back before me so that the king's justice may be done," EAdwig bellowed.

**

One cool spring morning, almost two years after Eric's death, a messenger arrived at StorEye. "The stork is needed at Deira."

PART 2
| THE BIRTH |

CHAPTER 14
FAIRNESS FOR NORTHUMBERLAND

NORTHUMBRIA, 956

I had not wanted to leave StorEye. I had been enjoying myself in the peace of my home for almost two years now. Boandi was now walking and I loved playing with him and showing him around our estate. He was a charming young lad with his curly golden locks and he stole the hearts of all of our womenfolk. For a while, I feared that he may never learn to walk, as his feet were rarely on the ground. The woman always flocked to pick him up and carry him around.

Eyja seemed to grow more beautiful each day. She had quickly regained her pre-pregnancy body, but her belly was now beginning to swell again from a new pregnancy. We spend many evenings snuggled together discussing our future family and how we both yearned to see it grow and thrive.

Eyja also took a great interest in our economic future. We were already financially well off. The entire estate of StorEye was tenanted and productive. We had experienced a drought the year before last but it was not a devastating drought. Our crops suffered, but StorEye was dependent much more on wool than on grain. Tenants had harvested enough of their crops to sustain themselves and though we had shortages of feed for the livestock, we had not lost any animals. Then, last year had been a good year and the larders of all of our tenants were full from the bounty which our land produced. However, we were not content with a purely agrarian existence. That would have created too great a dependency on the vagary of the weather and the occasional bands of outlaws who periodically swept across our land, burning and pillaging. We generally were able to track them down and punish them accordingly but they still threatened to drain our wealth. As a result we had begun diversifying our income.

We had built weaving and felling operations and as a result we now sent most of our wool to market as much more profitable finished fabric. We had several tenants who were exceptional smiths, and, in an exchange for the labour which they owed the manor they, instead, produced metal goods such as tools and weapons, along with many great works of art, which brought exceptional returns in the markets of York.

But I had been summoned by Torald and I must go.

***

We were sitting in the manor's great hall in Toraldesbi. Torald's messenger had been accompanied by a substantial armed escort. We had bedded them all down for the night. The next morning I had returned with them to Deira.

After exchanging welcomes we got to business. From the nature of Torald's message and the expressions of anxiety around the room, it was apparent that serious issues had arisen. Torald spoke first. "What I am about to say is treason. If we are caught, we might all be executed. I say this now so that any of you who wish to leave should do so now."

THE LEGEND OF STOR

I looked around the room. Aside from Torald, Ulph and I were the Earl of Orm, two nobles from Northumbria whom I had met before but did not really know well and two nobles from Mercia, which came as a real surprise. Torald had introduced the two Mercian's as Aelfric and Wulfheag. A greater surprise was the presence of a clergyman from Wessex, Bishop Dunstan. Nobody made a move to leave. Torald continued, "Our new king, EAdwig, has not only earned the animosity of Northumbria, but also that of the people of Mercia. He has even alienated the church in Wessex. There will be a revolt against him."

Dunstan then spoke, "This king is an abomination even in the eyes of God. I was there at the ceremony confirming his elevation to the throne. Just as the guests were arriving he left the room and failed to return. I was sent, by the nobles gathered there, to search for him. I finally him found in his bed with a woman named AEthelgifu and her daughter. All three were as naked as jay birds and cavorting shamelessly. I demanded that he return to his guests immediately, but he only laughed and hurled profanities at me. In a rage I dragged him back to his guests and demanded that he recant his behaviour. Upon realizing the rashness of my action I took my leave and fled to my monastery. EAdwig followed me and sacked the monastery. I was lucky to have escaped alive."

Aelfric and Wulfheag had tales of their own, although, however atrocious their stories, they scarcely compared to the outrage described by Dunstan. When they had finished it was obvious that there would be a large following for a movement aimed at removing EAdwig from the throne. Torald then got to the point of this particular gathering. "I have, of course, been talking to a great number of people in Northumbria, as have our friends from Mercia, and there is great support for an uprising. We have always favoured

Edgar's elevation to the throne over that of his half-brother, EAdwig. Where our problem lies is that we have not been able to judge the extent of support that might rally to EAdwig's banner. In particular, we do not know what our Earl of Northumbria will do. Oswulf was always a strong supporter of the Wessex crown, and he has been the greatest benefactor in Northumbria from Wessex's rule. But EAdwig might be a different story. However, we do not know. Therefore, we cannot take to the field against EAdwig until we are sure that we will not become ensnared between the army of Wessex in the south and the army of Oswulf to the north. I believe that there is a way to ensure the neutrality of Bamburgh but I am very concerned with the dangers which the plan holds."

"Go on," Orm urged.

"We have had contact with Bamburgh," Torald continued. "He is worried about the Scots. He knows that Northumbria is on the verge of revolt. He does not want to be caught in between a rebellion in Northumbria and a Scottish invasion of Bernicia. He may well desert EAdwig, but he wants some assurances and," Torald paused again, "He will only discuss it with you, Stor. This is why I sent for you. But it might be a trap. I am fearful of asking you to go to Bernicia. He may only want to lure you there so that he can extract vengeance for his humiliation at the hand of Eric. You played an active role in his surrender. Do not answer me immediately. If you decide not to go, it will not be held against you."

I sat there in shock, considering what I had just been told. "But why would he wish to only talk to me?"

"I have no idea. It must be something that you said or did during his surrender to Eric," Torald replied.

We all sat there speculating on Bamburgh's motives, but it was clear that we were talking in circles. I finally said,

THE LEGEND OF STOR

"Well I guess the only way we will find out is if I go there and talk to him."

"Then you will go?" Orm quickly added.

"Not so quick," Ulph jumped to my defense. "Let's discuss the possible downsides of this proposal, particularly the downside for Stor. It is his life that we are putting at risk."

And so we all talked some more, but in the end the conclusion was obvious. I would have to take the risk.

"This is a brave thing for you to do." Dunstan said. "All of England will be in your debt."

"I do not do this for England. I do it for Torald and for Ulphus. They are my family," I replied.

"And I will go with you," Ulph quickly added.

"No," I said. "If he means me harm, then two of us will die instead of just me. We will be amongst his army and at his mercy. But if he is speaking honourably, then it must be me he sees coming to meet him. I will only take what force is necessary to guard my passage against brigands on the way there."

BAMBURGH, 956

And so, several days later, I was again on the road to Bamburgh castle. But this time I did not have an army to protect me. I had brought only a dozen soldiers to protect me against outlaws along the way. But we encountered none. As I considered what might lie in wait for me upon my arrival, I felt none of the bravado that I had expressed when I agreed to this task. Actually, I was terrified then and I was more terrified now. But I knew that if I showed even a hint of that fear, I would likely get myself killed.

While I was still at StorEye I had made for myself a shield which was painted solid black and on its face I had depicted a likeness of a white stork, which Eyja and I had decided upon as a symbol of our estate. For this trip I was dressed in full armour, my father's sword slung on my back, my dagger at my waist and my shield proudly hung from my saddle.

Shortly after we entered Bernicia, a company of twenty four of Bamburgh's knights fell in beside us, forming equal ranks on either side of our smaller party. They did not speak a word, nor did they have to. Their presence spoke for them.

At last Bamburgh Castle came into sight. As we drew near, one of the earl's escorts signaled me to stop. "You will walk from here. And give me your sword. I will keep it safe for you," He said.

I snarled at him, "If you want my sword, then you will have to take it from me. But I promise you that at least half of your company will die in the trying. And as for my horse, I plan to ride right through the gate and possibly into the great hall before I dismount. Do you have a problem with that?"

He quickly backed away, and, with my party, we rode right up to the gate. Then I dismounted and indicated to one of my troop to do likewise. I bade the rest of my company to wait for us there and, accompanied only by that one man, I strode through the gate. When we reached the doorway to the great hall, I removed both my sword and my dagger and turned them over to my companion. Bidding him to wait outside, and armed only with my shield, I thrust open the door and strode through into the hall. "I am here at the bidding of Oswulf, Earl of Bamburgh, Earl of Northumbria and lion of Bernicia," I roared and stood my ground awaiting a response.

I remember Oswulf from Bamburgh's surrender to Eric. He was then a defeated man and had looked the part. I was amazed at seeing him now. What surprised me most was how different a man could look in defeat compared to the man I saw today. He looked younger, taller and fully in command. While not young, he was certainly not old. Grey was beginning to show in his beard and on his head, but his mane was full and his blue eyes shone with life. He was a stern looking man who looked like he would show no quarter. I felt a fear trickle through me but I quickly recalled my admonition to myself; show no fear.

"So, my young Viking minion, you are all grown up now and you have come," he bellowed across the hall.

"Minion maybe," I replied. "But this young minion left many of your best warriors dead on the battlefield the last time we met. And I am prepared to do so again, if that is your desire."

He was speechless for only a moment and then he roared with laughter. "Come, talk to me. I did not bid you come here to fight with me. We have other business."

I buried my rising trepidation and strode boldly across the hall where he bade me to sit with him.

"So your mother was a Bernician?" he inquired. As I nodded he continued, "And your father was a pagan Viking."

I bristled at that. "My father marched across this land with Ragnald and Guthric and carved out the greatest dominion that this land has ever known. And while he was at it he saved your Bernicia from falling into the hands of the Scots."

To this, he threw up his hands in surrender, laughed and called upon a serving girl to bring me some wine. Our conversation then turned amicable and we began to address the business for why I was here. I asked him straight forth why he had specifically requested that it be me that he would talk to. His face became serious. He replied, "I watched you closely when you were here with Bloodaxe. For a man so young and just fresh from battle, I was surprised that you demonstrated no illusions of superiority. You faithfully recorded what Eric and I had agreed upon. There are not many men who can read and write. Those who can do so are mostly either clerics who are too judgmental or poets and skalds who seek to curry favour from their patrons by colouring the truth to artificially enhance their images. You showed no bias, simply transcribing what was said. You struck me as a man who could be trusted. We have experienced so much treachery in Northumbria that I saw a need for someone who could be relied upon by all concerned to convey accurately the commitments that will be required to find our way out of the situation which we now face. Sometimes we must approach issues with the sword, but at times diplomacy is a more useful tool. But diplomacy without trust is as useless as a dull sword in battle." The sincerity of his response brought me to realize the degree of thought that had gone into his words and my admiration of him rose accordingly.

We then addressed the business at hand. We talked for several hours. What emerged was his initial belief that I would be requesting his support of an uprising. He was very guarded about revealing his strengths and weaknesses, but it became apparent that he was concerned about the strength of the Scots on his northern border and would be reluctant to draw troops away from that area even if he wished to support an uprising, which he was not completely inclined to do. The house of Wessex had treated him well, and even though he acknowledged the mistreatment of Northumbria by Wessex, he had not felt the effects of that mistreatment. To the contrary, he had benefitted. He acknowledged however that, with the support of Mercia, EAdwig would probably be overthrown. He recalled that the Northumbrian nobles had tried in vain to have EAdwig's brother, Edgar, named to the throne. He had supported Edgar's ascendancy and had shared Northumbria's disappointment when the Wessex witan had chosen EAdwig as their king. He finally agreed to keep Bernicia neutral in an uprising against EAdwig if the rebels would agree to have Edgar take the throne. He also wanted assurance from both Edgar and the Northumbrian nobles, that if they were successful they would guarantee his position in Bernicia and that they would support him against any Scottish invasion of Bernicia.

Once he had lain out his terms he dropped the business-like tone and with a warm smile inquired, "Last time that we met you were committed to your pagan religion and opposed to both Christianity and Wessex rule. Has your view on these issues changed?"

"Odin and the other Norse gods are the gods of my father and, as such, I owe them respect", I replied. "However, I have been taught that they are capricious with the affairs of man and would rather we imitate their warlike ways. If a Viking dies with a sword in his hand, then he is welcomed into the banquet halls of Odin to eat, fight, debauch and brag about the glory he has wrought on the field of battle. I, on the other hand, having tasted war, see no glory in it. It leaves warriors maimed and crippled; it deprives women and children of the support that they need to survive; and it causes fields to go fallow for a lack of labour. There is no glory in any of that.

"Your Christian God makes every joyful human activity a sin, but your church preaches peace over war. So while I have serious doubts about the whole of Christianity, I am inclined towards the teachings of peace. My desire in life is to stay home and enjoy my family and see them prosper. To the extent that your church supports me in this then, it has that much of my allegiance."

Oswulf smiled and replied, "That is not a bad philosophy to live by, young Stor, but what of Wessex? Have your views upon a united England under the rule of Wessex changed since we last met?"

"There I have greater conflict in my views. I have seen the destruction that Eadred and his father have visited upon Northumbria and in particularly upon Ripon. That was a Christian community. It was home to the relics of St. Wilfred. Many Christian priest and other Christian men and woman lived there. Eadred slaughtered them without mercy and leveled Ripon to the ground. This was a greater atrocity than was ever carried out by those whom you call pagan Vikings.

"On the other hand I am impressed by the approach to the development of fair and unified written law which I understand was developed by your King Alfred and has been propagated by all of his successors. Maybe the issue is not whether I support Wessex or not, but whether or not I support any given king who sits on the throne in Winchester. But of course, that is why I am here. From what I know, Edgar would make a good king and, if so, he will have my blessing. But with his brother on the throne, it will set back all of the good things that the House of Wessex has accomplished."

Oswulf nodded his agreement. "Perhaps we can become allies after all. Maybe even friends."

Oswulf fed me well, provided comfortable sleeping arrangements and in the morning wished me God's speed on my return to Deira with his proposals. Before leaving, however, he asked me, "and what is in this for you, Stor?"

I answer quickly, "Nothing my lord. I seek only to raise my family in peace on the land that my ancestors spilt their blood to acquire. That land is StorEye and this great bird, on my shield, is its symbol."

YORK, 956

When I returned to Deira and reported to the small band of conspirators who had sent me to Bamburgh, they were ecstatic. Torald thanked me over and over and proclaimed my abilities for successful completion of my assignment. They then turned to the issue of Byrniulf. "Before I support any excursion against EAdwig, we must ensure that the sons of York, and from my perspective, my son Byrniulf, are free of the reach of EAdwig should he attempt to retaliate against his hostages."

Dunstan's words gave Torald a needed assurance. "Byrniulf is in the hands of Prince Edgar's foster parents and his release should be easily obtained. The other hostages are mostly in East Anglia, where the same AEthelstan Halfking is Ealdorman or in Mercia where Halfking's brother is Ealdorman. Both of them supported Edgar's ascension to the throne. The releases of the hostages should all be easily achievable as will be their safe return to York. With those assurances in place, the company turned its attention to the demands that they would make as conditions of bringing York into the planned insurrection.

I reported that Oswulf had shared his discomforts with EAdwig. "Under his rule he has also suffered the diversion of exports and imports through London to the detriment of all of northern England. He is also outraged by the surcharge on Wessex minted coins. He supports monastic reform as he believes that the church in Canterbury has grown too wealthy and he has no vested interest in maintaining Wessex's financial discriminations against the North." Everyone assembled agreed that Oswulf's demands mirrored our own and could be accommodated if Edgar were king.

Our reservations, however, were best expressed by Torald. "I have come to Christianity reluctantly, and then only due to my trust in our Bishop Wulphstan. Because of his support for Bloodaxe, Wessex, with the support of the church at Canterbury, deposed him and to this day, deny him the right to return to York. In principle, I support the concept of English governance, with codified written laws and equal administration of justice. But our witan has been disbanded and the witan in Wessex has become the witan of all of England. We are far from fairly represented there. While we might place our trust in Edgar as king and your influence within the church at Canterbury, Dunstan, neither you nor Edgar can live forever. We have all witnessed the chaos of succession at the death of a Wessex king. Half of them have murdered either father or brother to create the vacancy on the throne to which they aspire. And the neutrality of the church at Canterbury cannot be assumed. The Roman Church in York must have a prelate capable enough, and inclined enough, to represent and support the interests of the north. We must have a native-born bishop of Scandinavian origin in the Archbishopric of York." All heads nodded in agreement.

They then agreed that I would go with Ulph, Dunstan, Aelfric and Wulfheag to Mercia where we would meet with Edgar and present our proposals. The northern nobles had one other demand of Edgar; that if he became king he would support the appointment of a cleric familiar with, and sympathetic to Northumbria to the Bishopric of York. As a result, we made plans to travel as soon as the worst of the winter weather had run its course.

MERCIA 957

One of the things which had aided the late King Alfred in bringing Mercia into an alliance under Wessex was the marriage of Alfred's daughter to a Mercian noble man. As a result, there were still close family ties between the royal family of England and much of the nobility of Mercia. Aelfric was one such relative. As such, he had easy access to Prince Edgar.

Our meeting was to be held in Chester, well away from the Wessex border. As Wulfheag explained, "the movements of people necessary for this meeting were too great to escape the notice of King EAdwig. As we were not yet ready to confront the forces of Wessex, where EAdwig still commands considerable support, the less he knows of our activities the better.

As we approached Chester, the spires of the cathedral were the first things to come into view. Flying briskly from the highest spire was the blue diagonal cross on its flaming yellow banner, representing the colours of Mercia. Emblazoned across this background was the ferocious dragon of Mercia. Travelling in England was still a dangerous undertaking and relief was obvious amongst our party as the solid façade of this walled city came into view. Chester was an old Roman fortress city whose fortifications had remained intact and impenetrable for centuries. It had been well maintained and appeared to be able to withstand the most serious of assaults.

Our arrival was greeted by a soft spring breeze which ushered in the change of season and caused the snow to begin to melt. It was also cause for great celebration. Neither Ulph nor I had seen Bryni since he left York a hostage several years ago. He had matured into a handsome young man and was ecstatic to see us and share his adventure. Dunstan was again reunited with his great friend and colleague, AEthelwold, as well Edgar, AEthelstan Halfking and, of course, Halfking's wife AElfwynn. The greetings accorded our Mercian partners by Halfking and his wife spoke to the close family relationship between them. All and all, our arrival was cause for a great feast.

After brief introductions, and delivery to our quarters, Ulphus and I met with Bryni in order to receive assurances of his good treatment at the hands of these Mercian and Wessex men. He quickly gave us that assurance. " They have treated me with great respect and I have become a fast friend of Halfking's son, AEethelwine, who is my age, and to a lesser extent with Prince Edgar himself, though he is several years my junior."

"Tell me about Edgar." Ulph demanded, but before Bryni could begin, Ulph explained the nature of our seditious plans which would see Edgar become the King of England.

"Well," Bryni began, "I like him and I have said as much in my correspondence to you. He is just turned sixteen years of age, but, except for his uncontrolled lust for women, he is very responsible. He has known all of his life, that, as second in line to the throne, it is very possible that he may succeed to that responsibility. Halfking, Dunstan and AEthelwold have all seen to his education with that possibility in mind. And Edgar is an excellent student. I have had the pleasure of joining his instruction and have well benefitted myself. I have had the pleasure of watching him develop. He has a very quick mind and takes very seriously the possible responsibilities which could await him. We also have enjoyed each other's company and so I can confidently describe him as a good man."

"What is this about women?" Ulph was quick to ask.

"I should be the last one to criticize him on this account, given my own attraction to wanton women, but he has been an unrepentant wencher since he was old enough to do so. Last winter he finally married AEthelwine's sister, AEthelfleda, who is a year younger than him. It was about time. He's been all over her since I met them. I am surprised that she wasn't with child long before they wed. But his relationship with her did not hamper his wenching, nor has his marriage. In all else, though, he is a good man."

In our subsequent discussion it became clear that Edgar would be the kind of king we needed. He saw previous Wessex policies of discriminating against the economy of the North as being short sighted and was committed to removing all barriers to trade throughout the kingdom.

On meeting Edgar, I was first surprised by his youth, regardless of the report by Bryni. He was a full year younger than I. But he was a man of deep thought and wisdom for his age. There was no frivolity in our discussions. I, for the most part, kept my own counsel and spoke only when asked to report on my discussion with Oswulf. When we were through with that discussion Edgar simply said, "I have no problems with Bamburgh's request, except that I will not support him in Edinburgh or the Lothian. Those territories are now in the hands of the Danes and the Scots are fighting them for it. That quarrel is between them and I will have no part of it. But everything south of the Lothian is legitimately part of Bernicia, and under my rule, England will defend every acre of it as our own."

When we had sorted out the issues around the alliance against EAdwig, and I thought we would adjourn, Dunstan suddenly spoke up, "When you become king, sire, you must address reform of the church. Corruption runs wild and must be curtailed." He went on for a time in this vein, making it apparent that this was a major issue with him. Edgar heard him out politely and asked the others there for their thoughts on this issue. In due course he turned to me and asked, "And you, Stor, my friend, Byrniulf speaks highly of your opinions. What are your thoughts on this?"

I was momentarily taken aback on being asked to speak on an issue upon which I pretended no expertise. Composing myself I replied, "The church must be independent and held in high moral respect. With all respects sire, kings are merely men and not beyond fault. The church is the only authority that is able to curb their excesses. If the church is corrupt or held in contempt then they have no authority to call the king to account when needed. Pious monks, trained in the words of God and committed to live up to those standards are so much more desirable than an aristocratic clergy who swell their own pockets at the expense of their parishioners"

Silence fell like thunder on the room. Then Edgar applauded, "Well-spoken Stor. I will take your counsel seriously."

CHAPTER 15
EDGAR: KING OF ALL ENGLAND

STOREYE, 963

Seven years have now past since I travelled back and forth between Bamburgh, Deira and Wessex brokering the details of the alliance which would challenge King EAdwig's throne. As the armies of Northumbria, East Anglia and Mercia prepared to march against EAdwig I returned to StorEye.

The armies of the rebel nobles marched against EAdwig as they had planned. They met EAdwig's army near Gloucester and defeated it. This did not result in a decisive victory, but it was sufficient for EAdwig to agree to allow Edgar to rule Mercia and Northumbria and the Five Boroughs. Two years later, in 959, EAdwig died at the age of twenty. Edgar became king of all of England.

To the north, King Indulf of the Scots managed to drive the Danes out of Edinburgh and the Lothians, but in an ongoing struggle with the Danes, in 962, Indulf was killed. Our old Cumbrian King Dubh succeeded him as King of Scotland and Indulf's son, Cuilien, became our king in Cumbria and Strathclyde. While Cuilien has probably no knowledge of my existence, I am well aware that it was his cowardice that caused my father's death and, often late at night, as I lay in my bed, I would become overwhelmed by a sense of shame that I owed him a blood debt which I had not repaid.

Generally, however, I have been enjoying myself with my family and my land at StorEye. Eyja has born me three more children, another son whom we have called Gyrdh and two girls, Aasta and Liv. Eyja lost one child at birth and, as she is again pregnant, I worry for her health. But she is feeling fine and we are basking in each other's company.

I am the thane of StorEye. A thanet is comprised of five or more hides, each hide being a size that it should support one family. Taxes are levied against a thanet rather than against the individual family hide. This allows the thane to adjust the tax for each of his tenants so that if one hide experiences a bad crop, lost livestock, poor birthing or any other mishap the thane can distribute the tax burden amongst the more fortunate thereby saving the individual family from ruin. Our land is fully tenanted. With ninety seven hides to oversee, the job keeps me fully occupied.

Thanes are also called upon to provide counsel to the king or earl as the case may be. Cumbria has enjoyed relative peace for the past decade and so we mainly concern ourselves with issues of crime and land disputes. We have a sheriff in Carlisle; however, out in the countryside, we generally provide our own law and order. I try to administer our estate fairly and with mercy, but if a man takes or destroys the property of another he must pay compensation and if he kills or seriously injures another person, then I will have him hanged.

Occasionally raiders strike StorEye and carry off livestock and other goods. Depending on their numbers we either send all, or part, of those doing garrison duty, or, if it is a large raiding party I raised the fyrd, track them down and deal with them. A fyrd is a call-out of all of our able bodied tenants for the purpose of defending StorEye. Our land occupancy agreements requires for every adult male tenant to respond to the fyrd when it is called. Where we cannot track the raiders, it usually means that they have crossed over into Strathcylde and there is very little that we can do unless we have followed them there in hot pursuit.

If one of our tenants refuses to live up to his tenancy agreement or continually commits crimes against others then generally I will evict him from our land. This is actually quite a harsh punishment, because a man without land has little option but to sell himself into slavery. Many estates continue to be run solely on slave labour, however, I believe that the system of land tenancy, established by my grandfather for our estate, is much superior and is rapidly being duplicated by most of our neighbours. In southern England, I am told, that it is almost universally utilized. For our part, this system is making my family very wealthy.

Most villages in England now have their own licensed market and a water wheel as well as their magistrate, church, fortifications and garrison. At StorEye, I have followed suit, adding two water wheels; one to drive our woolen mill and one to grind flour. Both have added substantially to our income.

* * *

Since Edgar has come to the throne of England, the whole country has known a relative peace. Certainly there continues to be sporadic raids by Vikings or Scots but none have been an invasion and therefore have not led to ongoing warfare. I do not know how much of this peace is attributable to Edgar's administration or how much has been his good luck to be king at the right time but whichever; he has basked in the reverence in which his subjects hold him. He has also made great strides in his monastic reforms, which have been popularly received by all but the most senior clergy and a few nobles whom had been in league with them.

I have prospered since returning to StorEye. Peace is good for business. All of my land is tenanted. The tenants are now known as serfs. For ten years now our land has enjoyed fair weather with mild winters and summers of brilliant sunny days interspersed with sufficient rainfalls to ensure healthy crops. Our livestock has been relatively free of pestilence. As a result, rents have rolled in continuously swelling our treasury beyond imagination. I have invested much of it in other commerce. I own thirty two vessels, eleven of which ply the Irish Sea and return to Carlisle ladened with the wealth of Dublin. The other twenty-one sail to all ports of Europe, including those in the Mediterranean Sea and North Africa. The proceeds of this trade are adding substantially to my already burgeoning wealth. I am without physical needs.

We have been expanding our manor house so that it now resembles a small stone castle with room for many guests to be housed comfortably. I have furnished it with the finest furnishings and tapestries Europe has to offer. Fine wooden tables, chairs, cabinets and cupboards are all complete with decorative figures of angels, people, plants and other objects, all tooled with the skilled hands of talented carvers. Plates, candlesticks and hangings of hammered gold and silver litter the living areas. Many items are inlaid with precious stones. I have many caches of buried gold but I can barely keep abreast of the wealth which keeps pouring in. I have become a man of considerable substance and many refer to me as Lord, but in truth I am simply the son of a sword Viking, who has been blessed with great luck on the returns of investments of the plunder which my forbearers accumulated.

THE LEGEND OF STOR

I continue to adore Eyja as much now as when we first met. She is my anchor. She has produced fine children for us and they are my joy. Boandi is now ten years of age. He is a big, strong lad. He has done very well in his training in the arts of a warrior, but his inclinations seem to be towards our land. This pleases me greatly. We are no longer a family of warriors. He loves the soil and has developed an extensive knowledge of how to coax out the maximum of its bounty. He is also enthralled with animal husbandry spending all of his spare time amongst the livestock, aiding them in birthing and administering to their ills.

Gyrdh is our scholar. While only seven years of age he buries himself in papers. He is constantly reading and writing and calculating sums. He shares none of his brothers desire to dirty his hands with rich thick soil or animal droppings. Brother Leo, who tutors all of the children, is fascinated with Gyrdh's inquiring mind, his cleverness and his ability to grasp a complex problem, and store all of its aspects for retrieval at his pleasure. The girls, Aasta and Liv are now six and three. While still too young to demonstrate more permanent traits which may follow them into adulthood, both are of a pleasant disposition and pleasing appearance. Liv might prove a little headstrong at times, but they are both generally promising daughters.

I feel contentment that I have accomplished the mission set for me by my grandfather so many years ago. My family is growing in size and I am beginning to imagine grandchildren. Peace prevails in the land and our financial wellbeing is as sound as is possible.

This new peace in England has allowed me to travel extensively, establishing financial enterprise across the land. The peace allows me to make short trips, returning home within days of my departure. I am constantly in York, but also travel to London and other parts of Mercia. Eyja patiently awaits my returns, eager to hear all of the news and gossip of the realm.

On returning from one trip to Mercia I brought with me some truly astounding news. We were all aware of the strides being taken by Edgar in his monastic reform. While the wealthy clergy and many of their noble patrons resented the reforms, they have too much fear of Edgar's determination to openly oppose him. AEthelwold, whom had been consecrated as Bishop of Winchester, had banished all of the wealthy clergy of Winchester and replaced them with monks from Abington. Edgar's support had included obtaining the Pope's agreement before the expulsion took place. He also founded monasteries at Chersty, Milton Abbas, Peterborough, Ely and Thorney. Edgar also supported AEthelwold in his recovery of church lands which had been appropriated by the aristocracy.

So with all of this selfless support for church reform, it came as shocking news to learn of Edgar's absolutely lecherous lack of marriage fidelity. He had become enthralled with a nun named Wulfrith. She, in turn, had rebuffed the king's royal advances and, in response he had her kidnapped and held as his personal sex slave. She eventually bore him a child. When Queen AEthelfleda died in 963, Edgar again approached Wulfrith and proposed marriage. Her contempt for him led to another rejection. Edgar had then turned his attention to a married woman, the beautiful EAlfryth. Edgar arranged to accompany EAlfryth's husband on a hunting expedition. During the hunt Edgar "accidentally" hurled a javelin which pierced the husband's back and protruded out of his chest. Edgar married the widow.

Bishop Dunstan was so outraged by Edgar's shocking behaviour that he refused to preside at Edgar's coronation until he had concluded seven years of penance.

THE LEGEND OF STOR

***

It was a pleasant summer day, and Eyja had just called the children and me to come for our noonday meal when I looked up to see a group of five mounted men passing through our gate. One, who appeared to be their leader, dismounted and, handing his sword to one of his company, strode towards me. He was a man of about my age, tall with a full head of flaming red hair and a beard to match. Something about him seemed familiar but I could not remember seeing him before. As he drew nearer he shouted, "Well my little cousin, it is good to see you alive and well."

I stood there in shocked silence until his words finally registered. "Ian MacFairburne, is that really you?"

"It Is I, but it is no longer MacFairburne," he replied.

We embraced and I made introductions to my wife and children. After making arrangements for food and drink for his companions, we invited him to join us for the meal which Eyja had spread out on a table in the yard. There he told us an amazing story. "My name is now Ian of Harmstrange.

"My father, Fairburne, continued as Duhb's weapon bearer after Dubh became king of Scotland. He followed Dubh into battle against the Danes. That was two years ago. He met them in battle near Edinburgh. As they rode into battle, Fairburn was at the king's side.

"In the heat of the battle, Dubh was struck in the leg by an invader's sword and knocked from his horse. Before the Dane could complete the task of dispatching the king, Fairburne, sword in one hand to ward off the attacker, had reached down with the other hand, scooped Dubh off the ground and swung him onto his own horse. Fairburn then carried the king to safety. When the battle was over, Dubh was victorious, alive and well, save for the nasty, but non-lethal, wound to his leg.

"After throwing a massive feast to celebrate the victory, Dubh summoned Fairburne forward. Before the assembled host, the king announced, 'Behold my fearless and faithful arms bearer and servant, Fairburne. In the heat of battle, when I was unhorsed and would surely have been struck dead by our enemies, Fairburne raised his mighty sword in my defense. While driving the cursed heathens into disarray, he reached down with his free hand and lifted me into his saddle as if I were a mere child. Fairburne', he addressed the arms bearer directly, 'from this day on you will be known as Strong Arm so that your deeds will be remembered. I am granting to you and your family forever, thirty hides of land in the valley of Liddell Water, in our kingdom, to use as you and your heirs see fit. And everyman here will bear witness to the promises made here.'"

And so he now bore his father's new name, Armstrong, but he pronounced it with his broad northern accent "Harmstrange"

"So have you moved to Liddell Valley?" I asked. The Liddell Valley drains into the Eske River, was just up river from StorEye where the river turned north as it flowed out of the hills of Strathclyde, down past our land and spilled into the sea at Solway Firth.

"I am only just now moving my family here. I do not know if news has reached you. A few months ago Dubh was murdered and my father along with him. We believe that he was killed by friends of Cuillen, the son of Indulf. Cuillen has now been declared king. Cuillen is a wicked, wretch of a man and I do not believe that my family would be safe living in any close proximity to him."

I felt a twinge of anger at the news of his father's death at the hand of the coward Cuillen. But rather than revealing my thoughts, I ask instead, "So, do you have a house to live in?"

"Only a very temporary shelter," he replied.

"Then I will organize a crew from amongst my tenants and we will get you a house built immediately. You cannot live in a temporary shelter come winter."

We talked and ate for the rest of the afternoon. I was so excited at the prospect of having kinfolk living nearby. But beneath my excitement, I concealed a surging feeling of guilt over my unpaid blood debt to Cuillen, which I struggled to not reveal. I think he was quite thrilled at the prospect of becoming my neighbour. He sat in awe as I told him of my adventures with Bloodaxe and Bamburgh and I was equally intrigued with his tales of life amongst the Scots.

After he had left, I rambled on and on about our afternoon, while Eyja simply sat smiling, amused by my feigned enthusiasm. She knew that behind my joy at having Ian Armstrong living close by, something was troubling me. "I know you too well, Stor. What is it that bothers you?" She finally asked.

"Ah! I have no secrets from you, do I? I did not know Ian's father, but he was my mother's brother. From what I have heard, he was a good man. It bothers me that this new king of Scotland is responsible for his murder and is now sitting comfortably on the Scottish throne."

"There is more, isn't there?" she asked.

An uncomfortable silence settled around us as I hesitated at responding to her question. I finally uttered, "Cuillen." I had never discussed the details of my father's death, but when I had returned from Bamburgh after hearing Oswulf talk of his fears of Bernicia being invaded by the Scots, Ulphus thought that I should know the whole story of how my father died. I finally spoke, "When our fathers were fighting to help Olfa Guthrithson retake the Kingdom of York, the Scots were their allies. Olaf was married to King Constantine's daughter. Ulph told me that when they engaged in a shield wall to face the enemy, a company of Scots were responsible for guarding their flank. Cuillen was the commander of that company. He was too young and inexperienced for that responsibility, but he was the grandson of the Scottish king and therefore was given command. In the heat of the battle, Cuillen panicked and ran. His troops followed him, leaving the flank of our fathers' shield wall unprotected. And to make things worse, in his flight, Cuillen took all of the horses, so that no one else could retreat. My father died as a result and your father was lucky not to have died with him. Ulph told me this because, with Cullien's father, Indulf attacking the Lothian, Cuillen again was in command. Ulph and I discussed joining Bamburgh's forces for the chance of meeting Cuillen in battle and making him pay for his cowardice. We decided against doing so, but my blood still boils when I hear Cullen's name mentioned."

* * *

It was late summer when I received the royal invitation. Oswulf of Bamburgh had passed away in the spring, and King Edgar of England was about to honour several of the promises which he had made in obtaining Northumbrian support in his struggle with his brother for the throne of England. Edgar intended to divide Northumbria into two earldoms, one in York and one in Bernicia. He had left Oswulf in peace as the Earl of Northumbria but now that Oswulf was dead Edgar was about to appoint a Northumbrian Dane to the position of Earl of York. That person would be a hitherto minor and unknown noble, Oslac, who had the blessing of Northumbrian nobles and a loyalty to Edgar. He also intended to appoint Oswulf's son, Waltheof, Earl of Bamburgh. I had received an invitation to attend the confirmation of Oslac as Earl of York.

We began planning the trip to York immediately. Eyja had given birth, two months ago, to another son, whom we named Haberd. While she had suffered miserably in the last months of her pregnancy and I had taken to constant prayer for her well-being, the baby had been born healthy and they were now both thriving. I considered this a very special outcome, as Eyja had lost two children, after Liv was born, before having this birth.

Eyja was excited at the prospect of visiting York and Toraldesbi and was rushing about in preparing for the trip. Boandi was now eleven years of age and Liv, the youngest of our children, aside from our new baby, was five. So, only Haberd required constant care. We planned to take all of the children with us so that they could become acquainted with all of Eyja's relatives. I had finalized with Steinar all of the arrangements for the maintenance of StorEye in our absence and we were now ready to leave.

YORK, 967

Our reception in York was one of enormous pleasure. The joyful re-acquaintances seemed to carry on throughout the entire feast which Torald had arranged in our welcome. After the death of Eric, Torald had closed the house in York and retreated to Toraldesbi. But, for this occasion, he had commissioned the house reopened. Servants had spent months scrubbing, painting and polishing until it regained its entire former splendor. The evening felt like it could just keep going on forever. Eventually, though, we tired and sought out our sleeping quarters.

On arising the next morning, it dawned on me how changed York had become in the last decade. While there was always new people arriving from other places, and bringing with them the language of their homeland, the majority of people spoke only one language now and that language was English. Certainly there were Danish and Norwegian words in their dialogue but those now seemed to be part of the English language and were used by Anglo-Saxon and Scandinavian alike. Because both Eyja and I spoke all three languages, and at StorEye we seemed to move between languages fluently, I had not noticed at first, and when it struck me, I resolved to ask Torald about it.

When I arrived at the breakfast table, the question immediately followed my opening salutation. "Alas," Torald replied, "we are all one people now. And it is not just the language. Go out in the street. If you don't ask people their names, you will never guess their place of origin. They talk alike, they dress alike, they eat the same food, and they worship the same God. They all think alike. We are all alike." He thought for a moment, and then added with a chuckle, "Well, not completely. Back at Toraldesbi we keep a few traditions which are strictly Danish. But not many," he added quickly. "Even Toraldesbi has its own English name now; Toraldesby," he stressed the difference in pronunciation.

As we began breakfast, Torald quickly moved into his favourite topic, politics. While he harangued, as always, about Wessex rule of Northumbria, he seemed genuinely pleased with Edgar's rule. England no longer attempted to restrict trade to her southern ports but instead encouraged the importing and exporting of trade goods all the way north to Bamburgh. Edgar's coins were in universal use, but York was no longer charged an extra fee for their minting. And most importantly, the new Archbishop of York, Aelfsige was sympathetic to Northern needs in the administration of secular ordinances. Now, the appointment of Oslac as Earl of York would address the last of the major grievances of the men who had supported Eric Bloodaxe.

THE LEGEND OF STOR

* * *

The ceremony in York was a spectacular event, designed as a confirmation that, while Edgar held absolute authority in all of England, he would exercise that authority fairly and in the interest of all of his subjects. He was magnanimous in his praise of the northern nobles but he did not extend his magnitude beyond the promises that he had made to gain their support. It was clear to all that he had done what was necessary to become the undisputed king of all of England, but, having done that, he would not be pressured into special concessions that would not otherwise be made.

After the ceremony, Edgar hosted a feast in the royal hall. While it was an event worthy of a king in its sumptuousness and generosity, it lacked the frivolity and irreverence which had generally accompanied Eric's great feasts. Torald, Ulphus, Ulph's sons, Norman and Achill, Byrniulf, I and my sons, Boandi and Gyrdh, all attended. None of the boys had before attended such a spectacle and were all impressed. We all enjoyed ourselves immensely and Edgar was generous with his attention, taking time to acknowledge all who had attended.

Edgar, no longer the boy who I had met in Chester, had grown into his role as king. He struck me as a mature, thoughtful man; fully capable of the command he had been given. With all of the responsibility that he carried on his shoulders, I was surprised that he remembered me from our encounter so many years earlier. He greeted me with a smile and asked, "How has life been treating you, my young peace broker?"

I chuckled, given that we were both aware of the age seniority which I held over him. "I have been busy raising a family and tending my land since we last met," I replied.

"If I recall, you told me that that was all you really wanted." He smiled warmly and inquired further, "So how is your family? Are these two lads your sons?"

I introduced Boandi and Gyrdh and assured him that Eyja, the girls and our new baby were all fine.

He then surprised me by asking, "And do you still believe that an authority is needed to temper the excesses of kings?"

I was amazed that he remembered the detail of our conversation. I paused to ensure that my embarrassment was hidden and would not betray my awareness of his sexual philandering. "Sire, some kings, like yourself, do not seem to have excesses, but that is not true of all of the kings whom I have met."

His eyes twinkled as he said, "It is good to know that I have a subject, with such extensive knowledge of kings, in my kingdom, to draw upon when I require it."

Waltheof of Bamburgh was also present at this event although his elevation to succeed his father as Earl of Bernicia had happened several weeks earlier. When I saw him, I immediately approached to offer my condolences on his father's passing and to congratulate him on his appointment. We renewed our acquaintances and, after concurring that his father had been a good and honourable man, he said, "Well Stor I guess we were both right in supporting Edgar to become our king. He has served us both well. So I suppose this now makes us both Englishmen. That should also make us political allies."

"No," I replied politely. "I am not English. I do support the principals and system of laws created over the years of English monarchy, but only so long as England represents those laws and leaves me in peace. I might even go to war in support of England and may well find myself your brother-in-arms. But it will only be to further my own goal which is to see my family grow and prosper. In its adherence to Alfred's law and administration, Wessex supports me. But my loyalties do not lie primarily with England. They lie with my family.

"You, on the other hand, are in constant war with the Scots. The Scottish throne technically holds sway over Cumbria on England's behalf. That relationship is too fragile to last. Some day they will war over Cumbria. When that happens, I will not be drawn into that struggle. So I will not now be drawn into the struggle over the northern boundary of Bernicia and the southern border of Scotland." While the line between the borders of England and Scotland was an often varying thing, Hadrian's Wall caused both kingdoms to view themselves as having an inalienable right to the land on their respective side of it. The Wall separated Cumbria from Strathclyde in the west. Northern Cumbria was technically under Scottish dominion, but that existed only at England's pleasure. In the east, Bernicia's northern border ran many hundreds of miles north of the Wall. This was a constant irritant to the Scots, even though the issue was moot since Danes continued to control most of the disputed land.

Waltheof smiled and said, "Well, for the present, we are both on the same side so we might as well be friends."

We shook hands on that and I took my leave.

* * *

After leaving the city we retired to Toraldesbi for several weeks before returning home. Ulph and Bryni spent most of their time commanding Boandi, Gyrdh, Archil and Norman in the use of those terrible wooden swords which had completely exhausted me so many years ago. Archil and Norman demonstrated the greater effectiveness of Ulph's training over the years than mine had been with my own sons. I made a mental note to talk to Steinar about remedying this situation when we returned home.

Eyja and her mother spent their time ensuring that Aasta and Liv received an appropriate set of lessons of their own. In spite of now being married, with her own children, Kari was relentless in her care of Haberd and, as usual, I spent my time arguing politics with Torald.

I always maintained that the English system of written law was good law because it could be administered fairly, unlike the old Scandinavian approach which permitted kings to rule capriciously. "As long as your Danish ways prevail"' I told Torald, "we will always be on the brink of civil war. A man can find no security under such rule, because if he loses favour of the king, his life and lands can be forfeit. Under English law there is at least some guarantee of impartiality. If the king steps outside of his own law, the church and the witan can pressure him to conform. But only a Christian Church would do that. Your pagan gods don't care what our kings do. We all only exist for their amusement." We had engaged in this same discussion many times before.

As if on cue, Torald responded, "But your Christian god is a god of surrender with nonsense such as 'turn the other cheek'. Our Gods were Gods of Warriors," he chuckled good-naturedly at his own provocation.

"Their Christian Gods did not refrain from giving us some terrible lickings when we warred against them."

"So you think that their god is a better war god than Odin?" Torald rebutted.

"No, "I replied, "I think that their wisdom to garrison burhs and create a localized responsibility for maintaining them was why they were able to defeat us so decisively. Their troops were more motivated because they saw themselves defending their land and their families. The Viking invaders were basically mercenaries, fighting for booty."

The following morning Torald picked up our conversation where he had left off the day before. "So we are now all Englishmen," Torald declared decisively.

Not missing an opportunity to catch Torald with a political jibe, as he so often did to me, I replied, "So let me get this straight; you were born a Dane, became a Northumbria/Yorkishman, and have now transformed into an Englishman?"

Torald responded thoughtfully, "I have little control over the outcome of battles which set different people on our throne. We now have an English king. I supported him obtaining his crown and I bowed the knee to him once he had captured it. I speak their language, wear their clothes, practice their religion and follow their customs. How can I consider myself to be anything but an Englishman? But you, Stor, have gone through the same transformation, so do not criticize me for the same experience"

"But I disagree with you," I said earnestly. "I too speak their language, wear their clothes and follow their customs and religion. I too have bent my knee to Edgar and I appreciate his rule. I will also concede that I have prospered by collaborating with my many Anglo partners and I feel safer living under the fairness of English law, but all of these things do not make me an Englishman.

"Who I am is determined by where I place my loyalties. I support Edgar and I will support England as long as she maintains her present approach to governance. I do so because it is in my interest to do so. But my first loyalty is to the promise which I made to my grandfather; that I will build my family. That is where I place my loyalty and will die for it if necessary. I will not throw that away to further the vain glory of other men. Therefore, regardless of my Norse or Anglo ancestry, my Scottish king in Carlisle or my English overlord in Winchester, I am, first and foremost Stor, son of

Eye. And I will try my hardest to instigate those same loyalties in my children and my children's children."

Torald leaned back in his chair and smiled broadly. "You have become very wise for one so young. So I too have fulfilled a covenant which I gave to Vidar. At his insistence, and at my pleasure, I swore to help prepare you for the tasks which he has placed on your shoulders. I believe that that goal has been attained"

CHAPTER 16
WHEN COWARDS DIE

STOREYE, 971

After returning to StorEye following Oslac's appointment, I have not had reason to travel further than my cousin's home in Liddell Valley or to Carlisle for the markets and to meet with Father Leo regarding my children's education. The children have grown quickly and are showing signs of being promising adults. Boandi would be a warrior if allowed. I have tried hard to convince him away from a life with the sword. Steinar has engaged a couple of old warriors to train my sons and ensure that they can protect themselves. But that is only a tool; not the purpose for our lives. I think that I am getting through to him, but time will tell. Gyrdh is our scholar. He loves books. Leo would steal him away for the church if I were not vigilant. Again I believe that Gyrdh shares my purpose, but, like his brother, time will tell. Both of the older boys, and their sisters, are betrothed and Boandi will marry next summer.

We have spent much time with the Armstrongs, either taking the family up to Liddell Valley or having them come down to StorEye. I enjoy having family close by and we have grown fond of the Armstrongs. I am somewhat troubled by

Ian's preoccupation with his father's murder. I envy him that he knew his father so well that he could not let go of his memory, however I thought that his brooding on vengeance was both unrealistic and maybe not good for him. I was also troubled by the thought that maybe my reactions to Ian were striking just a little too close to my own, long forgotten, thoughts of avenging my own father's death.

In spite of the numerous occasions on which I had visited Liddell Valley in the past, it had never been under such mysterious circumstances as the summons that called me there this night. My instructions were clear. Travel only after dark and do not be seen on the road. These instructions were all the more incomprehensible given the difficulty involved. The road to Liddell Valley is a narrow tract following the river, which I must also ford. It would be easy for a horse to lose its footing and fall, causing its rider serious injury. While we have made the trip many times in the light of day, it is not easy even then. So why Ian had me coming this evening I found perplexing.

I have come to like and trust my cousin. All the way to his place I could only think that he must have good reason for his request. I finally arrived safely and was quickly ushered inside. Ian was not alone. He quickly introduced me to a tall, dark-haired man whose face was twisted in an angry scowl. "This is Amdarch, Prince of Strathclyde. The time has come when I can exact my revenge against Cuillen for the murder of my father, but I need your assistance to do so. If you do not wish to assist me then I will find another way to do it. But remember, he was your uncle as well as my father, and, much as you tried to hide it, I saw how it pained you when you heard of his death."

"Before we discuss this further, what is the role of this man?" I asked nodding in the direction of Amdarch.

Without waiting for a response from Ian, Amdarch spat out his reason for being here. "Cuillen viciously raped and murdered my daughter. I want revenge as badly as Armstrong does and I can make it happen. But I need your help."

He went on to explain that Cuillen was usually well guarded. Armdash's plan was to lure him to a place where he would be unguarded and therefore vulnerable. He went on to talk about Cullien's desire to annex all of Bernicia to Scotland. The obstacle for Cuillen was Bamburgh Castle. He believed the castle to be impregnable and that if he attempted to take it by siege, England would come to Bamburgh rescue before the siege would have a chance to be effective. If Cuillen could be made to believe that the castle could be taken by stealth, then he would jump on the opportunity. "This is where you come in Stor. With the exception of known Bamburgh allies, you are the only person that both Cuillen and I know, and will trust, who has been inside Bamburgh Castle. You supported Eric Bloodaxe in his war on Bamburgh. Cuillen could easily be convinced that you remain an enemy of Bamburgh and would be prepared to ally yourself with anyone to bring about the defeat of Bamburgh. It should be easy for us to get Cuillen to believe that you would be willing to lead a sufficient number of men into the castle through a hidden entrance, and once inside, sabotage the defenses and have the gates thrown open to a frontal attack. Once Cuillen realizes that you were once a foe of Oswulf of Bamburgh, he will believe that, for a sufficient reward, you would be prepared to become part of such a plot"

"But I know of no such entrance," I protested.

"Maybe not," Amdarch replied, "but Cuillen does not know that you don't." Cuillen only knows that you were there with Bloodaxe when the old Earl surrendered. We could convince Cuillen that you were a friend of Bloodaxe and that you hold Bamburgh responsible for his death and desire revenge against him. We could convince him that you do not want your participation known and therefore he would have to meet you surreptitiously. If we play it right, we could lure him into a position where he would be vulnerable and we could then hold him accountable for all of his crimes."

My mind was racing. I do not believe that I had betrayed my knowledge of Cullien's role in my father's death, so I could only believe that it was an incredible coincidence that Ian would believe that I would be interested in his conspiracy. But then, maybe those old pagan spinners, who sit at the root of the tree of life, really had been sitting there spinning the thread which included my fate to deliver Cuillen to his just reward. We discussed Amdarch's proposal over the next several hours, groping for shortcomings and planning logistics. In the end I agreed to be part of their conspiracy.

We spent the next several hours working out the details. My role was to simply meet with Cullien's man, identify myself and convince him that I could give Cuillen the information which he wanted. I was not even required at the ambush. I protested my exclusion, but Amdarch was adamant. I would only get in the way, and it would be too hard to get me out of Scotland once the ambush was done. I do not know how Amdarch succeeded in getting word to Cuillen that I was willing and able to help him gain access to Bamburgh Castle, but word came that I was to meet a person named Eochaid at a small inn in a town named Hodden in southern Strathclyde. I was given the time and day for the meeting. When I arrived at the prescribed spot, and entered the inn, a cloaked figure approached me and beckoned me to join him outside. He introduced himself as Eochaid, the person I was to meet. It turned out that Eochaid was Cullien's brother. I played out my role as we had agreed. I claimed to be a mercenary, mostly motivated by money. I was also confident in my abilities and required only a small payment in advance; the remainder payable after Bamburgh Castle was in Cullien's hands. We talked for a while, mostly haggling over my fee. At the conclusion, and at my insistence, a meeting was scheduled with Cuillen himself, at a hall in the Lothian near the Bernician border.

When the details of my alleged meeting with Cullien were concluded, I took my leave, and returned to meet with Ian and Amdarch where I passed on the details of the arranged meeting. With that, my role was complete. They set off to carry out the ambush while I returned home to StorEye.

***

Three weeks had passed since I had last seen Armstrong. Today he arrived at StorEye, his horse perspiring from the pace to which it had been pushed. Ian dismounted, and with a wave to Eyja, who was standing in the doorway, he led me around a shed which stood in our courtyard. "It is done," he announced conspiratorially. "We are avenged."

I was surprised that I did not share Ian's elation at the news of Cullien's death but as he related the details I became increasingly aware that vengeance is indeed a bitter meal. Apparently Cuillen had arrived at the proposed meeting place with a larger guard than Amdarch had anticipated. Not seeing me, Cuillen had grown suspicious. Amdarch, Ian and the men they had brought to the ambush were forced to strike prematurely. The fighting had raged for an hour, while Cuillen and his brother had cowardly escaped to the hall and had barred themselves inside. Amdarch and Ian had eventually prevailed. But Cuillen would not surrender himself to them. Not being able to get Cuillen and Eochaid outside, Amdarch had set the hall to the torch. Both brothers had perished in the fire.

After Armstrong had departed, I brooded over my complicity in Cullien's death. Eyja was very supportive of the actions I had taken, and while I must confess to feelings of satisfaction at having played a role in avenging my father, feelings of guilt accompanied my thoughts of the manner of Cullien's death. Those thoughts followed me into my dreams for many weeks afterwards.

Subsequent to Cullien's death, the late King Duhb's brother became Kenneth ll, King of Scotland. His son assumed the crown prince's honour, and became King Malcolm of Cumbria and Strathclyde.

CHAPTER 17
ENGLAND HER OWN

CHESTER, 973 AD

I stood looking northward over the Eske River Valley towards the gentle hills which rose from the valley floor and crept ever higher as they ranged past Hadrian's Wall and into Strathclyde beyond. The sun had begun its climb but had not yet burned the fog from the valley floor below. It was a warm spring day and I had every reason to feel pleased with myself. My lands, here in the valley, were prospering and my family was growing. My horse stood saddled beside me and his saddle bags bulged with provisions for the journey which lay ahead of us.

I was waiting for my cousin, Ian Armstrong, whom I expected to see riding up the valley to join me on the trip. As expected, Armstrong came trotting out of the mist which still clung to the valley floor. He was riding tall and proudly, astride his fine black mount, red hair flowing in the wind behind him. Dressed in an elegant blue cloak over a leather tunic, Armstrong looked every bit a member of that proud family who called themselves Harmstrange. He was accompanied by five of his sons

The Armstrongs had been residing in Liddesdale since he had first announced his move to me so many years prior. He had raised a large family of eight sons and five daughters. While the use of surnames was not yet common, all of the Harmstranges had clung to the name proudly. Most of Ian's generation was known by Harmstrange, *a name that was to reverberate through Liddesdale for many generations yet to come. Spelled Armstrong, it is a common surname in that area even today.*

As he drew near, Armstrong called down to me, "Well Stori, if your party is ready we should be on our way."

"You're in a hurry to get to this circus", I chuckled in response.

"You don't trust our noble lords to resolve things?" Armstrong asked.

"If they don't, we will know no peace."

"You may well have reason for concern, but you'd best not share them with Malcolm until we see how this thing goes. If they don't resolve things and you're labeled as the naysayer, you might not be around to see the outcome."

Ian and his sons had come to StorEye to join us on our trip, first to Penrith at the summons of our King Malcolm, and then all of the way south to Bath to attend the coronation of King Edgar of England. Edgar had ruled all of England since his brother's death in 959. He was yet to be crowned. Dunstan, now Archbishop of Canterbury, had been so incensed by Edgar's role in the death of AEthelwold, and his subsequent marriage to Aethelwold's widow that he had ordered him to seven years penance. During this period Dunstan had refused to crown him. The seven years had now elapsed and the coronation was planned to be held at the ancient Roman city of Bath. This would be the first coronation of an undisputed king of all of England and the ceremony planned for the celebration was expected to surpass any previous extravaganza ever held in Britain. Every noble in the realm had been ordered to attend.

The coronation was to be followed by a second ceremony to be held at Chester, in which Edgar was to demand consolidation of his realm. Our King Malcolm, as a vassal of Edgar's, had been summoned to this event also. As a result, he sought to consolidate his own position and had therefore demanded that his thanes attend a ceremony, for that purpose, at Penrith as they travelled south to Bath.

Our small retinue left the path leading up to the farm house. Boandi, Gyrdh and even little Haberd were joining us for this occasion, along with our servants and armed escort. I turned and waved to Eyja, and the girls who had gathered in the doorway to see us off.

We rode in silence for a while. I was contemplating the potential dynamics of the coming gathering. While Edgar was the undisputed king of all of England, vassal kings still reigned at his pleasure in the westerly Celtic kingdoms and in the northern Scottish kingdoms. Vassal kings were seldom long content to serve as vassals. They wanted their kingdoms in their own rights. Edgar planned to use his coronation to reassert his undisputed claim over them all.

"So what do you think Malcolm really wants from this conference?" Boandi inquired as we rode side by side along the narrow dirt roadway, which was well packed from years of usage.

"Malcolm, first and foremost, wants Edgar's blessing for his reign over Cumbria." I replied. "But he has a problem. As you know, Kenneth still is of the opinion that all of Bernica north of The Wall rightfully belongs to Scotland. He may well be tempted to take it by force. If he does, he will demand that Cumbria and Strathclyde join him. Malcolm does not believe that Kenneth can win. He knows that England will send its entire army to defend Bernicia.

Malcolm is caught in the middle. He has everything to lose and he knows that he probably will. But Kenneth is both Malcolm's liege lord and father. Edgar will expect Malcolm's loyalty even though he might be Kenneth's son and heir. Malcolm may also be looking toward the future when he ascends to the throne of Scotland, and the further south that eastern border extends, the greater benefit it will be to him. So in the meantime he will attempt to appear to be loyal to England. For now, though, he will want to convince Edgar that his fealty to England is solid."

The Scots had always viewed The Wall as their rightful border. Long before the House of Alpin had welded the warring tribes of the north into a Scottish kingdom, Ida Flamebearer, and his Anglo successors had incorporated all of the land south of the Firth of Forth into their Bernician Empire and eventually into the mighty Kingdom of Northumbria. The Danes had conquered Edinburgh and The Lothian and still held sway there. AEthelstan, when he conquered Northumbria, had marched into Scotland and forced Kenneth's fore- bearers to bend the knee to him. In return, he had granted them Edinburgh and The Lothian but had insisted that Bernicia's claim south of that point would continue to be part of Bernicia. Edmund had reinforced that claim but in return had granted the vassalage of Cumbria, south of The Wall, to Scotland as part of the reward for helping to subdue the Celtic kingdom of the late King Dunmail.

"If he wants to be seen as neutral, why does he not simply ignore this event and stay home?" Ian prompted.

"He is fully aware of the fate of King Guthric of York when he ignored AEthelstan's summons." I replied. These Wessex kings expect attendance when they summon."

During this discussion Gyrdh had ridden quietly on my other side, allowing his elder brother to ask the questions and then listening intently to my answers. I loved telling my sons about the history and politics of our country. Years ago I had related in detail all that Vidar had taught me about our family history and the task that he had given me. I emphasized that this task would fall on their shoulders when I was gone to wherever whichever God had in mind for me.

The first leg of the journey was uneventful. The weather had been mild for early spring and the road had been good. We had chatted comfortably, deliberately avoiding the more serious conversation about my apprehensions concerning our reasons for making this journey. Ian had appraised us about the doings of his large family at home at Liddesdale. My children, along with Ian's, joined in the discussion about the landscape, the weather and many other pleasant, but mundane topics.

My sons were now growing into manhood with Boandi already married and a father of two children himself. Boandi and Gyrdh helped with the farm land and the management of our estate. The estate was fully tenanted and, as a condition of their tenancy; our tenants contributed labour to the upkeep of our manor. The land at StorEye was more fertile than the Valley of Liddisdale and therefore a greater portion was under cultivation than the Harmstrange lands. My manor still personally maintained a considerable herd of sheep, along with pigs, horses and goats. My daughters, while both married with children of their own, continued to assist Eyja with maintaining the manor house and its provisioning. All of these things provided good fodder for conversation, while the Armstrongs contributed many antidotes of their situation at Liddesdale.

It was mid-afternoon as we approached Caer Luel, now pronounced Carlisle. As a boy, Stigandr had taught me well the history of this country. The ancient town, built by the Romans to garrison their defenders of The Wall, lay mostly in ruins. This had been Luguvalium, the site of a mighty Roman fortress, which had been demolished in Anglo-Celtic wars several centuries earlier. The rubble from this demolition was still evident, and a closer inspection would reveal the still existing foundation on which the fortress had been constructed. This had not always been the case. In ancient times, Caer Luel had been the capital of the Kingdom of Rheged. The old Roman fort had been restored to splendor by the early Celtic kings. *Many current scholars believe that the fortress at Carlisle was the inspiration for the myths of King Arthur's Camelot.*

At Carlisle we intersected the route of the ancient Roman Highway. The highway which the Romans had built had overgrown over the centuries since Roman rule and was now buried far beneath the present surface of the road. But the route had remained unchanged over time. It was now well packed with only traces of ruts left from the winter dampness which had softened the surface. Here we turned south and followed this route which would lead us to Malcolm's Cumbrian capital at Penrith and eventually all the way through Chester to our destination at Bath. At Penrith we would assemble with the rest of Malcolm's retinue and together we would all complete the journey south to Bath.

We arrived at Penrith as preparations were being made for the evening meal. What a magnificent sight lay before us. Malcolm would be attended on this trip by a retinue of fifty of his thanes, including both myself and Armstrong and all of the family members who accompanied them, an additional twenty five members of his court, sixty servants, a guard of one hundred foot soldiers along with accompanying trades people and priests to minister to the host while we travelled to Bath and then back and during our stay in Chester. Our journey to Bath and Chester would be under the protection of King Edward of England, but none the less, two companies of foot soldiers would accompany us in order to insure that we were not harassed by bandits along the way.

Tents had been erected at the outskirts of the town to house this entourage. Hundreds of these red and white striped structures shimmered under the glistening sun as it began its evening descent in the heavens. Above the tents fluttered the arms of the various nobility and above them all, the standards of Malcolm and of the Kingdom of Cumbria, with its three white roses gleaming on their brilliant green background underscored by three alternating stripes of white and blue. Conspicuously absent were the banners of the clans of Strathclyde. The nobility of Strathclyde would side with Kenneth if it came to a dispute with Cumbria and so Malcolm had not invited them to join him. His entourage was almost completely Cumbrian.

I was a thane, and as such I was entitled to fly my family crest. I proudly unfurled the standard bearing the magnificent crest which identified my presence. It was composed of a shield divided into six sections in two rows of three. The sections were alternately coloured black and white. On each one of the three black sections, stood a white stork. At the very top of the standard, stood a fourth stork, holding a serpent in its beak.

We were shown to our respective tents. After unpacking our supplies and ensuring that our horses were cared for, we were all escorted to Malcolm's castle for the feast which Malcolm had arranged for his retinue before they embarked on the road to Bath. The castle was a grand stone structure, with an easily defensible wall surrounding an interior courtyard. While sentries manned the walls the massive wooden gate, for this occasion the gates were wide open, as if an unspoken invitation for guests to enter. Once inside, we crossed the court yard, crossed a draw bridge and mounted the large stone stairs that led to the castle itself.

The size of the hall into which we were ushered left me in awe. My grand manor house at StorEye, in which I took such great pride, could easily fit in its entirety within this hall. The wall soared thirty feet to an arched oak ceiling above. They were adorned with brightly coloured banners of every description, heralding the glories of Malcolm's ancient family. At the far end of the hall was a long wooden table set to accommodate thirty people seated on one side and facing out towards the guests in the rest of the hall. Malcolm and his court would be seated there. Stretching down the hall from the head table were two rows of tables which would accommodate the remainder of the retinue. The soldiers and servants would be fed elsewhere, at a tent set up for that purpose.

The tables themselves were laden with food and drink. There were haunches of venison, mutton and pork. Large platters were overflowing with a variety of fish. There were bowls of steaming vegetables and chilled fruits and cheeses. Great jugs held wines and ales. No restraint was evident in Malcolm's attempt to ensure this journey would commence in good humour. Malcolm and his queen were not yet in attendance and the guests stood, chatting amicably with each other while awaiting the royal arrival. Once they arrived the guests would be shown to their respective seats, which would be based on a strict protocol of rank and importance. Because I was a thane of some importance, my sons and I would be seated closer to the head table than the Armstrongs.

A silence fell over the great hall as Malcolm and his queen made their entrance to a fanfare of trumpets. They were resplendent in their attire. Malcolm was draped in a flowing purple robe trimmed with ermine and embellished by his crest of office. On his head was a golden replica of the ancient crown of Rheged which, upon Dunmail's death had been thrown into the Grisdale Tarn and never recovered. The queen wore a pale blue gown with jeweled necklaces and a jeweled tiara in her hair. When they were seated, the rest of his guests took their assigned places.

During the banquet, I made the acquaintances of many of my fellow guests and renewed acquaintances with those I already knew, proudly introducing my sons to all. Dinner conversation was light and cordial and accompanied by musicians and minstrels singing ballads commemorating the glories of old Cumbria, its heroes and its myths.

When the dining was complete and the tables clear of plates and platters, Malcolm rose to address the assembly. "Fellow Englishmen", he began, "We are gathered here to begin a journey to meet with all of the kings of this island of ours. The outcome of this meeting will have major ramifications for our Cumber homeland. Our kingdom is a direct succession of the Kingdom of Rheged established by Cole Hen so many centuries ago. I have summoned you all to join me at this council so that we may demonstrate to all of these kings, that we are all, regardless of our origin, Cumber men and that we are also Christian English men." Malcolm paused and then proceeded to introduce each member of his retinue in order of their rankings.

When he came to me he announced, "This is Styr." He deliberately used the Saxon pronunciation of my name." He continued," His ancestors were Norsemen. His grandfather fought for Ragnald and his father fought for Olaf Strithson. Stori has settled in our country and is raising his children as God fearing Christian Cumber men. Those are his sons beside him to witness this. They are Englishmen." As he proceeded around the room he ended each introduction with this same phrase. When he came to Ian he said, "This is Ian Harmstrange. He lives right on our northern border with Strathclyde. His father's ancestors were Anglos and his mother's were Scottish men. The Harmstranges are a god fearing Christian family of Cumber. Ian Harmstrange, and his sons beside him, are all Englishmen."

When he had finished the introductions, he introduced himself. "As you all know, I am your king, Maol Colum." This time he used the old Celtic pronunciation of his own name. "On my head is the ancient crown of the Kingdom of Rheged. I am a direct descendant of Cole Hen. But my ancestry also includes Scottish men, Englishmen and Norsemen. I am now the god fearing Christian king of Cumber. I am an Englishman.'

"But our kingdom has been given to Scotland. At this conference my father, Kenneth II of Scotland will want Edward to give him Bernicia, but Edward will not. This will lead to war. Kenneth will lose, but if we are his vassals, he will summon our support and we will be defeated along with him. Cumbria will be left in ruins. We must insure this does not happen."

Malcolm finished to a great applause that shook the hall, but beneath this was a gentle snickering. While none of the assembly disagreed with Malcolm's assessment of what lay ahead, they were amused by his emphasis on their nationality. They would be loyal to Malcolm's aspirations, but not out of a sense of national patriotism. These men were, first and foremost, family men; their loyalties lay with their families and clans. National patriotism registered a long way down their lists of conscious priorities, if it registered at all.

When the banquet ended, Ian, I and our sons made our way back to our tents unescorted. On the way, we discussed the position taken by King Malcolm. "So what did you make of the king's performance?" Ian inquired.

"It was as I thought", I replied. "Malcolm is right in believing that Kenneth will demand Bernicia as part of Scotland. Edward will, of course, refuse." The portion of Bernicia which Kenneth desired stretched along the eastern coast, north of Hadrian's Wall. Kenneth felt that it was properly part of Scotland's birth right. Bernicia, however, had been an Anglo-Saxon kingdom and at one time was part of the Kingdom of Northumbria. As such, Edgar felt that it would be a betrayal of his Anglo-Saxon responsibility to surrender the territory to Scottish rule. Both monarchs were intransigent in their positions.

As we parted to our respective tents for the night, Ian observed, "None of this will likely come up during the coronation at Bath but when we come back to the conference at Chester who knows what will be said."

*　*　*

BATH, 973

The following morning we all prepared for the journey to Bath. Ian had obviously been considering our conversation of the previous evening long into the night. He approached me and, in a stern voice, but in a near whisper, he declared, "My family will not participate in a war between England and Scotland." In spite of Malcolm's bold proclamations, we have family on both sides of The Wall but we are neither Scottish men nor English men. We are Harmstranges. We will not go to war against each other. While we live tight against The Wall, it does not automatically follow that we must choose sides. The Border is a flexible thing and we will choose whether it runs north of our lands or south of our lands and we will fight anyone who dares to make that choice for us." *And so began a process which would dog the entire border area, resulting in it becoming known as the "Debatable Lands" until England and Scotland became united six hundred years later.*

That morning Malcolm's entire retinue organized themselves for the journey to Bath. Instead of moving south, however, Malcolm had ordered a short detour to the west. The voyagers made a splendid spectacle spread out in a column moving down the road west from Penrith. Leading the company was a company of foot soldiers. They were followed by carriages carrying Malcolm and his court. Then came the Armstrongs and my family and the remainder of the retinue, mounted on our dark Fell ponies, a breed of horse found only in Cumbria. Following them were wagons carrying supplies and accompanied by servants and musicians. Bringing up the rear was another company of foot soldiers. We moved slowly, but steadily away from the rising sun.

After an hour's trip, the parade stopped and Malcolm stepped out of his carriage. He walked to a nearby cairn of rocks where he stopped and turned to address the now dismounted entourage. "This cairn of rocks is called Dunmail's Raise," he said, indicating the cairn beside him. "On this spot Dunmail, the last great ruler of a truly independent Cumbria was foully slain. As we proceed through whatever lies ahead we should always remember with pride that we are Cumber men." He continued in this vain, and ended by proclaiming, "… so we should always keep in our heart this spot where Dunmail lies."

The company then reassembled and returned to the old Roman road way, where we proceeded southward. The road continued to follow the old Roman road, providing a solid foundation for the hooves of our horses and the wheels of our carts. Much of the original paving stones were still clearly visible, testifying to the incredible craftsmanship that went into the original construction. Regardless of the immensity of our entourage, we were able to make good time and within a week Bath came into sight.

Bath was a very ancient place. Long before the Romans, local Britons had recognized the healing powers of the natural hot pools of water which rose up from deep within the earth. The Romans had built a city there, known as Aquae Sulis, along with a temple to their patron goddess, Sulis Minerva. Unlike most Roman cities this one was not built for military purposes. It was entirely for recreational usage. However, this did not cause the Romans to refrain from encircling the city with a wall. Despite the years of neglect after the Roman withdrawal, much of the wall, along with the now roofless buildings, were still standing and in reasonable repair. Much of the tons of marble which the Romans had imported to build the city still proclaimed the beauty of its former existence. In the past century much of Bath had been restored. Its grandeur provided a magnificent back drop for the approaching extravaganza. This would be the first coronation of an undisputed king of all of England. Others of Edgar's ancestors had claimed hegemony over all of England, but even his brother, EAdwig had never had the support of Northumbria even though they had bent the knee to him. Edgar was not about to allow the culmination of Alfred's dream to occur without the greatest of fanfare. The coronation ceremony would be the largest and greatest spectacle ever seen in Britain. This event would also be the first coronation of an English queen

Even at a considerable distance, it was obvious that the visiting population had swelled well beyond the city's normal confines and throngs continue to approach from every direction. Major caravans and lines of individual stragglers moved in a steady procession towards Bath. We would soon be swallowed up in a sea of humanity. Hundreds of tents surrounded the city. Above them flew a forest of poles, bearing the coats-of-arms of all of England's nobility. From a distance I could see the wolf of Toraldesby bravely proclaiming the identity of those who were residing beneath it.

I led our party directly to the spot where Ulph and his family were quartered. Ulph, Norman and Archil were milling about in front of their tent. Even Torald had made the journey, although age had forced him to make the trip by wagon, much to his chagrin. Ulph would later tell me that he had complained the entire way from York.

On approaching them I quickly dismounted, embraced Ulph and bid hello to Norman and Archil. I then turned to Torald and strode to where he was seated, my three boys trailing in my wake. I received only a courteous nod and his eyes carried past me. His face gleamed with a broad smile as he beckoned to the boys to approach him. He rose from his seat and declared in a booming voice, "So, these are the grandsons who you have created for me. Come; give your old grandfather a hug." He smiled his approval. "You have done me well, Stor. Now leave these handsome young princes with me while you attend to getting yourself settled."

Accompanied by Ulph, Ian and their sons, we led our party to the tents which had been assigned us. I quickly gave instructions for unpacking and caring for the horses and men, and then we all strode back to Ulph's encampment. On the way, Ulph turned to Ian, and with a mischievous grin asked, "Well Armstrong, what evil role did you assign to my son Stor in the destruction of Cullien?"

The expression of astonishment which crossed my face would have served as an admission of guilt to any sin ascribed to me, but Ulph was watching Ian. Without missing a beat, or revealing a thing, Ian responded, "Why, My Lord, whatever are you talking about?"

Ulph simply gave us both a knowing smile, "Enough said. We will talk no more of this."

There was much revelry as we took our evening meal. Torald was our host. He had arranged long wooden tables arrayed in the manor of a great hall. There was venison, wild boar, ducks and freshly caught fish along with all manner of vegetables. Wine flowed like rivers. Torald smiled with false modesty and declared the good fortune of his huntsmen during their journey to Bath.

FRED STOREY

After great frivolity and conversation, I was preparing to retire to my tent when Torald quietly said to me, "So I guess Vidar was right. Tomorrow we will all officially become Englishmen."

I replied equally quietly, "Country does not make you who you are. Blood does."

I did not need to look back at him to know that he was beaming with pleasure at me.

* * *

The coronation ceremony itself was as magnificent as all of its planning had promised. The ceremony was to be held outdoors. A large stage had been erected, standing at least six feet off of the ground and thereby enabling the throng of thousands to watch the proceedings. Crimson carpeting covered its entire surface and flowed down two wide staircases and well out onto the ground in front. Mounted on the stage were two enormous golden thrones inlaid with jewels of every description. They were flanked by two smaller thrones. Slightly to one side was the more modest bishop's throne. There were two expensively draped tables. One of these held the golden scepter of the king and beside it two crowns, one slightly more modest than the other, but both sparkling gold and heavily inlaid with diamonds and rubies. The other held the bishop's paraphernalia of office. The day itself was warm and sunny as if Edgar's priests had conspired with their God to ensure the success of this monumental event.

Directly in front of the stage were row upon row of benches on which the nobility were to be seated. On the front row, the benches were clad with soft looking cushions and were obviously intended for use by the subordinate kings of the realm. Ushers stood at the end of each row of benches to ensure that everyone was seated according to their rank. Torald, Ulphus and his sons and Byrniulf were seated six rows from the front. We were seated many rows behind them, but thankful, regardless, that we were not sitting on the ground like the common folk.

Shortly after we were all seated the air was broken by a fanfare of trumpets. From behind the stage came a grand procession. Leading it were two young altar boys, scurrying around to spread incense as if to ensure that the procession would not be insulted by nefarious odors which might be emitted from the ground. Next came Archbishop Dunstan in a flowing white gown and a tall pointed hat. It seemed to portray the greatest simplicity, but closer inspection revealed a wealth of tapestry woven into the rich cloth and rows of small matching pearls running down the seams from his neck all the way down and around the hem which hung only inches from the ground. It seemed in contradiction to the humble man who at one time inhabited the crude lean-to which clutched the side of AEthelstan Halfking's barn.

Behind Dunstan followed a host of senior churchmen in red and white robes followed by a hundred black and white clad altar boys. They were all joined in singing praises to their God in the tongue of the church in Rome. As Dunstan reached the nearest staircase he mounted the stage. The remainder peeled off to either side of the stage where benches awaited them. The two boys who had led the procession continued their mission of spreading the incense to every corner of the stage. Dunstan seated himself on his throne. The incense bearers scurried down to join their companions on the side benches.

The church people had barely been seated when the trumpets again began their fanfare. Four people came into view. Leading them was Edgar and, his soon to be queen, the lovely EAlfryth. They made a perfect couple, bedecked in all of their finery, walking hand in hand around the stage and mounting the stairs. Behind them came two regally dressed boys, one about eleven years of age, the other about five. They were the king's sons, Edward and AEthelred. Circumstances of Prince Edwards's birth were not widely known, but he was rumored to be the son of Edith, who had earlier chosen the nunnery over Edgar's proposed marriage. AEthelred was the son of EAlfryth by Edgar. They all mounted the stage and took possession of their appointed thrones, Edward on Edgar's right and AEthelred on the left beside his mother.

Dunstan rose and began the proceedings with speeches and prayers imploring his God to bless this event and to protect the realm of England. He then turned to face Edgar and EAlfryth. They both rose and then knelt on cushions which had been provided them. I could not make out Dunstan's words as he faced away from the gathered throng, but as he spoke he raised each crown and placed them on the heads of the now crowned King and Queen of England. A thunderous cheer resounded from those gathered to witness this happening.

Edgar then rose to his feet, raised his arms calling for quiet, and addressed his subjects. The wind muffled part of his speech but I clearly heard him make three promises to the people of England. "I am your king and I hereby promise you that the Church of God and the whole of Christian people shall have true peace at all times by our judgments. Second, I will forbid extortion and all kinds of wrongdoings by all order of men. Thirdly, I will employ equity and mercy in all our judgments." When he finished the whole land seemed to explode with the cheers which seemed like they may never stop. *England had just received its first declaration of human rights.*

THE LEGEND OF STOR CHESTER 973

Three days later the delegation from Cumbria arrived at Chester. What a marvelous city it was. Nestled in a bow in the River Dee it was naturally protected on three sides. Nonetheless, the entire inner city was surrounded by a high wall of red brick construction. Its red brick spires soared above the walls. The city had long before spilled the confines of its walls and spread out across the surrounding countryside. This was a very ancient city, predating the Roman occupation. The Romans refortified the city and it remained a central garrison throughout their occupation. Located on the Northern border of old Mercia, it had been maintained and expanded under Anglo-Saxon rule. On the outskirts of the city stood the old Roman amphitheater, which could seat seven thousand spectators. Nearby were the tents of the retinues of people who would be attending the conference. The conference itself would be held in a large hall within the city.

At Chester we were joined by all of the nobility of England and the sky was again a backdrop to all of the coats-of-arms flying gently above us. Our storks joined all of the others, fluttering softly in the pleasant breeze and keeping their watch over our wellbeing.

The morning after we had arrived, the entire assembly was summoned to the banks of the River Tees. We had no pre-knowledge of the purpose of this gathering. We stood on the river bank discussing with our fellow travelers what might be about to happen. But our shared ignorance made me realize that much covert planning must have gone into this event.

As we stood milling about at the water's edge, a vessel appeared rounding the upriver curve of The Tees and speedily making way in our direction. The boat was an open structure and was propelled by oars. As it drew near a gasp of astonishment ran through the assembly on the shore. At the forward right oar sat Kenneth, King of Scotland. Beside him on the forward left oar sat our King Malcolm. Immediately behind them was King Maccus, an Old Norse pirate who ruled the Isle of Mann and several smaller islands and Prince Dufnall of Dyfed. In the two rows behind them were King Sifreth of Wales, King Huwall of Gwenedd, King Jacob of Galaway and King Juchill of Westmorland. All eight kings were bent pulling the oars even though the boat travelled easily, propelled largely by the current of the river. Standing at the tiller, in complete command of this vessel stood the newly crowned King Edgar, directing the steering of the boat. The symbolism was obvious. While all of the royalty on the boat were garbed in their finest royal regalia, Edgar was definitely the one in charge. He was the one supreme ruler.

The conference lasted for four days and held little surprises. In the centre of the hall sat a large round table at which the regal delegates were seated. Directly behind each monarch, benches had been placed. Their closest advisors were seated there. Directly behind them, numerous more benches had been set to accommodate each accompanying retinue.

King Edgar of England opened the meeting and called on the Bishop of Chester to provide a prayer for them. He then introduced each of the monarchs, describing their titles and the realms which each ruled. He included a history of when each of them or their predecessors had acknowledged the supremacy of his throne and had sworn oaths of allegiance. He then went straight to the reasons for which he had summoned them to this gathering. "I believe that you all heard the oath which I made at Bath. I promised a reign of peace to all of our Christian subjects under my law which shall be equitably applied. For this to happen, you shall all again come before me and pledge your allegiance, not only to me, your sovereign but also to the laws and judgments to which I affix my seal. We will tolerate no defiance of this oath.

When he was finished he resumed sitting and one by one each noble rose, knelt before him in their turn and gave him their oath.

Over the following two days, each king, in his turn rose, introduced himself and his retainers, and outlined issues arising along common borders. These issues were discussed and resolved, often with Edward, in his capacity as overlord, acting as a referee and ensuring resolution or compromise as might be required.

As this process neared its conclusion, Malcolm of Cumberland rose and outlined his case as to why Cumbria should be an independent kingdom within a united England. In this, he found strong support from Huwall of Gwynned and Sifreth of Wales which countries were themselves remnants of the old Celtic Kingdoms. While Kenneth of Scotland raised objections, this was not the issue to which he was committed and he quickly conceded to Malcolm's position and Edward concurred.

Kenneth then rose to put forward his main agenda. He talked extensively about Hadrian's Wall as being the ancient northern border of the Roman Empire and how his ancestors had fought to defend the territory north of the Wall. He pointed out that he had, just now, graciously agreed to surrender his claim to Cumbria, as it lay south of the Wall, but in return he should receive all of Bernicia north of the Wall. Edgar rejected his position out of hand. He spoke elegantly about the history of Bernicia and its Anglo-Saxon past. He reminded Kenneth that Bernicia had been part of the Anglo Kingdom of Northumbria, stretching all the way north to Edinburgh. He reminded the assembly that Edinburgh had once been the Anglo-Saxon capital of Bernicia. He conceded, however, that should Scotland successfully expel the Danes, who now ruled most of that area, England would not challenge Scotland's claim to it. He then announced with a threatening firmness, "England will never surrender the remaining territory of Bernicia. It is, and it will remain, a part of Northumbria and therefore a part of England."

Kenneth realized that his aspirations would not be met in this forum and that here in England it would be foolhardy for him to persist further. He conceded to Edgar and took his seat. Edgar graciously confirmed Kenneth in his procession of Edinburgh, Lothium and that the Kingdom of Strathclyde would remain a client kingdom of Scotland, all of which were already in Kenneth's procession. The conference adjourned with each of the kings pledging their allegiance to Edgar, King of England.

As they walked down the path leading from the hall, Ian Armstrong leaned over, and in a hushed voice said to me, "Kenneth will never hold to the terms of this peace". I nodded gravely in agreement.

Before leaving Chester, I made a point of meeting with Waltheof of Bamburgh. "I was surprised to have not seen you in Bath," I started.

"I was detained," he explained, "but I am here now. Was this not a marvelous event? We now have a truly united Christian England with a monarch committed to fair and equitable laws. All of England should sleep peacefully tonight."

"But do you think Kenneth will adhere to his pledge?" I asked.

"Of course he won't. But when he breaks his vow and sends his army against us, he will find a strong and united England and we will crush him."

THE LEGEND OF STOR

We then talked about business interests. I was looking for a pact with Bernicia for us to jointly protect each other's shipping in the North Sea. We both had a mutual interest in such an agreement. We agreed to put our senior sea captains and our scribes to the task of working out protocols which would make such an agreement operational.

Business concluded, our discussion turned to the more intimate news of the wellbeing of each other's family. Waltheof confided that his tardiness in coming south had been caused by his wife being in child birth. The couple had been barren since marriage and he had become desperate in his desire to leave Bernicia an heir. He proudly announced that he was now the father of a newly born healthy son. "We have called him Uhtred."

Little did I know then of the entanglement the future held for Uhtred and my family. Looking back I sometimes wonder if the spinners, sitting around the roots of their tree of life, had, in fact, spun our fates.

PART 3
| INFANCY |

CHAPTER 18
PIRATES AND TRAITORS

A VIKING WARRIOR

STOREYE, 975

It was in the mid-summer when news came of the death of King Edgar. His death ended the most peaceful reign that England had known. The Scots had kept the promises made at Chester and the Viking raids had been minimal, probable due to the strength of England's naval forces. Tranquility had been maintained in the north, largely due to Edgar's policy of limited interference with northern politics so long as they abided by English law. Edgar had even used his army to mete out justice to the Saxons of Thanet in response to their harassing Danish born merchants of York.

StorEye had prospered incredibly under Edgar's stewardship. Not only did our crops and livestock enjoy the peaceful existence, but the peace was very good for business. I was now heavily involved in trading, continuing to maintain a substantial fleet of trading ships in partnership with Waltheof of Bamburgh and my brother-in-law, Ulphus. Our combined efforts allowed us to defend our ships at sea which plied the waters all along the European coast and the Mediterranean Sea. Wealth flowed to us in such large measure that I was often referred to as a magnate, signifying a person of great wealth.

I now devout much of my time to our mercantile ventures, leaving Boandi and Gyrdh, who are both young men with families of their own, to manage our estate. Boandi sometimes expresses a desire to be a warrior, but in the long run, he loves the land and is content to see it produce its bounty. While we have enjoyed a long period of peace, we are not without quite regular raids from bands of outlaws seeking easy pickings. They do not find it at StorEye. In most of these incidences Boandi takes over from our sheriff and is quick to chase down these raiders and subject them to a swift justice. Gyrdh, on the other hand, continues to be our man of letters. He not only manages the finances of the estate, but also the other ventures into which I have invested. He is the shepherd of our wealth and under his watchful eye, it grows steadily. Both boys continue to live in the manor at StorEye with their wives and children. Boandi has given me a grandson, Leifer, and a granddaughter, Hallerna. Gyrdh has given me my grandson, Hrolfr. All of these children are still infants, and their constant demands keep the manor house in a constant state of uproar. Aasta has also born me a grandson, but she lives with her husband in Carlisle.

The peace of Edgar's reign has created a much safer environment for travel in northern England. Eyja and I, along with our youngest, Liv and Haberd, now spend most of our time in York. With an escort of only one hundred soldiers to ward off small bands of bandits, we travel regularly between StorEye, York and Toraldesby. I spend a majority of my time in the city while Eyja and the children reside at Toraldesby. The safety of today's travel, however, allows us to also spend much time together with our offspring in Cumbria.

The City of York is a much more convenient residence for me, as it is the hub of commerce for northern England. Here, I am in close contact with my brother-in-law, Ulph and Waltheof of Bamburgh. We have developed an extensive partnership in trade and shipping. Between us we have more than one hundred vessels plying the water with cargos from all over Europe. While Edgar has brought peace to the land, piracy runs rampant off of our shores. Small fleets of vessels are easy prey for pirates so we are forced to form convoys of many merchant ships always accompanied by a number of sleek, swift, fighting vessels armed with well-trained warriors.

But with Edgar's death, the peace on the land has begun to fracture.

***

The nobility of England was divided over the succession of King Edgar. Edward was the oldest son, but he was born out of wedlock. AEthelred's birth was clearly legitimate in the eyes of the church but Edgar had steadfastly recognized Edward as his first born and heir. As a result, Edward became the king. One of the early casualties of this conflict was our Earl of York, Oslac. He had unsuccessfully supported AEthelred, and Edward was quick to banish him from England as soon as he ascended the throne.

This was far from the only conflict to grow out of the issues of succession. While he was king, Edgar had followed through on his promise of monastic reform, leaving many nobles and senior clergy feeling unjustly denied of both lands and power. Fearing Edgar's strength of purpose on this issue, none of these would protest while Edgar remained on the throne, but their anger did not dissipate. Upon his death it again rose to the fore. So the conflict for succession was not only a struggle between two infant princes, who were both too young to be parties to the dispute, but between the interests of the nobility who were in a position to manipulate the exercise of royal authority.

While the nobility and the clergy maneuvered to recapture lost lands and to settle real and imagined grievances amongst each other, the two princes appeared unaffected by the struggles that broiled around them, often in their names. So it was not surprising when, only two years into his reign, the young King Edward accepted an invitation to visit with his brother, AEthelred at his stepmother's estate, Corfe Castle. Upon entering the castle keep, a dozen armed men appeared to assist him to dismount and care for his horse. His foot had only touched the ground when the conspiracy unveiled itself. The armed escort fell upon him with daggers drawn and quickly stabbed at him until he was mortally wounded. It was widely believed that the dowager Queen, EAlfryth was behind this plot, but no charges were ever laid against anyone. AEthelred, at the age of ten, became king of England.

***

YORK, 980

The conflict within England had not gone unnoticed by her neighbours. Raiding parties from Scandinavia had increased in both number and intensity, as had raids from Scotland. While these raids were troublesome they created no real damage. It was the increase in piracy, which seemed more and more organized, that created real havoc for me and my co-adventurers. Our shipping losses were increasing. To address this issue I was meeting today with Waltheof of Bamburgh and my brother-in-law Ulphus of York. At the meeting it was agreed that I would take responsibility for the shipping decisions, while Waltheof would arm our fighting escort vessels and Ulph would be responsible for gathering intelligence on the pirates and their plans. Byrniulf would serve as captain of our fleet and Haberd would serve as his first mate. We agreed upon a number of strategies which would maximize our trade into areas which were relatively safe from attack, and increase the size of our fleet and its convoy where threats were greater.

The greatest threat to our shipping was along the southeast coast, up into the Irish Sea. But those shipping routes brought us the greatest returns. From southwest England we carried both Iron ore and slate, both of which were in great demand throughout Europe. Pirates from the Old Norse kingdom of Dublin held military superiority over those sea lanes. So it was a considerable relief that we received news that the Celtic chieftains, Malachy ll and Brian Boru had joined forces and had driven the Vikings out of Dublin. With shipping now much safer on the west coast, we could direct our energies to dealing with the Scandinavian pirates in the North Sea.

* * *

Liv was now married and our youngest, Haberd was off at sea with Byrniulf. We now have seven grandchildren with two more on the way. Eyja and I had prepared to slip quietly into old age, content in our grandchildren, so it came as a great surprise when Eyja found that she was again pregnant. She was now forty-two years of age and we had assumed that her child-bearing years were behind us. But we were wrong. Throughout her pregnancy I was terrified. Woman did not often get pregnant at her age and those who did were usually plagued with health problems, often fatal. But she was now in her ninth month and had known no ill effects. To the contrary; she was active and cheerful and quite looking forward to bearing me another child. She was with her mother and sister at Toraldesby, with Kari fussing over her until Eyja ordered her from the room. I rarely left her side, and then only in an emergency. I refused to travel at all unless I could be guaranteed to be able to return the same day.

Finally, in early spring, Eyja gave birth to a beautiful baby girl. We decided to call her Sigen. The labour took a toll on Eyja, but now she was out of danger and recovering nicely. The warm spring mornings allowed her to sit outside while she nursed Sigen and enjoy nature's beauty, as Toraldesby became alive with its bounty of blossoms,. The warm sun tanned her face and dissipated the paleness from her skin. In my view she was radiant.

Sigen's birth now allowed me to turn more attention to business issues which I had been neglecting during the later months of Eyja's pregnancy. In spite of the reprieve that we had experienced since the destruction of the Dublin-based pirates, the North Sea piracy had intensified and we had suffered extensive losses. So today I found myself in York, meeting with Ulph, Waltheof, Byrniulf and Haberd, searching for a strategy to combat the Scandinavian pirates. Ulph spoke first. "These pirates have great knowledge of our shipping schedules and the cargos which we are carrying. We know that they have spies hanging around the docks at York. I have caught a couple of them and executed them accordingly. But I now believe that they are acting in concert because, rather than the pirates having less knowledge, they seem to have more. I believe that we are dealing with coordinated actions which are undermining our shipping ventures."

"Have you tried questioning them?" Waltheof asked.

"No. At the time I did not yet realize what we were dealing with. But you can be sure that when we catch another one, he will tell us who he is working with."

"Maybe we can set a trap for them." I suggested.

"What do you have in mind?" Ulph asked.

"The pirates always attack our ships when we are in a convoy of ten ships or less. They send about the same number of ships against us, but they are filled with heavily armed, well trained sword warriors. Maybe if we send a dummy cargo in several ships secretly manned with our own warriors, instead of simply seamen, we can catch them unawares and defeat their fleet at sea." I suggested.

"And how are we going to get all these warriors aboard without them knowing?" Byrniulf asked.

We tossed this dilemma around for several hours and finally settled on a plan.

We decided that we would load our warriors aboard in Bernicia, where we could operate with greater security. The warriors would be dressed in rags and chained in the holds of our ships so that they would appear to be slaves heading for the continental slave markets. We would disguise five ships in this manner and sail them along the coast to York, where we would bring them up the Ouse River into the York's city harbour. At York we would bring on more trade goods and provisions for our voyage to the continent. We would leave the hatches off of the holds so that our provisioning merchants could see the "slaves" in chains, but not examine them closely enough to determine that they were in too good a health to be slaves. Word would soon spread through the harbour that these were indeed slave ships.

We would also bring cargo aboard loaded in crates. Instead of cargo, however, the crates would hold clothing, armour and weapons for our troops. We would also erect a slave pen alongside our piers. For several months prior to enacting our charade, we meticulously gathered felons from Cumbria, Bernicia and Deira, whose crimes might otherwise result in death sentences, and condemned them instead to be sold as slaves. We had them marched overland to York where we locked them in the holding pen. Once we had a dozen such slaves, to give our charade legitimacy, we sailed our five trading ships into the harbour. There we loaded the slaves aboard to join our mock slave inventory. We then set the ships assail to act as bait for the pirates. We also set two small flotillas of five ships each, all heavily armed, to harbour in seclusion along the coast to the south. From there, upon a signal from our bait ships, they could sail to their assistance, hopefully entrapping the pirates.

We knew that we would have to perform this charade several times before the pirates actually believed that we had entered the slave trade and would therefore take our bait. On each sailing we stopped at slaving centers along the Spanish coast and sold the felons, whom we had rounded up for this purpose, in very public markets, knowing that rumours of these actions would find their way back to York. Sure enough, on the fourth outing of our little charade, the pirates attacked.

***

BAMBURGH, 981

Waltheof, Ulph and I gathered at Bamburgh to receive the report of our ambush. We had already received a brief report by way of a rider rapidly riding overland to give us the news. While the ploy had worked and we had successfully surprised and overwhelmed the pirates, Byrniulf had been killed in the fighting. Ulph and I were beside ourselves in grief. Bryni was Ulph's brother but I also had considered him as a brother ever since I was a lad coming into Torald's guardianship. We had grown into men together and had enjoyed each other's company in all of the adventures that had accompanied our adolescence. We had been brothers in life and now he was gone. Aside from Vidor's death, I had not before experienced this level of sorrow. A piece of my heart will always be with Bryni.

In spite of the depth of my sorrow, I believe that it was only a fragment of the grief felt by Eyja at the death of her brother. The entire family experienced this devastation and Ulph swore vengeance. He called on me to share this blood debt and I willingly agreed.

Haberd had accompanied me on the ride to Bamburgh, but, except for a short overview of the battle, he refrained from giving me details until we were joined by my partners. And I did not press him with questions. But, now that we were all gathered, Haberd began his report.

"We sailed our five decoy ships, *York Princess, Pride of Bernicia, Cuthbert's Glory, Fine Lady* and *Sea Witch*, down the coast from York. Our fastest ship, *Sea Witch* remained wide to our windward side, off of our starboard, so as to remain close enough to shore to relay a signal to our undisguised warships which were harboured in concealment. We were not yet at the mouth of the Humber when the pirates struck. Our closest concealed warships, *Serpent, Noble Warrior, Blade, Thor's Thunder* and *Swift Spear* were harboured about ten miles to our stern, so when we signaled *Sea Witch*, our spotter, it turned and retreated several miles to ensure that our warships received the message. The pirate fleet was only seven ships strong, but they were on us before our reinforcements could arrive. We had locked in combat and they had managed to board one of our ships, *York Princess*, by the time our fighting fleet arrived, *Sea Witch* arriving first and the other war ships close on her tail. We caught them completely by surprise when our sword warriors appeared on deck, fully armed and ready for battle. Since they believed that they outnumbered us seven ships to four, they pressed their attack, but instead of engaging us all simultaneously, they concentrated their attack on our lead ship, *York Princess*, and successfully boarded her. *York Princess* was captained by Bryni.

"Their attack came from up wind of us, so that their approach was slower than it might have otherwise been. Our reinforcements were racing to our rescue with the wind to their stern and therefore they quickly joined us. On *Pride of Bernicia, Cuthbert's Glory* and *Fine Lady*, our three other decoy ships, the pirates had thrown grappling hooks aboard us and therefore believed that they had us captured and would board us one by one. This maneuver was their downfall. The three of their ships locked to us were entrapped. *Serpent, Noble Warrior* and *Blade,* our war vessels, simply came along their seaward side and grappled themselves to the pirate vessels so that they were each entrapped between two of our ships, all heavily armed. *Thor's Thunder* and *Swift Spear* quickly joined *Sea Witch* to support *York Princess.* But we were too late. *York Princess* had already been boarded and their crew was outnumbered four to one. Many of their crew had already been slaughtered, Bryni amongst them.

"We were on them like banshees. Catching them by surprise, we sank two of them and killed most of their crew. One ship however, managed to escape. *York Princess, Sea Witch, Thor's Thunder* and *Swift Spear* did not pursue it. At my command we returned to aid our other three decoy ships. But they did not need our help. Two of the pirate ships surrendered without a fight. The third we set to the torch and stood by till she burnt to the waterline and then sunk to the bottom with all hands on board.

"We then turned to questioning the crew of both of the two ships which had surrendered as well as the few surviving captives from the attack on *York Princess*. We sought the name of who had sent them against us. From them we learnt that the overall commander of this attack, and most of the preceding attacks had been a Norwegian pirate named Olaf Tryggvason who claimed to be a descendant of Harold Fairhair, the one-time king of Norway. They were aided by a local noble of Danish ancestry, named Thurbrand of Holderness. Holderness is situated in southeast Deira."

Ulph interrupted scowling, "I know of that surly dog. He has long deserved killing and I swear that his last day will be at the end of my sword."

We murmured support for Ulph's sentiment, pledging our support. Haberd then continued his report. "We separated the crews whom we had captured into two groups: the pirates from the two ships that had surrendered and those who had resisted. We then hung every last one of the latter group. The remainder we chained with the original real slaves which we were carrying aboard. We then placed all of the slaves on two of the captured pirate ships along with a sufficient guard, comprised of our warriors, and sent them off to be sold in the French slave markets. The pirate captains and mates we placed in chains and, after redistributing our crews and warriors amongst our vessels and the four prizes captured from the pirates, we returned home. We tied all of the vessels at the York city harbour so that all would know what had transpired. The prisoners are all being held at York for your disposal."

We left the fate of the prisoners in Ulph's hands. But we all knew that after he had extracted any further information which they might have, the lucky ones would be executed immediately.

CHAPTER 19
VENGEANCE DENIED

TORALDESBY, 983

Even after two years had passed, the grief which accompanied Byrniulf's death was unabated and Torald's demand for vengeance was unfulfilled. Over the past two years we had set many ambushes attempting to ensnare Tryggvason, so that he might answer to Torald's justice, but our attempts remained in vain. He had simply stopped his piracy off England's shores and disappeared. I, Eyja and Sigen had returned to StorEye where Sigen could be raised in relative peace. But after two years of unsuccessful attempts to avenge Byrniulf, Torald had summoned me back to Toraldesby to help devise a plan to avenge the death of my brother-in-law.

At Toraldesby we were now seated comfortably around the great hall. With us were Ulphus, Haberd, Thored, the Ealdorman of York, and two representatives of Waltheof of Bamburgh and, of course Torald and myself. Ulphus had just finished reporting on the unsuccessful attempts to ensnare Tryggvason and the apparent disappearance of his pirates from our coasts. "So where is that scoundrel?" Torald demanded.

Thored began, "Not much is known of Olfa Tryggvason. He claims to be the son of a Tryggva, who in turn claims to be a direct descendent from the late King Harold Fairhair of Norway. Apparently his father was murdered while Olfa was still a child. He was whisked out of harm's way, but the boat in which he was travelling was captured by pirates and the child, Olfa, was sold into slavery. After being sold several more times, he was recognized, and purchased out of slavery, by King Vladimir of Kievian Rus, a Norwegian monarchy established by Vikings deep inside continental Europe. As Olfa reached adulthood, Vladimir came to distrust him and banished him. Tryggvason turned to piracy and ended up on our shores. A couple of years ago, he met and married the daughter of a minor German King from a place called Wentland and he became the governing force of that kingdom. To my knowledge he is still there."

Thored's information was to be trusted, not only due to his access to intelligence from his position as Ealdorman, but also because of the strength of his relationship to the court of England. Thored's daughter, AElgifu was married to King AEthelred and, as such, she was the Queen of England.

After much discussion we concluded, that, at least for the time being, Tryggvason was beyond our reach. Upon finally accepting that conclusion Torald declared, "Then his English accomplice, Thurbrand of Holderness, must be held to account."

"What are you suggesting?" Thored inquired.

"I'm not suggesting anything." Torald responded sharply. I am demanding that we march on Holderness, drag this piece of horsemeat, Thurbrand, out of his lair and send him to Valhalla."

"The king will not take kindly towards a civil war within his kingdom." Thored exclaimed.

"This is not a war between us and Holderness," Ulphus joined in. "Thurbrand is a traitor and a pirate. We are not suggesting a private battle. My brother died defending, not just our shipping, but the coast of England. My only question for AEthelred is whether or not he will send troops to support us in administrating the King's justice."

Waltheof's representatives joined me in applauding Ulph's position.

"Well we all know that AEthelred is far too concerned about Viking raids in East Anglia to send troops, but I am sure that he will not object to your enforcing his Peace. But we should ensure that it does not become too messy," Thored conceded.

And so it was decided. Next summer we would send an army into Holderness to administer justice upon the warrant of Thored, Earl of York.

***

HOLDERNESS, 985

Our army had been camped at Holderness for two weeks. We were two thousand strong, all sword warriors from York and Bernicia. Thurbrand's stronghold was a massive stone structure with solid fortifications. When we first arrived, Thurbrand had sent his forces out to meet us in battle, but almost as soon as our shield walls collided it was obvious to all that, while our numbers were near equal, the skills of our warriors were far superior to those of his. Our shield wall was able to push Thurbrand's soldiers back and we inflicted much damage. In less than an hour of combat he organized a retreat and he was now well entrenched inside his very defensible fortifications, leaving the corpses of his fallen dead to rot on the field. We had completely surrounded his fortress and had laid siege to it, planning to starve him into leaving the safety of his walls to either surrender or face our warriors in the field. We were well aware that it might be several months before we forced him out, but Ulphus' determination was sufficient to ensure that we would succeed.

We had invaded Holderness with our forces divided into four companies of approximately five hundred warriors each. Ulphus was in overall command and had led the frontal assault. Ulphus had been on the shield wall himself and had fought like a man possessed. It was hard to believe that he was sixty-two years of age as his mighty sword hacked and hacked until the enemy retreated. Even then, he chased them right to the gate of their fortress, with his mighty sword creating havoc, until they finally wrestled the gate shut in his face.

I had commanded our right flank, while Ulphus' son, Norman, commanded the left. His other son, Achille commanded our reserve which was not needed during the battle. I was surprised at how my own body had reacted to the battle. Adrenaline coursed through me, giving me the strength of a man half my age. It was exhilarating. This bore no resemblance to the methodical butchery that I had experienced so many years ago fighting for Eric Bloodaxe. This was personal. This was a blood debt for the life of my brother, Byrniulf, and I thirsted for vengeance. But now the fighting was over and the waiting had begun. Thurbrand was now penned up in his stronghold and we waited for his food and water to run out and force his submission. We knew our wait would be a long one as Thurbrand must surely know that only death awaited him when he finally opened his gate. But we would wait.

When we had first entered Thurbrand's lands, we had systematically overrun every one of his serfs' hovels, pillaging all we could carry and burning both crops and dwellings to the ground. Our path through to Holderness was a waste land. We had come well provisioned and could hold out longer than those trapped inside Holderness.

* * *

It was just after dawn, on the fifty-fourth day of our siege, when Thurbrand finally opened his gates. We were somewhat surprised, believing that he would hold out longer. But a sigh of relief swept through our forces. While we had kept them busy, training and perfecting their battle skills, a siege is tedious business and our men were becoming bored with the lack of real action. So we were ready when Thurbrand's troops finally emerged, forming our shield wall and waiting their attack or surrender. But they did neither. They simply formed a defensive shield wall in front of their gate and stood there as if expecting us to come to them. We hesitated in accommodating them. There was something amiss. Not only were they emerging too early in the siege, they were also emerging too early in the morning. Thurbrand's gate faced east so that the sun, just coming over the horizon, shone directly into their faces. A wiser commander would have waited several hours in order to neutralize the sun's blinding glare. But they simply stood there, squinting at us into the sun and setting up a cacophony of noise by banging their swords and axes against their shields and screaming insults at us.

Their uproar all but drowned out a commotion coming from our rear. But as it grew in volume we turned to see a vast horde of thousands of warriors, formed into a shield wall, advancing towards the rear of our formation. Achille was the first to recognize the gravity of our situation and wheeled his reserve troops into formation to engage the assault which was rapidly approaching our rear. It was obvious that this new army was planning to drive us into Thurbrand's shield wall, and, having us caught in the trap, hack us to pieces. It did not take long to determine the source of this new army. Flying high above the centre of the approaching wall was the winged wolf banner of Olaf Tryggvason.

Only Achilles's quick response, and the skill of his warriors, avoided our becoming completely encircled in this trap. His troops were able to hold Tryggvason's army at bay while we engaged in an orderly retreat. The sun helped disguise our changing tactics from Thurbrand's forces and they maintained their defensive stance while we organized a retreat, flanking the southerly end of Tryggvason's shield wall. We suffered heavy casualties, but the bulk of our army managed to escape the trap and was now heading south to the safety of our home. Ulph and Norman escaped without harm. However, my company was on the most northerly end of our shield wall and since our retreat was southward we were the last to leave the field. As we retreated, we joined Achilles's command in a defensive rear guard to ensure the retreat did not become a rout. The fighting there was ferocious but our shield wall held until the enemy began to tire and we were able to make our escape. Both Achille and I suffered serious wounds, but we would both survive.

It was several months before we would learn the full story of our defeat. For my part, in our retreat, one of the enemy warriors managed a glancing blow off of my shield and his sword cut deep into the flesh of my arm just below the shoulder. I was almost killed and had to be carried from the field. My wound later became infected, but as I teetered on the edge of death, Ulph's wife, Torete, and his sister, Kari, never left my side, administering poultices until my fever broke and I began to heal. As I recuperated at Toraldesby, Ulph and Torald organized an extensive intelligence campaign to determine how and why Tryggvason's army had appeared at Holderness.

The full story finally emerged. Tryggvason's wife, Queen Geira of Wentland, had passed away early that year. With her demise, Olaf's stewardship of Wentland evaporated. He then returned home to Denmark. He had sent a messenger to advise Thurbrand of his return. The messenger had arrived at Holderness to find our siege underway. He managed to retreat undetected and made his way back to Tryggvason with the news. Tryggvason had turned his fleet to Holderness and brought them to shore in Bridlington Bay, off of Holderness. Because our siege was aimed at keeping people from leaving Thurbrand's stronghold, we failed to notice Tryggvason's couriers slip inside. Once there, they advised Thurbrand of Tryggvason's plan, and the latter organized his grand exit from his stronghold to coordinate with the timing of Tryggvason's attack. Only our ill fortune at the untimely death of Queen Geira, and Olaf's subsequent decision to return to English waters, had caused our blood debt to go unpaid. But secretly I wondered if maybe the spinners, weaving our fates at the Tree of Life, were more responsible than simply bad luck.

In my delirium, while fighting the claws of death which threatened to transport me to whatever fate awaited in the afterlife, many visions swirled through my mind. Most of them involved vicious battles between pagan Norse gods and Christian saints. As night closed on their battles, the Norse gods would retire to their great halls for a night of drinking and debauching while the Christian saints gathered in marathon prayer sessions. On the following mornings, the Christian prayers seemed to have no greater effect on the next day's battle than the impact of the night of carousing by the Norse gods. The battles would go on and on with never more than a draw being achieved.

CHAPTER 20
A WOUNDED WARRIOR

STOREYE, 987

It has been two years since our defeat at Holderness. I returned home to StorEye as soon as I was able to travel. I had to be transported by wagon as I was still too injured to straddle a horse for more than a few minutes at a time. My arm was still tightly bandaged and held in place with a sling attached securely around my neck and my waist. In spite of being forewarned of my injury, Eyja paled when she laid eyes on the crippled survivor who had replaced the valiant warrior who had ridden forth from our home only a few months ago. She quickly organized a party of men to lift me from the wagon, carry me into the manor and deposit me gently into a softly padded lounge near the blazing fireplace. She immediately assumed command of my nursing, feeding me, washing me, changing my clothing and every other personal activity of my existence. She allowed me to expend no energy, only to sit there and receive her ministrations. While I was coming to realize that I would never fully recover; never again wield a sword and a shield, I was restless for some kind of action. But, I relented to her will, realizing that a lack of motion was my best medicine. Only after several months did she permit me to rise from my sick bed for a few minutes' exercise each day.

I did not fully suffer during my recuperation. In truth, I secretly enjoyed the pampering I received from Eyja. It was as if she anticipated my every need and desire and attended to it immediately. I was surrounded by children and grandchildren continuously. Both Aasta and Liv visited often with their children. Even Haberd had returned with me from York, leaving Norman and a fully recovered Achille, in charge of our fleet. I was unable to use my right hand to guide my writing and Haberd served as my scribe while I dictated this chronicle. My youngest child, Sigen, who was now seven years of age, spent most of her days by my side with endless questions about every imaginable subject. She was a very cute little girl, with long curly hair, which her mother often kept braided to give it some sense of order. Through her quick wit and deep intelligence I came to adore her more and more.

My evenings, however, were for Eyja. We would sit by the fire caressing and talking about our lives, our hopes, our dreams and our fears. No topic went unexamined. Our love and devotion for each other emerged in every conversation. She had thought that she had lost me to that Viking sword and the thought terrified her. Given my flirtation with death, neither of us was prepared to let anything of importance go unsaid. On many of these occasions we reiterated our deep love and commitment to each other and to our family. I often recounted the mandate my grandfather had committed me to and the joy we both experienced in making that undertaking the most pleasurable events of our lives. She still poked fun at my youthful shyness and how terrified I had been when we first met. We would fall into such fits of laughter that she would worry that I might reinjure myself.

Eyja had fully embraced the Christian God, his church and the heaven which it promised. When I told her how deeply our war with Tryggvason and Thurbrand had shaken my faith in Christianity she became very troubled. Her initial fear was for my soul, but as time went on it became a debate between soul mates about the basis for our beliefs. I would ask, "How could the Christian god provide for Tryggvason's queen to die and for him to return to England just in time to rescue that scoundrel Thurbrand from receiving the justice which he deserved?"

"The priests say that it is not for us to know the ways of God", she would reply.

"How is that secret unmerciful behaviour different from the Norse gods callously and uncaringly allowing the spinners to weave our fates at their whims?"

The theme dominated many of our discussions. One day however she responded to me by asking, "Christianity is the faith of England. How can you believe in England and not believe in her religion?"

Those are not the same thing," I replied. "First off I do not consider myself to be an Englishman." My first loyalty is not to England, but to you and our family. We happen to live in England and, to be honest; I support the realm of England. But I do not do so because I am English. I do so because England holds out the greatest prospect for our peace, justice and security. First of all, I support the notion that just laws must be committed to writing and that they should be written in a common language and applied in a common manner. I am aware that England has chosen its church to write the king's law, to educate its magistrates and to enforce much of that law. And, of course, the common language is English. But all of that could be done without the Church. Lay people could take on that responsibility."

FRED STOREY

***

YORK, 988

AEthelred has now been the king of England for a decade. While he has generally followed the policies of his father, Edgar, he does not command the respect that Edgar received. This is partially due to the absence of a strong witan made up of wise counselors. Many of Edgar's old council are now dead. The struggle for succession to the throne by the divergent supporters of the two boy princes, Edward and AEthelred, has resulted in many being expelled for not supporting Aethelred's accession. In the strong undercurrent of dissent from magnates whose land had been confiscated in Edgar's monastic reforms, AEthelred was forced to direct his attention towards breaking the stranglehold which these magnates had attempted to force upon his rule. In this he has been largely successful, but it came with a price to his overall rule of England.

Sensing a weaker capacity to defend its borders, England's adversaries had become more emboldened. In 980 Vikings had launched attacks at Hampshire, Thanet and Cheshire. In 981 they attacked Devon and Cornwall. In 982 they attacked Dorset. AEthelred had concentrated his military in defending his southern coast, and since then the attacks have abruptly ended. In the north we have been left to our own device. York and Bamburgh were sufficiently garrisoned to defend themselves against all but the most concerted assaults and were capable of providing defense for the surrounding territory. But the increase in the number of raids from across our Scottish border exerted an ongoing pressure on our resources.

THE LEGEND OF STOR

Our Earl of York, Thored, could give us only limited support. He was an appointee of King Edgar and had supported Edward as Edgar's successor, leaving him now in disfavor from AEthelred's court. He was also engaged in an ongoing dispute over the ownership of personal property which was claimed by our archbishop, Oswald. Oswald, also a supporter of Edward's successorship, received greater support from AEthelred, being the father of AEthelred's first wife, Aelfgifu. However, due to a lack of unity of purpose between our Earl and our Archbishop, neither was overly effective in obtaining military support from our king for the defense of the north.

Then, in 988, the attacks on the southern coast began again. Tryggvason had been engaged in most of the earlier raids. Now, he led an invasion force, but it was repelled by the thanes of Devon. In retreat, Tryggvason sailed his fleet to Normandy where he received a warm welcome. This led to serious tensions arising between the English and Norman governments. Eventually their dispute reached sympathetic ears in Rome, where the pope demanded a secession of hostilities and eventually brokered a treaty between England and the Norman court guaranteeing a peace between the two countries. This did not lessen the Vikings attack on England's southern coast. In fact they intensified. AEthelred responded by drafting every military vessel in England and ordering them south to enhance England's naval defenses against Viking attacks. This left pirates off our northern coast a free hand to pillage our shipping.

I joined Ulphus, Norman, Waltheof of Bamburgh, Earl Thored and Archbishop Oswald in a trip to Wessex to petition AEthelred to provide us some relief in the protection of the waters off York and Bamburgh. Thored had since been forgiven by the king for having earlier supported his brother in the struggle for the English throne. AEthelred was now married to Oswald's daughter, AElfgifu. As the father-in-law of the king, Oswald was our lead spokesman. Nonetheless, AEthelred dismissed our petition out of hand.

CHAPTER 21
THE VIPER STRIKES

We were returning to York when we spotted two riders mounting the hill in front of us and moving in our direction as if the devil himself were on their tails. Without waiting for his horse to come to a halt, the first of the two blurted out, "Toraldesby is under attack!"

Toraldesby, under attack. At first I froze; shock and disbelief contended for control of my mind. I heard my voice scream "Nooooo!" Eyja was at Toraldesby. Eyja was in danger.

Without a word to my companions, I spurred my horse into action and, at a full gallop, raced down the road towards Toraldesby. Eventually the rest of our party overtook me only to find me standing over the body of my dead mount. In panic, I had run the poor horse into the ground. His strong heart had failed to live up to the tasks which I had demanded of him.

"Get me another horse," I demanded of Ulphus.

"Wait," Ulph counseled. "We are still a full day's ride from home. If you take another horse, you will only kill it too. We must rest before we continue."

I began to argue with him, "I need no rest," I exclaimed. But the others had now dismounted and added to his counsel. I protested, but eventually conceded to a compromise. Ulph, Norman and a contingent of our bodyguard would continue with me to Toraldesby directly. The remainder would rest and then follow.

* * *

Long before I arrived, I could see smoke billowing above the hills from Toraldesby. As I crested the final hill the manor was still black with smoke. I could see the extent of the carnage and I spurred my horse forward, not waiting for it to reach a full stop before dismounting. Eyja was awkwardly sprawled in a pool of blood. I dashed to her side. Dropping to one knee, I raised her head to cradle it in my arms. I looked into her eyes, searching for the life that had once shone forth from them. But I was rewarded only by a dull blank stare revealing nothing but death. Tears burst from my eyes as I raised my hand to her face and gently closed her eyes, which would see no more. I remained motionless for a long time unable to grasp the reality which confronted me. I could not even begin to imagine a life without her. She was my rock but now she would be no more. Grief overcame me and I finally crumbled to the ground, still grasping her in my embrace.

Eventually hands took hold of my arms in order to free her from my grasp. I yelled, bring me a pillow. I placed it gently beneath her head and rose to my feet. I surveyed the carnage surrounding me. Torald's lifeless body lay sprawled at the gate, his bloodied sword still clutched in his hand as a testimony to his valiant attempt to repel the invaders. Other bodies, old and young, men and women, lay lifeless around him. I finally spoke. "Were there no survivors?"

"Only the two messengers," a voice answered.

THE LEGEND OF STOR

My hand flew to my sword, as I spun to face one of the messengers. His faced paled in fear as I growled, "So you two fled to save your worthless skins."

Before I could draw my weapon, a calmer hand stayed my wrath. The second messenger hesitantly exclaimed, "Steinar ordered us to flee. We had to breach the invaders line to carry our message, My Lord. They almost got us but we sent several off to meet their maker in order to make good our escape."

As my anger subsided my eyes roamed the yard in search of my old mentor and comrade. His body lay crumbled in a bloody wreck, his head near severed from his shoulders, his helmet crushed and bloodied beside his still corpse. Somebody had placed his mighty war ax in his hand. As grief again threatened to overwhelm me, reality took hold. "Where is Sigen?" I screamed.

"Fear not Stor," a kindly voice responded. "Torete took her to visit Kari before the raiders arrived. They are still safe there."

"Bring her to me immediately," I demanded. I then dropped back down on my haunches, my head hung between my knees, sobbing in sorrow.

I was still sitting there when Sigen arrived, accompanied by Kari and Torete. Sigen leapt from the wagon and dashed to me. I looked up and took her into a long embrace. "Mamma is dead," I whispered to her, as if believing that speaking it aloud might make it more acceptable.

She was only eight years old, but, in an almost adult like voice she whispered back. "I Know. They told me."

We sat there hugging and weeping for some time. Finally we broke apart and rose to survey the carnage which surrounded me. Grief was everywhere. Both of Ulph's parents had been slaughtered, Steinar was dead and the household staff and garrison had been decimated. All of the buildings were in ashes. The destruction had been complete. Our guards were busying themselves erecting tents to temporarily quarter us. Others were engaged in preparing food over open fires. Archbishop Oswald and Earl Thored were attempting to comfort the rest of us. A pall hung over Toraldesby where life and laughter used to reign.

* * *

Two days later, family and dignitaries from across Northern England gathered at Toraldesby. All of my children and grandchildren were there. Ulph's remaining family was all there. Steinar's widow and children had travelled here from StorEye. Waltheof had come from Bamburgh, along with his son, Uhtred, Uhtred's new wife, Ecgfrida and her father, Aldhun, the Bishop of Lindisfarne. Hundreds of people from throughout York, many of whom I did not know, were also in attendance. Both the Earl of York and the Archbishop were also there with a contingent of Christian clergy.

On the shore of the river were two small boats, both filled with kindling and firewood. On one bier lay Torald, robed in the finery which he always wore in life. The sun reflected brightly off the magnificent gold and silver bracelets on both arms and the jewels imbedded in the hilt of his massive sword which he clutched in his hand. Steinar lay on the other bier, also wearing many glimmering bracelets, his fingers wrapped tightly around the sturdy haft of his terrifying war ax. Slowly, the boats were pushed out into the stream. As the current caught them and pulled them into the flow of the river, a lone archer launched two flaming arrows into the air. Both biers caught fire and blazed away on their voyage to Valhalla. As the current bore the craft around a bend, a hawk screamed across the sky as if sent by Odin himself to guide his warriors home. The churchmen in attendance, out of respect for these two men, stood watching in stoic silence.

This was not to be the fate of my beloved Eyja. Early the next morning a procession led by Father Leo made its way towards a deep hole dug on a grassy slope of hallowed ground. Eyja's coffin was borne by Boandi, Gyrdh, Haberd, Norman, Achille and Aasta's husband Hrolfr. Her coffin was piled high with flowers of numerous fragrant hues. I followed, surrounded by Aasta, Liv and Sigen. The rest of the procession trailed behind us. Eyja had staunchly proclaimed her Christian beliefs in life and I was not to allow her to be denied them in death. Her remains had been handed to her church.

While I sat weeping silently, surrounded by my family, choirs sang and Leo intoned the glories of the Christian God, of resurrection and of the union with God in heaven, my beloved was lowered into the ground. As I looked on, I was amazed by my reaction. Byrni's death had left me incensed that a God could be so unjust to have allowed him to be murdered by the fowl hands of Tryggvason and Thurbrand of Holderness while permitting them to avoid his justice. To Eyja's death my reaction was the opposite. I could not imagine Eyja's existence being now ended. It comforted me to believe that eventually I would be reunited with her in heaven. I resolved to do whatever was necessary for that to happen.

The following day, before returning to StorEye, I met with Ulph, Waltheof and our sons, to assess our situation in the face of the tragedy. The raid itself was the first order of business. In the discussion it became apparent that the raid on Toraldesby had been led by our nemesis, Thurbrand of Holderness. Regardless of my commitments to God, I realized that this was a blood debt which I could never forgive.

My hatred of that man percolated in my heart all the way home to StorEye.

***

STOREYE, 992

It has been four long years now since I made that trip home to StorEye. Every minute of every day, my waking hours have been filled with a sense of grief over the loss of my beloved. The pain seems as great today as it did when I first saw her blood-stained body lying motionless in the dirt in the court yard of Toraldsby. I spent my days moping around our estate. The pain would not abate.

Sigen is my constant companion. She is twelve years of age and growing into her womanhood. She so resembles Eyja that my heart falters every time I lay eyes upon her. Still, she is the love of my life and the only person who can bring a smile to my otherwise grim countenance. She is fast becoming a woman and I should be considering my fatherly responsibility in finding her a suitable husband, but I procrastinate. I do not think that I could bear the thought of her leaving my side. She has Eyja's beauty and she has a very quick and inquisitive mind. Her questions seem unending. She demands that I explain absolutely all that I know of StorEye, of our family, of our business interests and of the totality of life throughout England.

I am also surrounded by the rest of my children and grandchildren. They provide me solace and I take great pride in them. My sons have taken over running our estate. Boandi is in charge of StorEye, all of our crops and livestock and those of all of our tenants. He is very wise in the ways of animal health and husbandry and how to maximize the yield from our soil. Gyrth manages all of our other business interests. When he is not away attending to those activities, he serves as our sheriff. He is shrewd in business and enforces justice with a firm, but just, hand. Haberd is our magistrate and our scribe. He takes more comfort in the pen than in the sword. The priests are continually attempting to lure him away from us and into the service of the church but he will not consider it. The children consult me continuously on all aspects of their activities, but I suspect that this is more of a courtesy and respect for me than in a real need to glean my input. I know, and I am sure that they know also, that I am becoming redundant.

I spend my days wandering around StorEye, usually accompanied by Sigen and her endless questions on everything and everyone we encounter. I would be very lonely without her company. Except when answering issues raised by Sigen, I spend very little time concerning myself with those things which are beyond our borders.

But I do have concerns for the future of England. The Scots still raid across the northern border. Their ambitions are aimed at acquiring the portion of Bernicia that extends north of The Wall. They have little interest in the lands of Cumbria. The Vikings have increased their incursions into England and they are almost a constant presence well inside of East Anglia. But since our sea battle with that pirate, Olaf Tryggvason, there has been little Viking presence on our northern shores. Still, we are not immune to invasion. Weaknesses in parts of England only serve to encourage more expanded hostilities. King AEthelred has done nothing but weaken our northern defenses. After demanding that all of our war vessels be deployed to defend England's southern coast, he has been raising increasingly larger taxes on all of our land.

I do not know if AEthelred has bad luck, bad counsel or bad judgment or some of all of them. He continuously seems to have his army and naval forces deployed at the wrong place at the wrong time. As a result, the Vikings often gain much greater victories than their forces should otherwise have been permitted. On many occasions they have been able to bring their fearsome warships along the rivers, deep into the English countryside. Now AEthelred has taken to paying the Vikings not to invade. These payments are called *Danegeld* and last year the *Danegeld* amounted to 10,000 pounds stirling paid to Tryggvason. And still Tryggvason recommenced his raids again this year. Tryggvason's army sailed up the Thames River and threatened to invade London. Only after a vicious, but inconclusive battle, AEthelred paid him an additional 22,000 pounds and offered him a treaty allowing these new Danes to settle in East Anglia.

Our Northern coast has been largely ignored by the Vikings, who have settled for plundering our ships at sea and we have managed to keep the Scots at bay. But AEthelred has so weakened both our land and sea resources, for the defense of his southern coast, that I fear a concerted effort by either Vikings or Scots would have a chance to overrun us.

Sigen was well aware of my concerns for I have voiced them often. One evening, while sitting enjoying the warmth of a blazing hearth she ask, "Is there nothing that can be done to bolster the defenses of the North?"

"What is needed," I replied, "Is a strong standing army located well inland so that it is safe from surprise attacks from sea and far enough from the Scots that they have sufficient warning of an assault from our northern frontier. That way we could quickly reinforce either Bamburgh or York, should either of them require assistance to repel an invasion."

"So why can we not create such a garrison?" she asked.

"I have raised such a concern with both Earl Waltheof of Bamburgh and Earl Thored of York and their replies have been the same. AEthelred does not trust us northerners. He would no more agree to such a standing army than he would permit a strengthening of the garrisons of York or Bamburgh. And if either of them created such a force, the king would demand that they march south to provide support there."

"But, Papa, you cannot just sit here at StorEye worrying about it. It is bad enough that you brood so over the death of my beloved mother, but adding this worry has paralyzed you into inaction. I can see you age before my eyes," she said, her voice near sobbing with concern for my wellbeing.

CHAPTER 22
THE PALATINE ARCHBISHOPRIC

BAMBURGH, 993

Two hundred years have passed since the first Viking raider had set foot on Britain's soil. Now, two centuries later, Tryggvason, with the largest force that he had ever commanded, landed at Bamburgh and attacked the castle, which we had all thought to be impenetrable. They were well equipped with catapults, siege towers, scaling equipment and battering rams. They overran Bamburgh's defenses, looted the castle and slew many of the occupants. As quickly as they had appeared, they withdrew to their ships and sailed home to Norway, carrying with them the treasures of Bamburgh Castle.

 Rumours of this disaster reached StorEye days before a detailed report reached us. We were already packed for travel. Sigen and myself, along with a substantial armed escort began our journey east immediately. As we approached Bernicia, more details emerged. The raiders were long gone and Waltheof was back in residence at Bamburgh. He had been wounded in the attack, but was expected to survive. Many of his subjects had not been so fortunate. Waltheof's son, Uhtred had taken control of Bamburgh while his father recovered. Uhtred, now a man of twenty years, had grown into a fine warrior. He bore a tall, muscular frame, an attractive face and a wild blond mane covering his head and cheeks. He looked every bit the fearless warrior that he was.

Uhtred provided Sigen and I with a tour of the damage done to the castle, which he accompanied with a running dialogue of the raid. Apparently the Vikings had brought with them precut timbers and planks, with which, after skirting the castle at a safe distance, they quickly assembled siege towers, mounted on large logs. They then rolled these towers up to the landward side of the ramparts. The siege towers allow the invaders to climb to the top of the ramparts, protected from the spears and arrows of the defenders by a roof of planks covering the top of the towers. While the invaders built and moved the towers tight against the castle's exterior fortification, they employed catapults to harass the defender with a steady barrage of massive rocks and balls of flaming pitch. Once in place, some 6,000 screaming warriors clambered up the towers and breeched the ramparts. Heavily outnumbered, the defenders fought a courageous battle in the castle courtyard but were soon forced to retreat to the keep. The keep withstood the attack until reinforcements arrived from the surrounding countryside and even from York. Once the reinforcements came in sight the invaders quickly gathered their pillaged booty and retreated to their ships, leaving the courtyard strewn with dead and wounded and their invasion machinery where it stood. I could not help but notice Sigen's fascination with Uhtred's dialogue. For myself, I was infuriated with the audacity of this assault on the bastion of my friends and allies.

THE LEGEND OF STOR

***

The next week was spent burying the dead, tending to the wounded and clearing up the wreckage created by the invaders. Sigen pitched right in, helping feed the survivors and finding them suitable shelter where they could rest and sleep. Norman busied himself organizing the clearing of structures which had been burned or smashed. The castle exterior, for the main part, was solid rock and had sustained the attack without much damage. But inside the castle wall there had been many wood and thatch buildings, homes, stables, sheds along with wooden doorways and frames. For the most part these had been destroyed. Furnishings were also mainly in ruin. Only the upper floor of the keep remained unscathed. Sigen and I, Ulphus and Norman and Earl Thored had accepted Waltheof's offer to share these premises with his family. Ulph and I aided Uhtred in planning how to carry out the repairs and rebuild the structures which were beyond repair. Waltheof had many highly skilled workmen to carry out this work and the rebuilding was quickly underway.

As the rebuilding proceeded, Ulph, Uhtred, Thored and I joined Waltheof and Uhtred to assess how the raid had been carried out and how we could reduce the chances of it happening again. Sigen joined us in all of these discussions and added many insightful suggestions which aided our deliberations. Only after we had shared our assessments of the state of the immediate tasks of restoring Bamburgh to make it habitable and full restorations had begun, did we turned our attention to assessing the raid itself.

Waltheof spoke first. "Thank you all for being here in this, our time of need. Your support has greatly lessened our sufferings.

"This assault was personally led by Tryggvason. Many people here saw and recognized him." Murmurs of disgust accompanied this announcement." Waltheof continued, "I am convinced that this was not an invasion. These marauders were intent on ravaging and destroying Bamburgh, looting us and then fleeing. Your assistance interrupted the completion of their goal, but I do not believe that they ever intended to stay. They simply sailed to our shores with a mighty force, breeched our ramparts and killed and looted as quickly as possible. There was no attempt to lay siege to our keep, nor did they establish anything more than the most temporary encampment outside of our walls. Their actions all speak to a very large scale raid bent on terror and pillage. It was not the vanguard of an invasion."

Heads nodded in agreement with this assessment. "But it may have been a tactical strike in order to test our defenses in the wake of a planned invasion," Ulphus offered.

"Well if that was their purpose, they will have learned that we do not have a sufficient naval presence to even see them coming, let alone impede their attack. They must have had at least a thousand war ships and we never saw them until they were on our shore. They would have been visible for miles on the open sea," Uhtred spat out the words in disgust. "And yet we did not have a land force capable of resisting their attack. We are vulnerable and they now know it."

We analyzed and discussed our weaknesses for the remainder of the afternoon. When we finally broke, Waltheof announced, "We will meet in the morning and explore our options."

True to his words, the following morning Waltheof resumed our discussion. His wounds prevented him from standing, let alone walking. He had been carried into the room and sat on a large couch, propped upright by numerous pillows. Still, he retained the dignified image of the noble that he was and his voice still carried the sounds of his authority. Thored suggested that we offer the Vikings *a Danegeld* to end their hostilities. Norman responded bitterly, "What good would that do? It hasn't worked for Aethelred and it will not work for us. It will only whet their appetites to demand more." Ulph winced at his son's bitter rebuke of the suggestion made by the Earl of York, but he nodded his head in agreement.

"Then what do you suggest?" Thored shot back.

"Not cowering in fear of this pirate." Norman retorted.

Our mutual frustration increased and threatened to doom our discussion until Waltheof spoke, "Sires, ours is a problem that we all share. Fighting each other will not solve it for us. Let us remain civil to each other."

We resumed a civil dialogue but no reasonable alternatives were put forward. Finally Sigen spoke, her voice soft and calm. "My father has put forward a plan which you have all heard before and rejected. You may wish to reconsider it," She ended demurely.

All eyes turned to me expectantly. "Well Stor, what is this plan?" Waltheof inquired.

Remembering that I had previously convinced these same men to accept my plan but King Aethelred had dismissed it out of hand, I started hesitantly. "I believe that we need a standing army located inland far enough from the sea that it would be safe from a surprise attack by sea. In that manner, it would not necessitate the support of a large naval force." Gaining confidence, based on my belief that this was the only way to proceed, I continued. "By locating this force away from our shores, an invasion from the sea would require the invader to establish and protect supply lines across your lands, allowing you to harass and disrupt his abilities to supply his army. If such a force was located midway between Bamburgh and York it could be called upon by either, as required. With the forces you would already have at both those locations, you could repel an invasion from a force far larger than Tryggvason has set against us.

Tryggvason has returned to Norway but those Scandinavian countries do not have sufficient arable land to support the populations which live there. They may spend years fighting each other over their insufficient land but again and again they will look outward for the land of others. The closest such land is England. They will eventually be back and we must be ready.

"Likewise the threat from Scotland will remain constant. They do not trust Anglo-Saxons ambitions towards their land. As a result they will always seek ways to extend their border ever further into England. It is only fear of the strength of England's army that keeps them at bay. When they sense weakness they will attack us. An army such as I have described will have the further benefit to protect our Northern border."

Thored responded immediately, "Aethelred has already heard and rejected this proposal. He will never trust a Northern noble with the power that such an army would bring. He keeps us weak, not only because of his needs for our troops in the south, but because it keeps us too weak to rebel against him. Edgar had sufficient strength to confidently appoint native northern nobility. But this king is not Edgar. Oswald is his father-in-law and he does not even give him that trust."

"With all due respect, my Lord," Ulphus spoke up. "Since we last discussed this plan of Stor's, I have given it much consideration. If King Aethelred fears to place such an army as Stor has proposed under the command of his northern nobility, then I propose that it be created under the authority of the church…"

"Archbishop Oswald would never agree to taking on such authority," Thored exclaimed, cutting Ulphus off

THE LEGEND OF STOR

mid-sentence. "Beside that, he would never agree to transfer the seat of his bishopric from the City of York to some backwater that you may decide upon."

Ignoring Thored's rebuke, Ulph continued, "I was about to suggest that a new bishopric be created and that it would replace the Bishopric of Lindisfarne."

Thored considered this possibility for several moments and then replied, "We had best include Archbishop Oswald and Bishop Aldhun of Lindisfarne in this discussion." We all agreed and messengers were sent to invite the two senior churchmen to join us.

Two days later we again assembled. Waltheof welcomed Oswald and Aldhun and then turned to Ulph, saying, "Ulphus, please review where our discussions have led us."

Ulph summarized the weakness of our present defense, the King's earlier refusal to allow us to further strengthen our sea and land forces and the dilemma which that created for us. Ulph then said, "Stor has developed a strategy which has the potential of resolving our problems while still working within the parameters of what King Aethelred might support. He proposes creating a new archbishopric at a place well inland and well south of our border with Scotland, yet, at the same time sufficiently close to both Bamburgh and York so that it might reinforce the forces of either as required. It could then also serve as a buffer between us and the Scots."

"The Archbishop of Canterbury will side with AEthelred if the king demands any surplus armies to reinforce his southern defenses. Canterbury is the senior archbishopric in England and that is how they have responded to any attempt which I have made to enlarge the army of York," Oswald observed.

"Then the solution lies in creating the new bishopric on an equal footing with Canterbury and endowing its archbishop the authority of an earl." I declared. "In doing so the king would have no need to fear an earl challenging his authority. The pope would never allow a prince of the church to challenge the authority of the King of England unless the king was excommunicated." On the other hand the church would never stand by and permit the king to overrule their own archbishop unless the Archbishop himself was guilty of treason against the crown."

Thored smiled and offered, "You have schooled yourself well in the relationship between the crown and the church here in England, Stor. If agreed to, both the church and the king must allow the new Archbishopric to arm itself as it requires and not interfere unless the Archbishop became a traitor or an unrepentant heretic."

At this point Aldhun, an ambitious man, never long forgetting his own self- interest, queried. "Where do I fit into this plan?"

"Why father," Uhtred announced charmingly masking his disdain for his father-in-law, "You would become the Archbishop/Earl."

***

After considerable discussion we all came to an agreement that a well garrisoned archbishopric, strategically located, and with the authority of an earldom, was the best method of ensuring an ability to reinforce either Bamburgh or York in a timely manner from attacks from the sea. At the same time, both York and Bamburgh could reinforce the archbishopric if it were to be invaded by land by either the Scots or the Danes who continued to hold settlements in Edinburgh and the Lothian. We then turned our attention to a suitable location for such a bishopric to be located. We discussed many options but rejected them all for one reason or another.

THE LEGEND OF STOR

I finally spoke. "I hold a piece of land located on the River Wear. It is known as Dun Holm. *Dun*, as you know, in English means hill. *Holm* is a Scandinavian word meaning island. It has the advantage, for purposes of defense, of being both a hill and virtually an island. It is located at a bow in the River Wear, so that the river provides a defensive barrier on three sides; East, South and West. At that point in the river, the banks soar up vertically at a very steep angle on all three sides. At the top of the cliffs is a hill that rises even higher. A fortress located at the top of the hill would be impregnable from three sides and only minimum ramparts would be required across the northern-most side to complete its defensive perimeter. It is located almost exactly where you wish it to be and it is close to Chester-le-Street which was the home of the Community of St. Cuthbert for many years after they were forced to flee from Lindisfarne. I am prepared to gift that land to the church if they desire to locate the bishopric there."

Most heads nodded in agreement at my choice but Bishop Aldhun expressed a concern. "I know of this place, and it is as you described. It will make a great location, but it must appear as formidable as possible. This can be accomplished by erecting a fine stone cathedral which would tower over all of the surrounding landscape proclaiming to all who approach that this is a most holy place of God and the resting place of our beloved St. Cuthbert."

Waltheof smiled in amusement at Aldhun's obvious self interest, but declared, "Bamburgh has always supported the Community of St. Cuthbert and Bamburgh will build your stone cathedral."

We then set out to demarcate the boundaries of the proposed Bishopric of Dun Holm and the lands over which the Earl/Bishop would be the liege lord. This discussion involved much bickering but was finally resolved to the satisfaction of Aldhun and Oswald with regard to the ecclesiastical jurisdictions of the Archbishopric of York and Dun Holm and the secular boundaries of the Earls of York and Bamburgh and the newly proposed Earl of Dun Holm.

Thored then pointed out what we all knew to be the case. "We must now convince the rest of the nobility and the thanes in our respective jurisdictions to endorse our proposal. Then we must seek the endorsement of King Aethelred, the Archbishop of Canterbury, and probably even the pope in Rome in order to secure the status of this new Archbishopric and Earldom. These tasks were all assigned and it was agreed, that once completed, Thored and Oswald would lead a delegation to Winchester to attempt to obtain the assent of the king and the church.

CHAPTER 23
SIGEN AND UHTRED

DUN HOLM, 995

In the two years following the finalization of our plan for the establishment of the Bishopric of Dun Holm, much time had been invested in developing a consensus amongst the lesser nobility of the North-west in support of the plan. Due to Aethelred's continuing distrust of all things Danish, we felt that we must have this consensus if we were to convince him to endorse our plan. Our task was exacerbated by the death of Archbishop Oswald in 993 and, in 994, Thored, the Earl of York, was slain in a skirmish with Viking raiders. Not only did we now not have their active support, but we had to convince their replacements, the now Archbishop EAdwulf and Earl AElfhelm, of the merit of the plan. Waltheof remained too infirmed to provide much more than moral support and his son Uhtred was occupied much of the time fighting back the ever-more emboldened Scottish incursions into Bernicia. The job had fallen largely to Ulphus who regularly called on me to assist him. In spite of these challenges, our mission was now complete and a consensus had been attained. A delegation had been dispatched to obtain the endorsement from King AEthelred and Archbishop AElfric who had only months before been affirmed as Archbishop of Canterbury from his previous archbishopric of Winchester.

Travel in England was better than it had been for several years. Since Tryggvason had signed a treaty with AEthelred, as a condition of his last *Danegeld* payment, he had returned to Norway, converted to Christianity, and subsequently, had seized the throne of Norway from Sweyn Forkbeard. While he left much of his army in East Anglia, the attacks on England from Vikings had been greatly diminished.

My work in York, now largely complete, allowed me to turn my attention to my badly neglected personal affairs. Foremost amongst these was the need to find Sigen an appropriate husband. That evening I raised the subject with Sigen. "I am aware that I have delayed too long in finding you a husband. I am attempting to correct that situation and have identified several well bred young men, any one of which who make a very suitable husband for you. If you agree I will…"

Sigen cut me off mid sentence, "But Father, I already know the man who I will marry."

I was struck speechless. Sigen had always been a loyal and devoted child. She had never challenged my decisions regarding her upbringing. I could scarcely believe that she was doing so now. Women did not go about finding themselves a husband. This was their parents' responsibility. I finally stammered out, "So who is this man who you would marry without my approval?"

"I would love for you to approve, Father, but if I do not marry him quickly, I might likely be delivering you a bastard child," she responded calmly.

If her first declaration shocked me, this last one left me dumbstruck. "You have lain with this man?" I demanded. "Are you now with child?"

"I have known this man," she maintained her calm composure. "He is Uhtred of Bamburgh."

"But… but he is a married man and he already has a son," I stated, my level of distress rising sharply.

"He plans to set Ecgfrida aside, not for me, but because the two of them cannot abide each other's presence. They only married in order to meet their fathers' wishes to unite the House of Bamburgh to the church. All that Aldhun and Ecgfrida wanted from Uhtred is that he sire a son so that their heir would ascend to the Earldom of Bamburgh. They now have that heir, EAldred. They now have no further use of each other."

I did not know whether to react with shock or dismay as I processed all that Sigen had spoken in her calm but determined oratory. Wisely, I chose to say nothing. Sigen has always been a very clever girl and knows well her own mind. She is also still my very precious daughter. In due course, I regained my own composure and simply said, "I will speak to Waltheof."

As it turned out, all things were as Sigen had described. Uhtred and Ecgfrida had already begun the process of setting their marriage aside. Waltheof and Uhtred were both ecstatic about the prospect of Sigen marrying into the Earldom of Bamburgh and Ulphus was beside himself at the prospect of Uhtred marring his niece, Sigen and thereby creating a stronger bond between their two families. I alone had reservations, but I kept them well hidden and the wedding plans proceeded.

* * *

The wedding was to be held at Bamburgh castle. Elaborate plans were underway. I had reconciled my thoughts regarding my daughter's actions and decision and encouraged her in every way that I could, in order to do my part to ensure that the wedding and the subsequent marriage would be a success.

With only a few days remaining before the wedding, our delegation from Wessex finally returned. They had been gone for almost a year. Earl AElfhelm of York, the successor to Earl Thored, had led the delegation and it was he who summoned us all to gather in Waltheof's chamber to report the situation to us. When we were gathered, AElfhelm announced, "Our mission has been a success. King AEthelred and Archbishop AElfric have put their respective seals to the creation of the Archbishopric/Earldom of Durham (the name had been altered from Dun Holm in the process). The pope in Rome has received these documents and has also given his approval." Many questions followed this announcement. Several involved the length of time it had taken to obtain these agreements. AElfhelm explained, "AEthelred was reluctant to agree. Without his consent, the church would not be moved. As you are all aware, AEthelred is leery of a strong military force being garrisoned in the North and being largely under the command of men of Danish ancestry. I believe that it was the Viking attack at Chester-le-street that finally convinced him that the North, and subsequently his whole kingdom, was at risk unless he took action to strengthen the northern defenses." Six months earlier a Viking attack at Chester-le-street had forced Bishop Aldhun and the Community of St. Cuthbert to flee their home and move to Ripon.

AElfhelm surveyed the room and asked, "Is Bishop Aldhun not in attendance for the wedding?"

Ulphus answered, "He is not. He believes that it is an insult to him that Uhtred is taking Sigen as a second wife after setting Ecgfrida aside. He refuses to attend."

"Well he must attend," Archbishop EAldwulf declared. "We had planned to use the occasion of this wedding to announce the creation of his Bishopric/Earldom and Aldhun's translation to that position makes him the central figure in this announcement. He must be here. Send a message to him at Ripon, under my seal, demanding that he attend us here."

CHAPTER 24
A RESTING PLACE FOR A SAINT

DURHAM CATHEDRAL

It was the morning of the wedding when Archbishop Eadulf's messenger returned. Aldhun, it turned out, unaware of the decision of the king and the church had become doubtful that our plan would ever become a reality. Badly shaken by being driven from Chester-le-street he had decided that, if he could not rely on his secular supporters to protect his flock, he would place them all in the hands of God and return to the Holy Island of Lindisfarne where, in his words, the relics of St. Cuthbert, with God's grace, could rest in peace where they properly belonged. Using the excuse of Uhtred's wedding as a pretext he, and the entire Community of St. Cuthbert, had packed up all of their belongings and were now on the road back to Lindisfarne.

On hearing this news, EAldwulf screamed, "Has he lost his mind? He must be stopped."

Ulph, Uhtred and I were sent with a military escort and a sealed order from EAldwulf, to intercept the *Haliwerfolklond* and return them to Durham. When we caught up with them we were cordially greeted and led to Aldhun's presence. "What is the meaning of this?" Ulphus screamed.

Aldhun responded in kind and the whole exchange threatened to elevate into a major confrontation when Aldhun realized that we were there because his Archbishopric/Earldom was to become a reality. He quickly apologized to Ulph but he could not resist directing some final venom at Uhtred. "I gave you land as a dowry when you married my daughter. It is now forfeit and must be returned."

Uhtred smiled the winning smile of which he was so capable and replied, "Don't get foolish. You got what you wanted from our marriage. Your grandson will succeed me as Earl of Bamburgh and you are about to become the most powerful man in England, second only to the king himself."

Aldhun demurred and ordered his long train of wagons to turn and move towards Durham. We escorted him all of the way. When we arrived at the dusty little village at the base of the mighty hill on which Aldhun's church would be built, he clambered onto the box of the tallest wagon and summoned all villagers who were within hearing range. "I, along with my flock, the Community of St Cuthbert, was on the way to take St. Cuthbert back to Lindisfarne. Late at night, while I was sleeping, St. Cuthbert appeared to me and told me that it was his wish that his remains be put to rest here at Dun Holm. As a result, we are here. And here I shall build the Archdiocese of Durham and St. Cuthbert will rest in peace forever."

And so the Archbishopric/Earldom of Durham was established *and here it would stay for the next half of a millennium.*

* * *

BAMBURGH, 1001

In 997 the Vikings again escalated their hostilities in southern England. They raided heavily in Cornwall, Devon, Somerset and south Wales. The following year they raided Dorset, Hampshire and Sussex and in 999 they raided Kent. None of these attacks were of the stature of invasions. They were simply after pillage and plunder before retreating from mainland England. They did, however, maintain a permanent base on the Isle of Wight, from which they attacked England's southern shores time and again.

I have spent most of the past six years home at StorEye. We have lived in relative peace during that time, however, last year, our good king, AEthelred, decided that the descendants of Danish residence of Strathclyde had not been paying their fair share of the *Danegeld* and sent his army through Cumbria to lay waste to many of those estates in Strathclyde. We are well west of the old Roman road upon which his troops travelled and, therefore, were spared his wrath. However his credibility amongst his otherwise loyal subjects of Danish descent has been badly diminished.

Meanwhile developments at Durham have gone as planned. Aldhun is now the Archbishop/Earl and has raised a substantial standing army. Uhtred has kept his promise and now Durham is well garrisoned and fortified, with a temporary wooden church. Plans for the more permanent stone church and fortifications are now well underway.

I have made many trips to Durham to survey the progress. While my relationship with Aldhun remains somewhat strained, he is not the reason for my journeys. I have come east to visit Sigen. Marriage has served her well and she looks as radiant as ever. She has borne Uhtred two sons, EAdwulf and Cospatric. They are an absolute pleasure to me and are fiercely loyal to their step brother, EAldred. Cospatric is still only a toddler. But EAldred, while only a boy himself, has taken up much of the training of his younger brother, Ealdwulf in the arts of warfare. Uhtred is not much concerned with the cultivation of land. He is a warrior and is determined that his sons should all become warriors.

When Uhtred is not off defending Bamburgh from marauding Scots and Danes, we often spend much time together. He is an intelligent gentleman, a relentless warrior, and a good husband and father. I have great respect for him but this does not give us to necessary political agreement on the future of England. I, on the other hand, do not interfere with his plans for his sons even though I am the grandfather.

DURHAM, 1002

The Stone fortifications protecting Durham were in the final stages of completion and the stone church construction was well underway. The Scots did not take long to test its capacity. Scotland decided to attack the new episcopal city. Thousands of Scots, led by their king, Malcolm ll, our old Cumbrian king, now elevated to the throne of Scotland, streamed across into England and attacked Durham. The defenders, however, while outnumbered by a large majority, held their fortifications for two days. Then, Uhtred, leading a force of several thousand Bernicians, swept down on the attackers, thoroughly routing them. Joined by the defenders of Durham, Uhtred gave chase to the fleeing Scots and slaughter ensued.

The defenders of Durham were so incensed by this attack that they methodically combed the carnage beheading every Scot they encountered, whether living or dead. The severed heads were meticulously gathered and placed in wagons to be taken back to Durham. Once back in Durham, the severed heads were carefully washed and groomed by the womenfolk of Durham so that their bloodied countenances again became recognizable. The heads were then each placed on pikes which were then placed before the gates of the city as a warning to future invaders. Aldhun arranged for these women to be given a cow for each head that they had cleaned and a great celebration was held to acknowledge that the *Haliwerfolklond* was finally capable of defending itself and its holy relics.

After the carnage of the battle was cleared and some semblance of order was restored to the city, I commented to Uhtred, "It is fortunate that our plan prevailed. This time not even York sent assistance let alone our king."

Uhtred, as was his habit, leapt to AEthelred's defense. "The Vikings are again very active in the south. AEthelred has been busy giving them battle. He could not also support us."

"Giving battle," I challenged. "He paid them another 24,000 in d*anegeld* so that they would not continue their attack. If his army was busy, it was busying itself killing and harassing loyal Englishmen of Danish descent."

As we talked, we came to an agreement that AEthelred had made many mistakes in his tactics against the Vikings. This time those mistakes were irrelevant since we had quite capably defended Durham and that is what we had promised the king that we could do in exchange for his endorsement of our plan. Uhtred then went on the offense in his defense of King AEthelred. "While he might receive and follow bad military advice he has taken great strides in the development of the English law which you so admire."

Uhtred knew that I had to agree. He was well aware that my support for England had never been support for its king and realm. I supported the system of law started by Alfred and built upon by all of his successors. I had to admit that AEthelred had added to, and improved upon the laws of his forbearers. Most recently AEthelred had introduced a system of juries into English criminal law. He had proclaimed that, "...in every wapentake... shall go forth the twelve eldest thanes and the reeve... and they shall swear that they will never knowingly accuse an innocent man nor conceal a guilty man..." His father had introduced similar juries to witness property transactions but AEthelred had extended them to make decisions in criminal offences.

After exhausting our discussion on the pros and cons of AEthelred's reign, we turned our attention to the Viking situation. Uhtred advised me that Tryggvason had been killed in battle and that another pirate, Swend Forkbeard, had regained the throne of Norway. Tryggvason was now out of our hands forever and our blood debt against him could not now be honoured, but there remained our blood debt to that despicable Thurbrand of Holderness. I told Uhtred of Thurbrand's role in the death of his mother-in-law, Eyja, his great Uncle Bryni and his great grandfather, Torald. "I, Ulphus and your father are now too old to ensure that the blood debt is paid. The responsibility must now fall to your generation." *And so I set in motion a series of actions which would require a price in blood, that, had I known the extent to which it would flow, I may well have held my tongue on this entire issue.*

THE LEGEND OF STOR

* * *

OXFORD, 1002

AEthelred's fear of the Scandinavian Vikings continued to affect his distrust of all of his Danish subjects. As a result, he ordered an ethnic cleansing of all of England by issuing a decree, that all people of Danish ancestry living in England, be put to death. At that time, AEthelred was only powerful enough to assert this atrocity in the southern third of England, but in those parts where it could be carried out, thousands were put to the sword. In Oxford a group of Danes took refuge in the cathedral. AEthelred's soldiers were unable to dislodge them. So they barred the exits and burnt the cathedral to the ground, killing all inside. Amongst the victims was Gunhilde, sister of King Swend of Norway. Swend was so outraged by the death of his sister that he launched an invasion the following year and he sacked Norwich. The English forces, under the leadership of Ulfcytel Shillingr, met and fought Swend's army and, while Swend was eventually successful and Shillingr was slain, he inflicted such damage to Swend's army that the Danish king deserted his assault and retreated to Denmark.

AEthelred undoubtedly recognized the error in his anti-Danish policy and sought some reconciliation by recognizing the efforts of the Northumbrians in protecting the Northern part of his realm. In spite of the turmoil raging across his kingdom, he decided to personally come north and give recognition to the people who had planned and delivered his northern defense.

CHAPTER 25
THE HORN OF ULPHUS

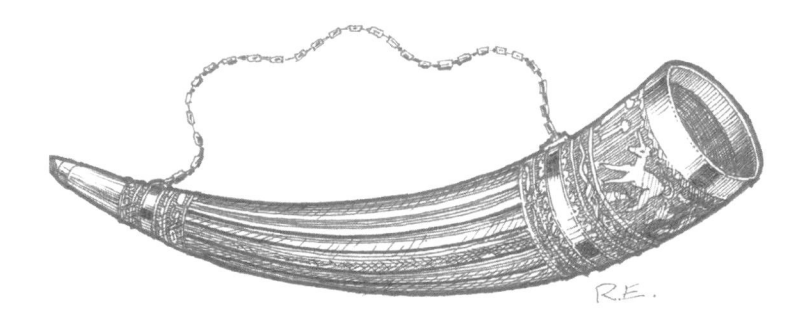

HORN OF ULPHUS

YORK, 1005

As part of the ceremony that AEthelred would preside over in York, Ulphus insisted that the contribution of my land, to make the Archdioceses a reality, must be acknowledged by the king himself. "You are the son of Vikings. As long as your contributions to the well-being of England go unnoticed by the king you are likely to become one of his victims in the manner that Gunhilde did. We must do all that we can to avoid that outcome. We must force AEthelred to witness your contributions.

The ceremony took place in the magnificent York Minister. AEthelred, in his full robes of office sat on a throne in front of the altar, above the bema and the nave. Petitioners then approached to a point on the bema, several steps below the throne. First amongst these was Wulfstan ll who had replaced EAldwulf as Archbishop of York a year earlier. He requested, and received royal assent to Aldhun's appointment to the Archbishopric of Durham.

AElthelm then rose and petitioned the king to recognize The Archbishopric of Durham as an Earldom and Aldhun as its earl with all of the authority that an earl would command. This also received royal assent to which the king added, you shall exercise the power to create your own witan, raise an army, appoint your sheriffs and justices, administer law, levy taxes and duties, create fairs and markets, issue charters, salvage shipwrecks, collect revenues from mines, administer forests and mint coins.

Ulphus rose next. In his hands he carried a finely carved horn which was about two feet in length. The horn was the end of an elephant tusk and was carved in Asiatic designs. A band about four inches in width circled the widest end of the horn and carried relief carvings of a unicorn, a lion devouring a deer, a gryphon, having the body of a lion and the wings and head of an eagle facing a similar creature which has the head of a wolf and three additional wolves' heads and above them a wolf in flight or pursuit. Ulph then spoke, identifying himself and his role in these affairs. He then turned to me, "This is our beloved son Stor. Stor was the rightful owner of lands in Durham, granted to his ancestors by King Ragnald and confirmed in his possession under the laws of England. He has freely gifted this land to the then Bishop Aldhun of Lindisfarne and upon which our Archbishop Aldhun of Durham has built his church."

When the applause ended Ulphus approached the altar and knelt before it. After a brief prayer he took a drink of wine from the horn and then placed it on the altar. "In the custom of my people, I present this horn to you, AEthelred, King of England, so that it may commemorate the gift that Stor has bequeathed to your church.

***

TORALDSBY, 1005

Ulphus has seen to the rebuilding of Toraldsby. It is now larger and grander than the old manor and so it is to there that we retired, after the ceremony at York. All of my family was there, as were Ulph's remaining kin. Uhtred joined Sigen and their three sons EAldred, EAdulf and Cospatric. I knew that a moment like this would probably never occur again for me. My health was too fast failing as age took its toll. As we all sat around the remnants of a sumptuous meal served in the great hall, Ulphus rose to speak. Age was also taking its toll on him but he still stood tall and his imposing appearance caused everyone to stop and hear his words. He raised his drinking horn in a toast, "To our beloved son, Stor of Eye in recognition of the contribution that he has made to the defense of England through his role in establishing the palatine bishopric of Durham."

Glasses were raised and applause ensued. My son-in-law Uhtred was next to speak. Like most of the men in his lineage, he was a tall, well-built, blond-haired giant of a man. "Father," He said respectfully "in spite of your Norse background, now, not only are you an Englishman, but you are a true hero of England. I salute you."

At that I rose. "While I appreciate your kind words, I am not an Englishman. My sword is pledged to no king, only to my family. I agree that a kingdom requires a king. And the descendants of Alfred of Wessex who have sat on his throne have implemented a system of law which, to my knowledge, is second to none. We have a written code of law that applies to all men. We have a legal system which provides for a jury to determine guilt or innocence and to resolve disputes between men. We have a process of registering land ownership and forbidding the involuntary alienation of that land for any reason short of treason. We have communities which are fortified and garrisoned, leaving them somewhat independent of standing armies which could as easily oppress them as defend them. All of these things are attributable to these kings from Wessex. And I support them for it. But my sword does not belong to them. It belongs to my family and it is my family to which my fealty belongs. My ancestors are both Norse and Anglo. My land lies within Cumbria which is sometimes claimed by Scotland and sometime by England. At the time of my birth it lay within the Kingdom of Cumbria. Kingdoms come and kingdoms go. My reality is in the land which my grandfather, my uncles and my father spilt their blood to obtain and for my family whom, I pray, will derive their sustenance from it, until the end of time. So I will raise my glass and toast to StorEye."

Uhtred responded, "I can appreciate the position which you have taken. It has not varied since I first knew you when I was still a child. But I am a descendent of the oldest ruling family of Northumbria. My ancestors created the largest Anglo-Saxon kingdom in all of Britain's history. We have recognized Wessex as our overlords since Aethelstan first raise the Wessex banner in our land. My allegiance is pledged to his successors and therefore to England and I will raise my sword in defense of the English realm for as long as I have the strength to do so. Regardless, I still see your actions as heroic in the defense of our country.

After we had left the great hall Sigen approached me saying, "Beloved Father, with your blessing, I have pledged myself to my husband. Whither he goes, I shall follow."

Giving her a kiss on her cheek I replied, "Go thou with my blessing."

STOREYE, 1007

I am back in StorEye. A plague has swept across England. On the good side, the Vikings curtailed their offensive and fled to Norway to escape the devastation from this curse. In Cumbria we have only a few cases of this dreaded disease, but I fear that I will be one of its victims. The sores appeared this morning and I fear that my time on earth will be now be numbered in days. Looking back, I have had a good life and have accomplished what my grandfather set out for me. I have gathered my children around me and have had Haberd prepare my last will and testimony. I have divided my estate equally amongst my children making appropriate adjustments for any gold or the value of goods given to my daughters' husbands as dowries. I have bequeathed the lands that Steinar was granted by Vidar to his remaining family. Our lands and tenancy agreements I have left in one package which will pass equally to my three sons to administer, along with caveats that the land may not be alienated without the agreement of all three. I have given over this chronicle to my son Haberd, with the request that he take up my pen and insure its completion.

I now listen to the priests drone over my fast failing body and eagerly await reunion with my beloved Eyja.

PART 4
| A COMING OF AGE |

CHAPTER 26
TREACHERY AND MURDER

**ANGLO-SAXON HELMET DURING
VIKING BATTLE FOR YORK**

ENGLAND, 1008

I am Byrniulf of StorEye, son of Haberd. My grandfather, Stor, asked my father, Haberd, to ensure the completion of his journal. He, in turn, has passed this responsibility on to me. This will not be my story. Nor will it be the story of my family. That history will be written on our land and by our descendants. Instead, I will attempt to ensure that the outcomes of those things that my Grandfather started in motion, and the impact that those things had on the history of England, will be recorded.

Grandfather passed away peacefully last year. He remained lucid to the end, although the plague ravaged his body. We were all there at his passing and, while we wept, he seemed fully at peace. I lost a brother to the plague and Boandi lost a granddaughter. Other than that, the plague passed us by. In southern England many families suffered much worse. Even many members of the royal family were taken. But the plague also drove the Vikings, at least temporarily, from our shores. But now they are back.

AEthelred again bought us peace at a cost of 36,000 *Danegeld* and used this peace to reorganize a much stronger military fleet. However, one of his commanders turned pirate and deserted with many of England's war vessels.

The following year the Viking leader, Thorkell the Tall, led the largest invasion force ever seen under AEthelred's reign, into England and harried the country until 1012. But again AEthelred bought us peace, this time at a cost of 48,000 *Danegeld*.

* * *

In spite of his initial reaction to Sigen's marriage to Uhtred, I am convinced that, in the end, Grandfather was very happy with this union. Initially the couple seemed immensely happy together and Father adored Sigen. Her happiness was his happiness. The birth of her two sons left Grandfather ecstatic. He often commented that, as the son of a simple sword Viking, the idea that his grandchildren would be amongst the nobility of England was far beyond the simple ambition that Vidar had given him in rebuilding our family. As a result, he would have been dismayed to have been here to see them set their marriage aside.

Uhtred was devoted to England and to the rule of the Anglo-Saxon House of Wessex. I believe that he and Sigen remained very close to each other, but when the opportunity arose for Uhtred to become even more closely allied to AEthelred, through marriage to AEthelred's daughter, his ambition caused him to sacrifice his marriage to Sigen. By the same token, Sigen fully supported Uhtred's ambitions and probably willingly agreed to set her marriage vows aside. Even after the dissolution of their marriage, the two remained very close to each other and, from my knowledge, showed no bitterness or regret over their official separation. And so, it came to pass that Uhtred married for the third time, this time to AEthelred's daughter, AElfgifu.

For his part, AEthelred was strongly in support of this relationship. Uhtred had been unrelenting in his defense of AEthelred's crown and kingdom, to the extent that people have taken to referring to him as Uhtred the Bold. AEthelred has appointed him Earl of Northumbria, combining the previous Earldoms of Bamburgh and York. Aside from his strong and competent defense of AEthelred and his throne, it serves AEthelred well to have this widely loved, northern Anglo-Saxon so closely allied to him.

Sigen meanwhile now plays the role of dowager Duchess of York. She has full reign in raising her children, as well as her step-son, EAldred, and she remains a trusted advisor on Uhtred's council.

ENGLAND 2013

Early this year, Sweyn Forkbeard again invaded England. Uhtred's defenses in the north were becoming legendary and so Swend launched his invasion in East Anglia and pushed his assault across the south towards London. Before the year was up he had completely overwhelmed the English defense. AEthelred fled the country to Normandy, where his brother-in-law, from his latest marriage, was Richard ll, Duke of Normandy. The English witan invited Sweyn to become their king. Uhtred, left with no monarch to defend, surrendered his sword to Sweyn.

But Sweyn's victory was short lived. Within five months of his coronation as king of England, Sweyn Forkbeard died.

Immediately upon hearing of Sweyn's death, AEthelred sailed back to England and the English witan returned his throne to him. Uhtred immediately again swore allegiance to his king and father-in-law.

Sweyn's son Cnut was elected by Swend's army and navy to succeed his father as King of England. AEthelred led an army against him and he fled back to Norway. The following year he returned to England with an army 10,000 strong.

AEthelred's son, Edmund, also returned to England from exile in Normandy and proceeded north to join forces with, Uhtred, Earl of Northumbria. In early 1016 AEthelred died. Edmund laid claim to his crown but much of England was now under the control of Cnut. They fought a number of battles against each other which resulted in a treaty giving Edmund control of the land south of the Thames and Cnut control of the remainder. Later that same year, Edmund died, or was possibly murdered. Regardless, Cnut became king of all of England.

THE LEGEND OF STOR WIHEAL, 1016

With Edmund's death and Cnut's ascension to the throne of England, Uhtred again had no choice but to surrender. Under a promise of safe conduct Uhtred, with a guard of forty men, proceeded to a little hamlet of Wiheal on the southern border of Northumbria. At the edge of the town stood an enormous tent with Cnut's flag flying from its top post. This should have indicated that the new king was within. It appeared that this must be his temporary great hall, erected to receive Uhtred's surrender.

Guards at the entrance to the hall, where the meeting was scheduled to be held, demanded that Uhtred and his men surrender their swords and axes, as was the custom in the presence of their king. Having come in peace, they did as they were bidden. They entered the hall, which, at first glance, appeared to be empty. Suddenly, from behind long curtains, draped from floor to ceiling, armed men rushed out, swords waving wildly as they came. EAldred and his party, being unarmed, were dispatched rapidly, leaving the ground sodden with Anglo-Saxon blood. The dead lay everywhere. None were left alive. We later learned that this murderous ambush had been led by our old family nemesis, Thurbrand of Holderness, but Cnut's hand appeared all over this assassination.

Norman Ulphusson of Toraldsby was the first to arrive at the scene of the massacre. The bloodied corpses lay everywhere, untouched since the slaughter. There were no traces left of the murderers. But local people had seen Thurbrand leading his cowardly warriors from the site of the carnage. Norman sent word to Bamburgh. He then sent for enough horse-drawn wagons so that the bodies of each of the victims could be born home in a separate carriage. The bodies were all washed and groomed and redressed in fine garments. *At this time, in England, the concept of Knights merely meant men who had been trained to fight while mounted and had proved this capacity in battle. The social status of "Knight" would not yet receive its full feudal grandeur until after William of Normandy brought that concept from the continent, but its origins were beginning to be seen in England.* The victims were given all of the recognition of lofty status, note-worthy of the honour which would be shown to them. Each carriage had a riderless horse whose reins were secured to the back of each carriage so that they followed their fallen rider on his return home. When the procession was underway, the carriages created a parade over half a mile in length, slowly proceeding towards Bamburgh. Norman had ordered his troops to don their full mail and helmets, all polished and glittering in the sun, and providing a full honour guard to accompany their hero and his fallen comrades. As the procession slowly made its way across Northumbria, thousands of local residents gathered along the route to show their respect for Uhtred and his men. Each mile of their trip to Bamburgh served as a testament to the love which the county held for its heroes.

Many Northumbrians joined the procession as it moved northward, so that by the time it approached Bamburgh Castle it had swelled to thousands and had grown in length to more than five miles. A grim faced EAldred, Uhtred's first-born son, led an honour guard out to meet the procession and had ridden beside Norman, at its head, when they finally reached and entred the castle.

* * *

Inside the castle the mass mourning was overwhelming. High ranking and low, wept openly, many inconsolably. The out pouring of loss at Uhtred's death spoke volumes of the love that so many felt for this most valiant of Anglo-Saxon sons. None was felt more than the grieving of his second wife, Sigen. To the end, she still truly loved him.

By the time of the funeral, however, much of this grief had turned to anger at the realization that Northumbria had now been deprived of this valiant warrior and Anglo-Saxon leader. The funeral was as grand as any state funeral England had ever witnessed. But the guests were grim faced and stoic as the remains of Uhtred the Bold, as he was known, were prayed over and then lowered into the ground.

After the guests had all been fed and had departed, the male members of Uhtred's family gathered around a table in the great hall of Bamburgh Castle. Stor's sons, Boandi, Gyrdh and Haberd along with their seven adult sons were there, as were Ulph's sons, Norman and Archil and their six adult sons. Eadulf Cutel, Uhtred's brother and the new earl of Bamburgh and Uhtred's sons, EAldred, EAdulf ll and Cospatric were all there. Sigen Storsdotter and the newly widowed AElgifu were the only women present.

Regardless of his young age, Uhtred's eldest son, EAldred took control of the meeting. He resembled his father, tall and handsome with an air of recklessness about him. "My beloved father has been foully murdered," he began. "I know that you all loved him as much as I did. We are his family and it is we who must avenge his death. We know that he was cowardly murdered at the hand of Thurbrand of Holderness. Our families have long owed a blood-debt to this scoundrel. We have been remiss in allowing that debt to linger unpaid for so long. And now my father has paid the price for our inaction. We cannot allow Lord Uhtred's death to go un-avenged. We know also that our new king, Cnut, was probably behind this atrocity, but proof of his complicity has, so far, eluded us. Cnut guaranteed my father safe passage as he travelled to lay his sword before him in surrender."

The new earl, EAdulf, a much more cautious man than either his late brother, Uhtred or his young nephew, EAldred, was the next to speak. "While I agree with the conclusions of young EAldred, Cnut has won the war. The witan have confirmed him as king. It would be folly to attack him. He is unassailable. Thurbrand, however, is a different story. It was his hand that smote my brother. He is also responsible for the deaths of Torald and two of his children, Bryniulf and Eyja. We all owe him a blood-debt."

After considerable discussion we all agreed. Cnut was probably responsible for Uhtred's death, but we could neither confirm it nor could we extract a vengeance, even if we knew it for a fact. Thurbrand was a different issue. We all swore to seek Thurbrand's death in retaliation. EAldred would take the lead in determining the manner in which we would extract that vengeance and the rest of us would be prepared to support him however needed.

CHAPTER 27
THE VIKING KING

1017 -1065

Cnut quickly consolidated his grip on England, divided England into four earldoms and named, from amongst his supporters, four men who would rule as earls. Erik of Hlathir became the Earl of Northumbria however, for all intensive purposes, EAdulf continued to rule in Bamburgh and his title, Earl of Northumbria was used by him and his successors throughout Cnut's reign. Much of the Anglo-Saxon nobility in the rest of England were brutally executed or driven into exile. Cnut extracted 72,000 *Danegeld* from England, paid off his army and sent most of them back to Norway, where they would aid him in gaining the thrones of Norway, Denmark and southern Sweden as well as holding the throne of England.

The terms of office of Cnut's Danish earls were all short-lived. Within several years of their appointments, they were all deposed and replaced with nobility from old Anglo-Saxon families.

Cnut also left much of the English Witan in place, and, under the leadership of Wulstan ll, they quickly took Cnut under their wing, convincing him to keep intact the laws and administration of justice laid down by England's Anglo-Saxon kings from Alfred to AEthelred. Cnut then, like so many English monarchs before him, made a pilgrimage north to Durham, knelt before the remains of St. Cuthbert and said a prayer.

After his initial blood bath, through which he consolidated his rule of England, Cnut became a very good ruler of England. He knew he needed Anglo-Saxon support and so, after the initial debacle of appointing his housecarls to senior positions of authority, he went out of his way to replace them with Anglo-Saxons. He listened to the advice of both the church and the witan and with that he brought about a gradual acceptance of his sovereignty. He even married AEthelred's widow, Emma of Normandy.

With England at peace, he turned his attentions to overthrowing the kingdoms of Denmark, Norway and much of Sweden, establishing himself king of all of these countries. This opened the way for a zenith of trade between England and continental Europe, to the great benefit of an already prosperous England.

***

Cnut was prepared to leave Bernicia unmolested under the control of the Earl of Bamburgh largely because it, along with the earl/bishopric of Durham, provided England with a line of defense against the ambitions of the Scots. In 1021 an important battle was fought between the Scots and the forces of Northumbria in which Earl EAdulf Cutel was slain and the Lothian surrendered to Scotland. Archbishop Aldhun died, reportedly of a broken heart over this loss. EAldred became the Earl of all of Bernicia. EAldred, true to his oath, carried out the promised vengeance of his father's murder and completed the blood-feud by murdering Thurbrand.

Thurbrand had been a supporter of Cnut, and of his father, Sweyn, during their invasion of England. Seeking to maintain a peace with Northumbria, Cnut allowed Thurbrand's death to go unpunished upon the agreement with EAldred that his daughter, EAlfrytha would be married to a housecarl of Cnut, named Siward, a Dane who had accompanied Cnut in his conquest of England. In 1031 Cnut appointed, the now married, Siward as Earl of York.

In 1038 Thurbrand's son, Carl, reopened the feud by murdering Earl EAldred.

Sigen's son, EAdulf, succeeded EAldred as EAdulf ll, Earl of Bamburgh. During his term of office disputes arose over individual possessions of land in Cumbria as to whether individual title followed from English law or Scottish. He appointed his younger brother, Cospatric, to carry out a review of land holdings in Cumbria. While there, he visited us at StorEye and ensured that our ownership of the StorEye family estates were beyond any form of legal challenge.

* * *

In 1035 Cnut died and was succeeded by, first Harold Harefoot, his oldest son, and then in 1040 by Harthacnut, Cnut's son by Emma of Normandy. In 1042 Harthacnut died unmarried. In the absence of a direct heir, the English witan invited Edward, the son of the late king, AEthelred, and Emma of Normandy, to return from his exile in Normandy and accept the throne of England, which he did. And so, the throne of England returned to a descendent of Alfred and Aethelstan of Wessex, where it remained until 1066, when Edward died.

Meanwhile, in 1041, Earl Eadulf was murdered, most likely at the hand of Siward, who had become his nephew through marriage to EAldred's daughter, EAlfrytha. Siward became Earl of Northumbria. Siward and EAlfrytha had two sons, Osberne and Waltheof. In 1054 Siward took an army north into Scotland to help in unseating the usurper, Macbeth. Osberne was killed in that battle and Siward himself died of natural causes that same year. His youngest son, Waltheof was only ten years old at the time and was therefore passed over to succeed his father. King Edward appointed Tostig Godwinson as Earl of Northumbria. Tostig was widely hated in Northumbria and eventually, under a threat of rebellion, was deposed by Edward and expelled from England in 1065. Siward's son, and Uhtred's great-grandson, Waltheof, was appointed Earl of Northumbria and his uncle, Cospatric, Uhtred's youngest, son purchased the earldom of York.

CHAPTER 28
COMES THE CONQUEROR

ENGLAND 1066

Gospatric and I are the last living grandchildren of Stor and Eyja. We have both grown old, our hair and beards have turned to white. We have our own children and grandchildren. Along with my offspring and those of my numerous cousins, StorEye is well populated by the children of Stor. Cospatric, the youngest son of Uhtred and Sigen, is now the Earl of York and continues to spend his time between York and Bamburgh. It would be a good time to end this chronicle of the life of Stor and the origin of StorEye but I would be remiss not to include aspects of the life of our nephew, Waltheof, the son of Siward and Uhtred's granddaughter, EAlfrytha, and the impact on England from the crisis created by our King Edward not having sired a direct heir. Waltheof has succeeded to the title of the Earl of Bamburgh.

Our late King AEthelred left his wife, Emma of Normandy, and their son, Edward, in Normandy after he returned to England to face Cnut for the final time. When Cnut became king he married the widow, Emma, but Edward remained with his mother's family in Normandy.

When Cnut died in 1035, his son, Harthacnut succeeded him. Although his claim was challenged and not formally resolved until 1040, he convinced his half brother, Edward, to join and support him. When he died in 1042, Edward succeeded him. Edward ruled until his death in 1066 but he was a committed celibate. As a result, he left no children to succeed him on the throne.

As King Edward lay dying, we knew that the question of his succession would pose a serious problem for England. I had joined Cospatric and Waltheof in a discussion of the repercussions that his death would have on northern England, and their respective earldoms of Bamburgh and York.

Cospatric announced, "Edward is dead. The witan has invited Harold Godwinson to take the throne. He is the son of a powerful Anglo-Saxon noble and the nephew of Cnut on his mother's side. He is also the brother of Edwards's wife and therefore Edward's brother-in law."

I replied, "But Harold's claim to the throne is not unchallenged. Harold's brother, that scoundrel, Tostig, was Earl of Northumbria before we were able to eventually force him into exile. I hear that he travelled to Denmark and convinced their king, Harald Hardrada, to challenge for the throne of England, in order to rebuild Cnut's North Sea Empire. The rumour is that, together, with an army of 10,000 and 240 ships, they are under sail to York to battle Harold Godwinson for the throne. As we speak, King Harold has raised an army and will call out the *fyrd* to support him against this usurper."

"We cannot allow Tostig to succeed," Waltheof declared. "When he was our earl, he increased our taxed without any benefit to the north. He executed his critics without trial even while they were meeting him under his guarantee of safe conduct. He does not understand

Northumbrians and his iron-handed rule gave no opportunity for us to raise our concerns. And, from what I hear, Hardrada is even more tyrannical than that dog, Tostig. Even if our king did not call for our support, we should give it regardless."

Our nephew, Waltheof, was still a young man. He had inherited all of the best traits of the Earls of Bamburgh who had come before him. He was tall, blond and well proportioned. He was fearless in battle and had the skills and strength to support him. He was quick to anger, but his skill with weapons, particularly the massive war axe which he favoured, was tempered by a sense of humour and a weakness for enjoying strong drink and loose women. Still, he was a natural leader of men, who would not hesitate to rally to his banner.

He was often brash in his decisions, but this time he was right. We must support King Harold against Hardrada and Tostig.

Hardrada and Tostig carried out some minor coastal raids before landing their fleet and proceeding by land to York. Cospatric, and his army of York, met them on the road and challenged them to battle. The army of York was defeated and the invaders attacked the city itself, and successfully overran its defenses. Meanwhile, King Harold marched his army north to face these invaders. On reaching Northumbria, he was joined by the army of Bamburgh under the leadership of Waltheof. After several substantial battles, the opposing armies met at Stamford Bridge. Waltheof led the attack, flanked by Cospatric on one side and King Harald on the other.

I was not there to witness this battle, but Cospatric described it to me in great detail. Godwinson was successful and Hardrada and Tostig were both slain. Upon the collision of the shield walls, Waltheof's warriors almost immediately breached the invaders' line. Their wall crumbled, and Waltheof led the screaming warriors of Bamburgh into the breach, where a systematic slaughter began. Waltheof's fearsome battle-axe sent numerous of these invaders to their bloody demise. Both Hardrada and Tostig were slain and their forces were massacred. Only 24, of the 240 invading ships, managed to escape the carnage.

* * *

Meanwhile, William, Duke of Normandy had long claimed that King Edward had promised him the throne of England upon his death. In his opinion Harold Godwinson had cheated him out of his rightful inheritance. While Godwinson was fighting Hardrada and Tostig in the north, William prepared to invade from the south. King Harold forced-marched his troops back to England's southern shore where, at Hastings, worn from their march and weary from their war, they formed in battle formation to greet William's invasion at Hastings. Both armies were similar in size but William was strongly supported by cavalry and archers, while Harold had only the foot soldiers that had just complete the forced-march from York. They formed a shield wall awaiting William's advance. William instead used a series feigned retreats and when Harold's men broke rank to pursue them, William's cavalry swooped in to decimate them. Meanwhile William's archers, who, equipped with long bows, darkened the sky with arrows. The results were a slaughter. William's victory was decisive.

William claimed that he had been rightfully named heir to the throne by King Edward in a message delivered by Harold Godwinson. Therefore all of those who had taken up arms against him at Hastings were traitors to the crown. While a large majority of them had died in the battle, William claimed for the crown the holdings of 80% of the Anglo- Saxon thanes. This he then distributed amongst his followers, creating a Norman nobility to rule England.

CHAPTER 29
NORTHUMBRIAN REVOLT

YORK, 1068

We had only just finished our meal and were relaxing with a glass of wine in a small room off the great hall of Bamburgh Castle. I was sharing my views with Waltheof regarding the Norman invasion when a servant appeared to at the doorway. "Earl Cospatric is at the castle gate," he announced.

"Well, show him in," Waltheof commanded.

Within moments, the bedraggled Cospatric was ushered in. He had obviously been travelling rapidly and his exertion had him gasping for breath. "What has happened?" we both demanded in unison.

Gathering himself he blurted out, "The Bastard has seized York."

We both were aware that he was referring to William of Normandy, not only with disdain, but in reference to his birth out of wedlock. Throughout England he was generally referred to by this title, reflecting the contempt which Anglo-Saxons felt towards him. "Sit down. Have a glass of wine, gather wits, and tell us what has happened," I ordered.

Once seated, Cospatric continued in a calmer manner. "William has appointed Robert de Comyn as the Earl of

Northumberland. His minions arrived with an army of 1500 men, announcing that they were here in the name of de Comyn, on the written order of King William. After producing a proclamation to that effect they demanded that I surrender the city of York to their castellan. Caught by surprise and badly outnumbered, I accepted their demand and fled here."

"But he cannot do that," Waltheof exclaimed. William is not our king."

"I am afraid that he well may be," I responded. "According to the Bastard, King Edward named him his heir to all of England. In his mind, Harold was a usurper and by defeating him, and killing him, at Hastings he expected that all of England would simply surrender to him and crown him as our king. He was obviously wrong, but, since then, the witan has surrendered and named him to the throne."

William's conquest of England was swift, brutal and complete. But the witan had initially named Edmond Ironsides' son, Edgar AEtheling as our king. After Hastings, William had been forced to fight several battles with Edgar's supporters, before the witan surrendered to him.

In Northumbria there were many Anglo-Saxon thanes and nobles who still retained their estates. They, like us, had been supporters of Harold Godwinson and had fought for him against the invasion attempt by Hardrada and Tostig, but they had not marched south to face William at Hastings, thereby preventing William from accusing them of treason and confiscating their lands and titles.

"Well, we might not be in agreement, the witan speaks for all of England. And they have now spoken for the Bastard," Cospatric added.

"But this does not give him claim against our lands and our titles," Waltheof declared.

THE LEGEND OF STOR

* * *

We had talked late into the night about De Comyn's seizure of York, before eventually retiring for the night, without having resolved how to deal with this latest affront. Early the following morning, however, our response became clear. A messenger arrived from Durham, his horse heavily lathered from having been pushed too hard. As soon as he was in our presence, he announced, " De Comyn has taken Durham. We welcomed him in peace, but once inside our walls, his troops began behaving as conquerors; wantonly raping and pillaging our citizens. They even desecrated St. Cuthbert's resting place."

"This is an outrage." Waltheof screamed. Turning to one of his warriors he commanded, "Make ready our army. We march to liberate Durham."

As they readied themselves for battle, Waltheof turned to me. "My most precious Uncle Byrni, with all due respects, you are not a warrior. You are a scribe. Return to StorEye. You will be much safer there."

Waltheof led his army directly to Durham. Along the way, many of our countrymen, hearing about the carnage at Durham, swelled our ranks. Waltheof first attacked the stronghold of William's newly appointed Earl of Northumbria, Robert de Comines and his army of 700. All of de Comines men were slain. Many of them were dispatched by Waltheof's terrible axe. De Comyn took refuge in a house in Durham, but he burned to death when Waltheof ordered the house be put to the torch.

Well after the battle was over, other Anglo-Saxon nobles and their warriors arrived at Durham, anxious to lend their support to any opposition to the Bastard. Emboldened by the success at Durham, the rebels then marched on York. At York they quickly seized the town, slaughtered William's garrison and the Norman castellan was put to death. Waltheof led the main attack and his mighty axe is credited with leaving scores of Normans dead in its wake. But the rebels could not breach the castle. They burnt the city to the ground and laid siege to the castle.

In response, William led his armies north. They pillaged their way to York. By the time they arrived many of the rebels had fled to Scotland, including Edgar AEtheling and Cospatric. Waltheof and several other brave sons of Northumbria were taken as a hostage against the good behaviour of the Anglo-Saxon and Danish populace of Northumbria.

All of the hostages, except for Waltheof, were chained in enclosed wagons for the trip back south. Waltheof, while bound at the wrists, was given a horse to ride. A rope was placed around his neck. The loose end was held by one of William's knights to ensure he could not escape. They did not start south, but instead took the road to Durham. As they were starting out, William beckoned for Waltheof to be led forward so that he would be riding beside him on this trip.

William addressed him, "Well young Anglo, I heard you fought well and caused the death of many of my men."

"Untie my hands and return my axe and I will show you how many Norman heads I can cleave from their worthless bodies," Waltheof replied. Waltheof shared his family's tall, muscular build, their handsome face and their golden manes and beard. He was a striking figure even in his restraints.

"I should hang you and cut out your arrogant tongue."

"So why have you not yet done so?" Waltheof asked.

"I still might. But, for the meantime, I want you to see first-hand the fate of those who rebel against my throne."

William then summoned one of his generals and ordered him, "We are riding to Durham. I want you to burn every building along the way. I want you to burn every crop and to kill every cow, sheep, goat, pig and fowl that you see. I also want you to kill every male person over the age of sixteen years. These vermin will learn the price of raising arms against me. And I want you to salt the fields when you have destroyed everything else. I do not want another crop to grow here in my life time."

As they proceeded across the country side, William's orders were carried out while Waltheof watched in horror. Women and children wept as their men folk were annihilated, but if they moved to intervene, they too were struck down. The bodies of man and beast alike were left to rot in the fields. More than 100,000 people died of starvation over the next decade and not a single village was re-inhabited during that time. Waltheof struggled to remain mounted as his stomach churned from watching the barbaric and wanton destruction.

After Durham, William continued towards Chester with the slaughter continuing unabated. Along the way he must have decided that he had made his point, for he abandoned his butchery and returned south with his army.

* * *

NORMANDY, 1070

Waltheof was sent as a hostage to Normandy. He received the good treatment generally afforded to hostages of the nobility. For the most part, he spent his time at King William's Normandy court. Waltheof had been there almost a year but he had seen little of William, whose time had largely been spent in England. But today the conqueror was back in Normandy and he had ordered a private audience with Waltheof. At the appointed time Waltheof was escorted to William's chamber. He was invited to sit and make himself comfortable.

William began the conversation. "Have you figured out my plans for you?" He inquired.

"Well, you've had me here for almost a year now and you still have not butchered me, so, no, I don't know what your plans are," Waltheof replied.

"Well you are aware that, with the exception of those who were killed in battle, I have not executed a single member of your Anglo-Saxon nobility. I am not interested in killing you all. I am interested in ruling my kingdom, both here in Normandy and in England. To do so I need the support of the remaining English nobility. It is not a secret that I am not popular in England. Some might even say that I am despised. But I am not there to be popular. Edward promised to make me his heir. Your witan betrayed me and gave my throne to Harold Godwinson. But I have successfully taken it as was my due. But I need the support of the remaining English nobility."

"Given that you have acknowledged that they hate you, how do you think that you can win their hearts?" Waltheof asked.

"I do not seek their love. I only seek their fealty. And I plan to achieve that by having the remaining English nobility marry my nobility or their children and then leave them to their estates, seeking only their fealty in return."

William never ceased to surprise Waltheof, but this proposition left him shocked. "Are you proposing marriage for me?" he stammered.

"That is exactly what I have in mind."

"And who then is the lucky lady that you have in mind for me?" Waltheof queried. Waltheof was an attractive man and he knew no shyness when it came to women, so his sarcasm was not without merit.

But William was all business. "I would have you marry my sister Adelaine's daughter, Judith de Lenz. She is a comely woman and of child bearing age. I would also return you to England as the Earl of Northumberland."

"So you plan to give me give me back my Earldom after you have laid it to waste," Waltheof replied, unable to completely disguise the bitterness which he felt.

"Don't be too quick to judge me badly," William countered. "I will be creating an Earldom of Huntington covering all of the land south of Northumberland. Once you are married, you will become the Earl of Huntington as well as Northumberland."

This left Waltheof speechless. "All I ask in return" William continued, "is that you marry my niece and pledge me your fealty."

Within a year Waltheof and Judith were married and he became the Earl of Northumberland and Huntington. Waltheof had sworn his fealty to William, King of England and Duke of Normandy.

* * *

One of the first undertakings of the newly installed Earl of Huntington and Northumberland was to track down Carl Thurbrandson. Thurbrandson resided within Waltheof's new domain and therefore he needed little stealth to locate the old family adversary. One evening, as Carl was enjoying an evening meal with his sons, Waltheof's troops swarmed into the room and put them all to the sword, thus ending this long running blood-feud.

While Waltheof was a fearsome warrior, he was not cut out for a life of peace. He was somewhat lazy, a drunkard with an unapologetic lust for women. While he carried on a normal civil marriage with Judith, they were not in love with each other and the marriage did little to inhibit his womanizing throughout his new domain. One of his favourite mistresses was an attractive young woman who lived in the village of Loxley which lay within the boundaries of Huntington, not far from Waltheof's manor. Waltheof spent many nights in her bed and from this relationship she was rumoured to have born a son whom she named Robin. *Robin of Loxley would later distinguish himself in English mythology.*

Waltheof also found time to father three children with Judith; a daughter Alice, a son Uhtred, who would be known as Uhtred of Tynedale, and a daughter, Maud, often known as Matilda.

In 1071 King William expressed his recognition of the strategic advantage of the palatine bishopric at Durham and elevated its prelate to the title of Prince Bishop of Durham.

***

HEREFORD, 1074

William the Conqueror was a ruthless tyrant. He implemented a full scale Carolinian form of feudalism in which he divided England into a dozen earldoms with each earl tied to him through oaths of fealty. While he permitted them to administer their sections of his kingdom autonomously, he played these nobles to suit his needs. Most of these earls were tied to William through kinship or marriage, and he arranged those marriages to create alliances to meet his needs or to balance their power relative to each other. He played little heed to their wishes in these matters. To defy William was both dangerous and sinful. Nobles languished in jails for speaking against him. Clergy of the old English church joined them in their cells while Norman prelates ran the church and the king's council. Many of William's nobles chafed over the harsh treatment towards any opposition, even the slightest perceived insult. The slaughter carried out in Northumberland would not be forgotten. The savaged land still left thousands starving to death while their new king bathed in the riches which had been taken from them.

In 1074 Ralph de Gauder, Earl of Norfolk and Suffolk, proposed marriage to Emma, the sister and ward of Roger Fitzosbern, Earl of Hereford. De Gauder was a Norman whose father had fought for William at Hastings. Ralph and Emma were very much in love. But William refused to allow the marriage. The couple, with the blessing of Roger Fitzosbern, decided to proceed with their wedding vows without regard for William's wishes. At the wedding ceremony a messenger arrived from William, who was in Normandy at the time, announcing that Lanfranc, the Archbishop of Canterbury, had declared Fitzosbern excommunicated for violating the fealty sworn to his king. Excommunication placed the Earl of Hereford outside of the protection of the laws of the church and of the king. The assembly was incensed.

How much the consumption of wine and ale played a role is difficult to determine, but the feast degenerated into calls for insurrection against the Norman ruler. Earl Waltheof was the guest of honour at the feast and he too joined his voice in the condemnation of William's treatment of his people. Soon the air was filled with pledges to take up arms to overthrow the king and place the pride of Anglo-Saxon England, Earl Waltheof of Northumbria and Huntington, on the throne. The combined forces of Northumberland, Huntington, Hereford, Norfolk and Suffolk virtually guaranteed success for the rebel cause, particularly with William detained in Normandy dealing with insurrection against his rule there.

The following morning, however, Waltheof had sober second thoughts. The role of his wife, Judith, is not fully known, but she obviously reminded Waltheof of his pledge of fealty to William, and of the foul consequence to Northumberland the last time Waltheof raised his sword against the rule of King William. What is known is that she wrote, and had delivered, a letter to Archbishop Lanfranc, revealing the planned insurrection. William had left Lanfranc in charge of his kingdom while he was in Normandy. On learning of this letter, Waltheof immediately rode to London where he confessed and recanted his involvement in the insurrection. Lanfranc absolved him and advised him to travel to Normandy and surrender himself to William and seek his mercy. Waltheof complied.

WINCHESTER, 1076

The desertion by Waltheof left the insurrection divided, as Huntington lay directly between Hereford to the west and Norfolk and Suffolk to the east. William sent his army, under the command of Bishop Odo, to first crush Hereford and then lay siege to de Gauder's castle at Norwich. De Gauder escaped into exile and Roger Fitzosbern was jailed for the remainder of his life. The last serious challenge to William's rule of England was over.

Waltheof languished in William's jail in Winchester with Lafranc pleading for his forgiveness and Odo arguing to have him tried for treason. Odo prevailed. At his trial, his wife, the king's niece, Judith, was a witness against him. He was convicted of treason and sentenced to death. On May 31, 1076, Waltheof was taken to St. Giles Hill to face his executioner. He arrived wearing the finery of his office, which he distributed to the poor. A large crowd gathered, many of them agitated by the fate awaiting their hero.

It is reported that before his death, Waltheof requested that he be allowed time for a prayer. As he knelt, and recited the Lord's Prayer, the crowd began to swell with Anglo-Saxon supporters. The executioner grew nervous, fearing the potential of the crowd to attempt to free Waltheof. As Waltheof spoke the words"…lead us not into temptation," the sword swung, cleanly severing his head from his body. But the severed head continued, "…but deliver us from evil. Amen."

His body was thrown into a ditch.

William crossed the cold channel and reddened the bright swords,
And now he has betrayed noble Earl Waltheof.
It is true that killing in England will be a long time ending;
A braver lord than Waltheof
Will never be seen on earth.
-Thorkill Skallason

EPILOGUE

Waltheof's death heralded the end of open rebellion against William's rule. The descendants of Boandi, Gyrdh and Haberd of StorEye continued to reside at StorEye where they flourished. The surviving offspring of Sigen Storsdotter and Uhtred the Bold all moved to Scotland to escape the wrath of the Conqueror.

    Waltheof's death left his widow, Judith de Lenz, a wealthy woman. She seemed to believe that she was now free to do whatever she pleased. To her dismay, William had other plans for her. He betrothed her to Simeon of St. Liz. St. Liz was a cripple and Judith was revolted by the thought of marrying him. When she refused, William was outraged and stripped many of her holdings including the title to Huntington. William gave the latter to the daughter of Waltheof and Judith, Matilda, more often known as Maud. Maud married Simeon of St. Liz, making him the second Earl of Huntington. Judith fled with her other children to Scotland, but not before having the remains of Waltheof transferred from the traitor's grave to be honorably reinterred at the Abbey of Crowland. Cospatric's son, also named Waltheof, after his renowned uncle, returned from exile to become the Abbot of Crowland. Many claimed miracles resulted from praying at Waltheof's grave and petitions were made for him to be sainted. But those honours were to fall to his grandson from Maud and Simeon, who became St. Waltheof.

After the death of St. Liz, Maud married a second time to David, the crown prince of Scotland. Their daughter, Isobel would marry Robert the Bruce IV.

* * *

It is rumoured that Waltheof's illegitimate son, Robin of Loxley retreated to live in the forest. He became an outlaw, separating many well-to-do Normans from their wealth. He was much pursued by a grandson of King William, William Peveril who had been appointed Sherriff of Nottingham and Chief Steward of the Royal Forest. Robin's legend lasted well past the end of his life and into the reign of King John. It became the name attributed to the leader of generations of English who were forced into a landless existence in the forests of England. For centuries they pillaged the ill-gotten gain of the Norman nobility and their greedy counterparts in their Norman clergy. With it, they kept alive the Anglo-Saxon dream of an England free of Norman tyrants.

But it was not to be swords through which England's Anglo-Saxon culture would survive and prevail. The dream was conceived by Alfred the Great. It was given life through his creation of law written in the English language, the spread of that literacy through church institutions and the encompassing of concepts of basic human rights. It was nurtured by fortified burgs with their own garrisons and magistrates through which villages came to see their taxes as supporting their peace and their justice and not simply adding to the majesty of their kings. And it was supported by thousands of people such as Ulphus Toraldson, Stor son of Eye, and Uhtred of Bamburgh and brought to fruition by Edgar, King of England at his coronation in 973, AD which gave the Anglo-Saxon culture the strength to absorb the early Britons, the Welsh, the Cumbrians, the Danes, the Norse and finally the Normans into a tapestry which would endure regardless of who sat on their throne.

THE LEGEND OF STOR

***

FRED STOREY

AUTHOR'S GENEOLEGY

Stor (Styr) c995AD
|
Alanue le Storey
|
Jordanus le Stori c1274AD
|
Galfridus le Storey (Sturis, Sturey) c1369
|
Ricardus le Storer m Cristine c1395
|
Bryan Storey c1476
|
Ricus Storey c1476
|
Gwalter (Wot of the Hove) c1484
|
Thomas Storey c1538
|
Thomas Storey c1608
|
Thomas Storey c1666
|

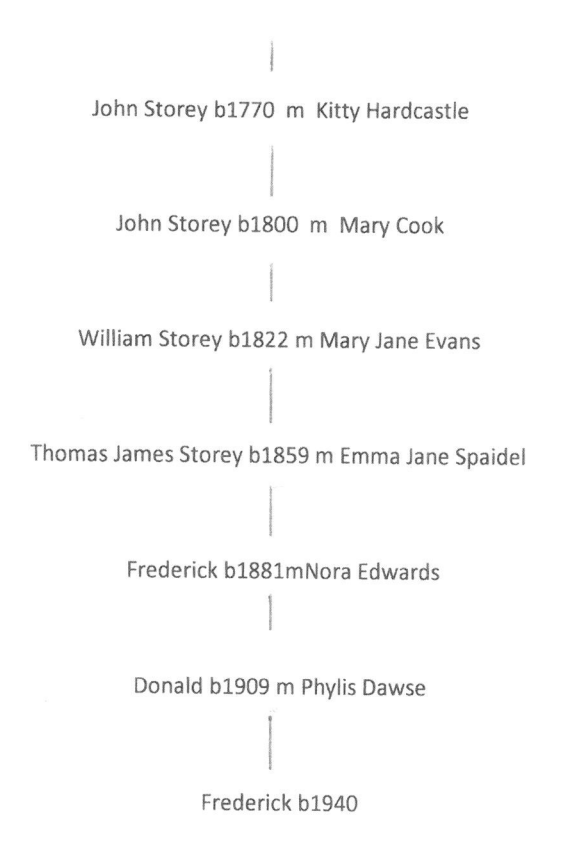

THE LEGEND OF STOR

John Storey b1770 m Kitty Hardcastle

John Storey b1800 m Mary Cook

William Storey b1822 m Mary Jane Evans

Thomas James Storey b1859 m Emma Jane Spaidel

Frederick b1881 m Nora Edwards

Donald b1909 m Phylis Dawse

Frederick b1940

ABOUT THE AUTHOR
FRED STOREY

With a Master of Arts degree from the University of Regina, Fred Storey spent most of his professional career working for various governments and aboriginal organizations, looking for sustainable solutions to issues relating to the oppression of aboriginal nations.

After retiring, he developed an interest in genealogy, looking into his family history and the origins of his own surname. As he uncovered information about his Viking ancestry, from the time of Britain's Dark Ages, he quickly recognized that what he was learning would be a solid foundation of a story well worth being told. *The Legend of Stor* is that story, based on his research, and is his first book. Storey lives with his wife in Langford, British Columbia.

Printed in Canada